FOR THE NATIONS

For the Nations

Essays Evangelical and Public

JOHN H. YODER

WILLIAM B. EERDMANS PUBLISHING COMPANY
GRAND RAPIDS, MICHIGAN / CAMBRIDGE, U.K.

© 1997 Wm. B. Eerdmans Publishing Co.
255 Jefferson Ave. S.E., Grand Rapids, Michigan 49503 /
P.O. Box 163, Cambridge CB3 9PU U.K.

Printed in the United States of America

02 01 00 99 98 97   7 6 5 4 3 2 1

Library of Congress Cataloging-in-Publication Data

Yoder, John Howard.
    For the nations: essays evangelical and public / John H. Yoder.
        p.   cm.
    Includes bibliographical references.
    ISBN 0-8028-4324-7 (pbk.: alk. paper)
    1. Church and the world. 2. Mission of the church.
    3. Christianity and culture. 4. Christian ethics—Mennonite authors.
    5. Sociology, Christian (Mennonite).   I. Title.
BR115.W6Y63   1997
261 — dc21   97-21623
                                              CIP

Contents

IV. Ecumenical Testimonies

Introduction

I. What This Book Is About

The theme of this book is the tone of voice, or the style and stance, of the people of God in the dispersion.

When the Jews who had taken Jeremiah seriously began to settle into Babylon as a place where they would maintain their community, raise their children and grandchildren, and thereby testify to the supranational authority of their God, they needed to decide whether to talk the local language.[1] That was part of the larger question of whether to make themselves at home there or to constitute an alien enclave.

"Decide" may well be the wrong word; the negative alternative would not have been viable for long. They had no choice but to work out, in response to the challenge of missionary existence, whether their acceptance of the Chaldean culture around them would be grudging and clumsy or wholehearted and creative. Would they continue to maintain the language of "back home" as their primary identity? If they did that, could they be effective participants in the Mesopotamian culture?

This is a question which our century again can understand. Chinese brought to the United States as cheap labor, Armenians scattered by Turkish persecution, Scandinavians brought to Minnesota by

---

1. I here anticipate one strand of the theme of chapter 3 below, which seems to me the best way to concretize the whole book's witness.

cheap land, Amish left over from the frontier age still speaking "Pennsylvania German" represent in our recent national memory other versions of the same challenge, to say nothing of the several forms of Jewish subcultural identity. Yet these analogies are not really very close to Jeremiah's Jews, since most of these groups in our time did not leave their homelands with a mission.

The general pattern, which Jews were to replicate a dozen times through the centuries, was to use three languages. They did not abandon the Hebrew enshrined in their Scriptures; in fact it was in the dispersion that the Scriptures first came into their own. It was for and in the dispersion situation that the writings later called "Bible" were copied and collected on a growing scale, and that the language was studied in an intellectual way.

They also entered fully into the host culture; they did it in Mesopotamia then, and they have done it ever since in the places to which they came. They became so good at the language game that in a few generations they were effective as translators, educators, diplomats, scribes serving the authorities. They became socially effective as merchants, poets, and sages in the social interstices not controlled by the rulers.

Yet beyond this double affirmation it usually happened that, when there was time, Jews created a language of their own between the other two. In America we know about Yiddish, a special German dialect taken from the Rhine basin to the East European world, still surviving there but also scattered all over the West and the former Russian empire and to Israel.[2] Yet before that the same kind of thing had happened in Spain and Portugal, whence Sephardic migrants took Ladino/Judesmo back to the Middle East. Yet long before that the same thing had been done in Persia, in China, and in Ethiopia.

My reference to that memory of Jewish polyglossia in this preface is more than a mere metaphor. Elsewhere I have written about Judaism for its own sake as the seedbed of the Christian movement.[3] Here I

2. Had it not been for the surprising creativity of Eliezer Ben Yehudah, creating modern Hebrew out of the ancient roots, Yiddish would likely have become the official public language of modern Israel.

3. In addition to chapter 2 below, cf. also: "The Jewishness of Early Christian Pacifism" and "The Nonviolence of Judaism from Jeremiah to Hertzl," chapters 2 and 3 of Joan B. Kroc Institute for International Peace Studies working paper packet 7:WP:1. Cf.

draw it in as a background image to illuminate the problem this text addresses. YHWH's command, through Jeremiah, "Seek the peace of the city where I have sent you," engaged the Jews to live *for the nations*.

A Christian minority group within the culture created by Christian majority groups faces a different form of the problem of the Jeremian migrants. Ever since forms of prophetic dissent arose in Europe, the thinkers in church and state who controlled the language called those protestors "sects," defining them not by what they believed but by their minority status. Sometimes the so-called sectarians were minimally tolerated; in other times and places they were killed. In the cases where they were tolerated, they had prima facie no choice, like the Jews described above, but to use the language of the dominators.

The posture I seek to interpret in the chapters that follow is usually called "sectarian" by its critics, and sometimes by social thinkers intending to be objective. The very choice of the term says that a priori the position to which someone applies it pejoratively has been measured and found wanting by the standards of the establishment.[4] That tends to impose on me, and on people who take similar positions (intentionally or not), the obligation to accept that label, and to explain why that is a justifiable position for Christians to take. I have sometimes done that, especially within the subconversation staked out by Ernst Troeltsch, who sought to make the terminology objective-descriptive rather than pejorative.[5] I have been interpreted in "sectarian" terms by others, by friends[6] and by

---

also *"Tertium Datur: It Did Not Have to Be,"* in *The Jewish-Christian Schism Revisited*, Shalom Desktop Packet, 1996; and "War as a Moral Problem in the Early Church: The Historian's Hermeneutic Assumptions," in *The Pacifist Impulse in Historical Perspective*, ed. Harvey Dyck (Toronto: University of Toronto Press, 1996), pp. 90-110.

4. "Establishment" does not mean the majority; it means the minority who are in dominant social roles and claim the authority to speak for everyone.

5. I did it in my programmatic essay "The Anabaptist Dissent: The Logic of the Place of the Disciple in Society," in *Concern: A Pamphlet Series*, no. 1 (Scottdale, Pa., 1954), pp. 45-68. At that time I assumed that the Troeltschian "objective" or "nonjudgmental" understanding of the term was established. I have since learned that that is far from being the case.

6. E.g., by Stanley Hauerwas, who maximizes the provocative edge of the dissenting posture with titles like *Against the Nations* (Notre Dame: University of Notre Dame Press, 1992), or *Resident Aliens* (Nashville: Abingdon, 1989).

friendly critics.[7] I have often accepted the challenge of explaining why this position is a more ecumenical and more "catholic" way to be Christian than are the various national and regional establishments that have become accustomed to claiming to be the main line.

Yet the Troeltschian attempt to make the language nonjudgmental will not ultimately hold. Troeltsch's American admirer H. Richard Niebuhr used the posture of above-the-melee, generous, descriptive objectivity to clothe his below-the-table advocacy of the establishment position.[8] Niebuhr's heir James Gustafson returned to making the adjective simply pejorative.[9]

My accepting the "sectarian" label for myself, for purposes of discussion within American Protestantism, 1950-90, is like the Jew in Babylon in 500 B.C.E. using Chaldean or like Buber, Landau, and Zweig in Germany in 1920 using German; I have usually done it, accepting having no choice but to play by other people's rules. Yet it routinely has led to misunderstanding and misrepresentation. The present book seeks to correct for that.

This collection may be described as an analogy to the development of Yiddish. I am expositing, not in my own ancient in-group language but in my own variant of the common idiom, the claim that the position I represent is the line of the gospel.

This is not a new project on my part. In 1955[10] I began expositing how followers of Jesus,[11] who in fact are an outvoted minority almost

---

7. Cf. Richard Mouw in his *Politics and the Biblical Drama* (Grand Rapids: Eerdmans, 1976), pp. 90ff. Since then Mouw has agreed with me about the limits of the usefulness of these categories; cf. our joint effort: "Evangelical Ethics and the Anabaptist-Reformed Dialogue," *Journal of Religious Ethics* 17 (fall 1989): 121-37.

8. Cf. my "How H. Richard Niebuhr Reasoned," in *Authentic Transformation*, Glen Stassen et al. (Nashville: Abingdon, 1996), pp. 31-89.

9. "The Sectarian Temptation," *Catholic Theological Society Proceedings* 40 (1985): 84-94. Oddly, the persons Gustafson accuses of falling into this temptation are his former colleague the Lutheran ecumenist George Lindbeck and his former pupil United Methodist Stanley Hauerwas. Gustafson does not name me.

10. This was the date of the first drafts of the text which later became my pamphlet *The Christian Witness to the State* (1964); it began with a reference to a still earlier paper.

11. I use "follower of Jesus" as a meaningful functional definition. Most admirers of Jesus, and most people who call themselves Christian, do not affirm that they are committed to following seriously either his example or his teachings. Cf. my *The Politics*

everywhere, can and should address to the wider society, including the state, and to the persons exercising power within it, the invitation, as good news, to participate, in their own best interest, in the cosmic meaning of the sovereignty of their risen Lord.[12] Others have preceded me in characterizing the stance I am describing here as "radically catholic."

II. What Kind of Book This Is

Despite a certain formal symmetry in the titles of the two volumes, this collection of essays differs from the previous collection entitled *The Royal Priesthood: Essays Ecclesiological and Ecumenical*.[13] That book brought together texts, some of them old, mostly once published though now out of print, the reprinting of which editor Michael Cartwright judged would have some continuing value for history or to fill out the outlines of my position. For that reason it was fitting that someone other than I should select and interpret them, as Professor Cartwright generously did.

This present collection, on the other hand, gathers more never-published materials. Some of the chapters are old, too, but more of the collection is recent, and some of it addresses themes so contemporary that five years from now they may be out of date.

A second difference between the two volumes is that, whereas the

---

of Jesus, 2d ed. (Grand Rapids: Eerdmans, 1994), pp. 4ff. and 15ff. The bulk of ecumenical moral discourse is devoted to expositing the strong reasons, which I respect intellectually, and which have constituted a large part of my concern as academic and as participant in conciliar processes, which they give for thus assigning Jesus a nonnormative role.

12. In the framework of a lecture series presented in early 1980, under the general title "New World on the Way," the theme essay was "How Ecclesiology Is Social Ethics," since published in my *The Royal Priesthood: Essays Ecclesiological and Ecumenical*, ed. Michael G. Cartwright (Grand Rapids: Eerdmans, 1994), pp. 123ff. Another affirmation of the paradigmatic or (even better) kerygmatic role of the people of God was spelled out topically in "Sacrament as Social Ethics," *Theology Today* (April 1990), and popularly in *Body Politics* (Nashville: Discipleship Resources Press, 1992). In the present collection this scheme is pursued most directly in the second chapter.

13. Grand Rapids: Eerdmans, 1994, edited and introduced by Michael G. Cartwright.

corpus of older writings in *The Royal Priesthood* can be seen as fitting within a vision of the mission of the Christian community some call "sectarian" or describe as standing "against the nations," the essays in this collection are intentionally devoted to demonstrating the wrongness of that characterization of my stance. That always was an inaccurate characterization, but in the past I did not usually argue that point, since some other, more precise issue (the ethics of violence, or whether to baptize infants, or how to take the Scriptures seriously, or the etiquette of ecumenism, or the shape of congregational life, etc.) seemed more urgent. Thus in the past I permitted some interpreters to ascribe to me the "purist" or "withdrawn" assumptions which they thought belonged with such convictions.[14]

My lecture on "Why Ecclesiology Is Social Ethics" in *The Royal Priesthood,* which first was presented as a lecture in 1980,[15] had already sought to make the point which I exposit further here. That date of origin should suffice to certify that the thesis of the present book does not represent a change of conviction on my part.

Each of the following essays argues, though each in a somewhat different key, that the very shape of the people of God in the world is a public witness, or is "good news," for the world, rather than first of all rejection or withdrawal. Where the attitude to the world needs to be rejection or retreat, that is determined contextually, because of the world's recalcitrant response to that initial noncoercive, yea vulnerable affirmation. I call these essays "evangelical" in the root sense of the term, having to do with being bearers of good news for the world.

That does not mean that I would disavow a relationship to the numerous other currents in recent church life whose self-ascription of the adjective "evangelical" has other foci. For some, the adjective "evangelical" belongs to those who read the Bible with a special kind of respect; some of them consider me as fitting in that realm.[16]

---

14. I write "permitted." I might have written "acquiesced," but not "agreed." I never thought that characterization was accurate. There were however dialogical settings where my self-defense against inaccurate characterizations would have distracted from more important issues, such as reading again the Gospel testimony to Jesus or renarrating fairly someone else's history or being fair to some other interlocutor.

15. It has since been expanded into a booklet, *Body Politics* (Nashville: Discipleship Resource Press, 1992).

16. I have been asked, by people who considered me "evangelical," to contribute

For others, "evangelical" links with "evangelism" and thereby with the Christian missionary enterprise. In much of our recent American experience "mission" means one particular kind of institutional activity, namely, sending especially mandated and supported individuals into foreign societies, usually in small numbers, since there are few such highly qualified people, and sending them is costly. They are sent to communicate a message and to gather their hearers into communities. That is part of what this book is about. I have been privileged to serve as staff of a denominational board of missions, supporting and interpreting persons with that vocation.[17] I have also been invited into the academic world of missiological studies.[18] I was assigned to offer at Eastern Mennonite Seminary and at Goshen Biblical Seminary courses on the theology of the Christian world mission, most of whose content was derived from that experience. I am glad to dedicate this collection to the memory of Joseph D. Graber, the elder brother who called me into that work in 1959.

But in a broader and deeper sense, into which the seminary-based instruction just referred to had already begun to point, beyond "missions" in the narrower sense, the entire Christian community is sent into the world to "communicate a message and gather its hearers into communities." There should then not be one theology for professional missionaries and the agencies which send them abroad and another for ordinary Christians with no such call. What we do about social justice or about education should then be no less "missionary" than what we do about crossing linguistic or political borders and communicating our convictions to unbelievers.

Most of these essays, for that reason, are not *especially* focused on

---

to conferences or to anthologies as a representative of that posture. I have been invited to teach at Regent College in Vancouver, at Wheaton College in Illinois, at New College in Berkeley, California, and at the Asian School of Theology in Manila. In that milieu, the essay (below chapter 9) on the biblical mandate for social concern was an assigned keynote address at the 1973 founding meeting of Evangelicals for Social Action. The *Christian Century* of 15 February 1989 included me in a cover story on "The Evangelicals."

17. I was called by the Mennonite Board of Missions and Charities to serve in marginal-time staff roles, 1953-57; as full-time staff, 1959-65; and part-time again, 1965-71 and 1974-76.

18. A set of more explicitly missiological writings is contemplated as a further volume in the present series.

"missions" in the classical institutional sense. They pursue other dimensions of the fact that Christians are "sent" to and for the world. Since the Christian community is normally a message-bearing minority in whatever world we are concerned with, there is no setting where the missionary dimension of being Christian should not demand (and reward) clarification. In their several different ways, these essays are about that definitional task.

The span of subject matter in this collection, from ancient Mesopotamia to the present, seeks to make a theological and practical point by its disciplinary breadth. The perspective being advocated here is not, as some have sought to see it, primarily or merely an idiosyncratic way to read the New Testament, or merely a minority bias within the repertory of models of Reformation in the sixteenth century.[19] This is a coherent posture which is pertinent up and down the centuries, just as the Hebrew and Christian story is all one story from Abraham to our own time.

The two ancient turning points represented by Jeremiah and Constantine have become, as the reader will see at greater length soon, the two most important landmarks outside the New Testament itself for clarifying what is at stake in the Christian faith. They are more basic than the more recent turns, which Western Christians call "the Reformation" and "the Enlightenment." It is because of what those earlier changes meant that Reformation and Enlightenment have meaning.[20]

Each of these defining events, like the New Testament itself, must be exposited in a larger-than-life way, i.e., as "legend," as something having to be recounted, bigger in its meanings than what the historians' questions about documents and causation can contain. I have already

19. The origins of radical Protestantism within the Swiss Reformation in the 1520s was my dissertation theme in 1957, and I have continued to publish, translate, and edit in that field, but I have intentionally not taken those events to be paradigmatic for these essays. Classifying my position as "sectarian" or "anabaptist" (in contrast to the references above at notes 6 and 7) has also sometimes been done benevolently, i.e., by friends who mean it as an act of respect, to identify the character of a view other than their own. I seldom reject the ascription, and I do not regret at all having studied the history of people called "Anabaptist." Nonetheless my conviction has always been that my normative testimony is "catholic," i.e., pertinent to any Christian. Michael G. Cartwright was correct in characterizing my intent as "radically Catholic" in his introduction to *The Royal Priesthood*.

20. This comment does not deprecate either reformation as such nor "the Reformation." As I already wrote, that has been the field of much of my scholarly effort.

written[21] about the difference Constantine makes; this book adds an interpretation of the Jeremian shift. The reader is thus invited to see each of those major turnings through the lenses of later times, in which again and again the linkage between God and power has come up for review.

III. Why This Kind of Book?

Some have said that I ought to write "a basic introduction" to my thought, or a summa, instead of publishing side by side a number of texts written at different times in the past for people who asked for them. In what field should I do such a primer? Some have said in social ethics.[22] What would that have looked like?

My then-colleague Stanley Hauerwas once set out to write something like that, which he called a "primer."[23] But that will not serve as a model for something I can do.[24] In choosing instead the pattern of bringing together things written occasionally I am in good company:

21. As to "Constantine" as symbol of a change in styles of moral discourse, cf. my "The Constantinian Sources of Western Social Ethics," in *The Priestly Kingdom* (Notre Dame, Ind.: Notre Dame University Press, 1984), pp. 135-47. Unfortunately the importance of that shift is confirmed by the ease with which references to the Constantinian posture can become cheap slogans. A fuller text on the man and the events of the fourth century is in preparation.

22. Ralph Potter said that in 1981 when, at Boston University, he responded to my lecture "But We See Jesus": Glen Stassen said it in 1976 in Kansas City in a colloquium on my *Politics of Jesus*.

23. *The Peaceable Kingdom: A Primer in Christian Ethics* (Notre Dame, Ind.: Notre Dame University Press, 1983).

24. The word "primer" has three meanings; Hauerwas's text, when finished, did not turn out quite to fit any of them. It is not a primer in the elementary-education sense, a book for beginning to read in the first grade, because it does not start at the beginning simply, nor does it track a curriculum. It is not a primer, secondly, in the sense of the first coat of paint, intended to fill the pores of a wood surface, or to heighten the adhesiveness of a metal surface, so that a later coat of the real paint will stick better. Nor is it (thirdly) like the first gallon of water poured into a pump to wet the leather around the plunger and thereby augment the vacuum drawing the water up from a well. (*Webster's* has two other meanings for "primer" which do not fit either.) *The Peaceable Kingdom* was as selective and as idiosyncratic as Hauerwas's earlier writings, even though it differed from them in having been written all in one piece. Were I to try to write a book like that, I do not know what it would be about.

. . . it does but supply another instance of [the author's] lot all through life, to have been led to its publication not on any natural plan or by any view of his own, but by the duties or the circumstances of the moment.[25]

One reason I do not start from scratch to do a book on just one subject is that there is no scratch from which to start. Every theme is already awash in debate. The artifice of beginning *as if* from scratch is useful for some educational purposes,[26] but hardly for these subjects.

A second reason is that there is no one subject. The themes I have been called to treat over the years overlap and interlock, each of them gaining significance from its connection to the others, but they are in several disciplines. That quality, which results from what I have had the privilege of being asked by others to think and write about, need not be a vice in my stance[27] but part of its integrity. Yet it does have the effect that in each field I am seen as an outsider, not an expert.

The truth claim and the internal coherence of one's stance is best displayed and best validated (are those two verbs different in meaning?) in the reciprocal supportiveness of the several statements, each in its own subdisciplinary setting. There would be less value, less substance, and less evident originality to a single, new, simple "introduction" written "from scratch" on any one subject, than in the unpremeditated interlocking of the several themes in this collection, each of them originally validated by some program planner, or some editor, who gave the assignment.

25. John Henry Newman, in the first issue of the *Rambler* which he edited, May 1859, introducing his own collection of "Lectures and Essays on University Subjects."

26. An authentic elementary "primer" does that. But then one must have a clear picture of one's first grader. I did once write a book called "preface," introducing the beginning seminary student to the nature of the discipline of theology (*Christology and Theological Method* [Elkhart, Ind., 1981], available in photocopy from Cokesbury Bookstore, Duke Divinity School, Durham, NC 29706). More often it is the case that to think that there is a bare baseline, to which one could dig down before doing anything else, is the mistake of foundationalism or methodologism, which I renounce in my essay "Walk and Word: The Alternatives to Methodologism," in *Theology without Foundations*, ed. Stanley Hauerwas, Nancey Murphy, and Mark Nation (Nashville: Abingdon, 1994).

27. "Stance" is of course a better word than "system" to describe the coherence, such as there is, of my various concerns. I do not deny that from this *in se* valid stance certain vices within the several disiplines might also be derived, such as my not being up to date on the very latest readings in each subfield.

The chapters which follow, each of them initially requested by someone for presentation to a specified audience, should then represent better what I stand for than what I would do if assigned to start over to write "my basic book" without knowing to whom I should address it. It may partially compensate for the failure to have all my ideas in one place if I cross-reference generously to other writings where I said things I do not repeat fully here.

A few of the texts reprinted here have been cited broadly enough that reprinting to make them more accessible would seem to be called for.[28] Others have circulated informally. Most of them, though, appear here for the first time. I am grateful to Wm. B. Eerdmans and his staff for assistance in bringing them out, and to students and colleagues at Notre Dame and in many audiences elsewhere for the stimulation their different perspectives have given me.

Notre Dame, Yom Kippur 1996

---

28. Three texts are described as "basic" in a double sense: (a) their themes are the simplest logical foundations of my position; (b) friends have told me they are the best introduction to my thought.

PART 1

Presence "for the Nations"

CHAPTER 1

Firstfruits: The Paradigmatic Public Role of God's People

A number of good, lively questions surface when academic thinkers preoccupied with questions of methodology set to work inquiring about how we should proceed to talk about "the public good."[1]

Some of these language games and subgames concern themselves with defining what identifies the kind of talk we should call "public," by contrasting it with other possible "nonpublic" realms of discourse.

- The "public" may be differentiated from the "private" by asking who knows about a topic or who has a right to be concerned with it. Yet even the notion of "privacy" has become public in our time. Since 1973 a "right to privacy" serves as a public legal justification for one kind of lethal institutional medical intervention. Thus even the private is public.
- The "public" may be differentiated from the "clannish" or the "sectarian" by asking how the community is defined that may properly participate in some conversation or some process of decision.

1. This paper was presented on 4 October 1992, at Christian Theological Seminary, Indianapolis, as part of an event inaugurating the work of the seminary's Institute for the Study of the Public Good, an instrument for continuing education and community service. The title was dictated by the event. The other guest speaker was Max Stackhouse.

15

- By "public" some mean those matters which are dealt with by the institutions of the civil order; i.e., "public schools" (except in Great Britain) are those paid for and governed by the state. The non-public would then be what is left to noncoerced and noncoercive initiatives, what Reaganism called "the private sector" and what George Bush, making the priority of this role of the private realm a matter of public policy, called "points of light."
- By "public" some mean to accentuate the pluralistic quality of discourse, in a society where numerous distinct value-bearing communities cohabit, with a concern to minimize violence and oppression while getting on together with our day-to-day business. Toward that end second-order game rules, which some call "civility" (whereby "civil" has a different meaning from when I used it three sentences ago), should operate to restrain the modes of decision and discipline which were at home under previous "established" religious regimes. To be "civil" is then to apply pluralism negatively. "Civility" forbids me to impose my values on you, except by polite and rational discourse. Yet "civility" may be taken positively as well. Members of different value communities need to talk together about overlapping concerns in the common society.

In response to the challenge of "pluralism" thus conceived, whichever of these dimensions we give the most weight, there are at least two standard conflicting strategies:

a. One strategy seeks a wider and, it is hoped, common wisdom. One posits that there must be forms of knowledge which we hold to be true because we have a wider way to know it. This "wider way" may be a tool like "reason," which we claim is more accessible to others than our particular "faith," so that we have a right to oblige people to assent to our views on other grounds than that they are our views.

b. On the other hand, one may seek a thinner common truth, easier to commend to neighbors over whom we have no power, because they probably already believe it.

Both of these tactics, the wider and the thinner, assume, as I would not, what might be called a kind of reflexive solipsism. They assume that the *other* party or parties in a multicultural setting are self-contained, making sense only to themselves, recognizing no truth other than what they already hold, just as I may grant that my values make sense only within my ghetto. That is why the "wider" or the "thinner" maneuver is thought necessary.[2] The faith stance would not reach them.[3]

But I had not finished listing the possible meanings. By "public" some Protestants mean what some Catholics call "common"; namely, those goods whose bearers are nonvoluntary relationships.[4] Also, by "public" some mean the visible and verifiable, what no one can deny, as contrasted to the "spiritual" or "subjective." This is what the sciences deal with, and journalism and history. Its credibility is "out there," "objective."

The reader may properly sense in this sketch a certain skepticism on my part about whether in conversing about "the public" we all mean the same thing. That does not decrease my interest in the discussion, but it does illuminate my priorities as I need to decide, after this first round of stocktaking, where to begin a discussion of what Christians have to say about "the public good." I do not assume, as some do, that we already know what the discussion is about.

These several lines of definition and potential debate are important. Among other values, they give work to academics like me. There are recent good book-length treatments, notably by the divinity school deans of Harvard[5] and Drew,[6] with the word "public" in their titles,

---

2. In my essay "On Not Being Ashamed of the Gospel: Particularity, Pluralism, and Validation" (*Faith and Philosophy* 9 [July 1992]: 285-300) and in "But We See Jesus" (*The Priestly Kingdom* [Notre Dame, Ind.: Notre Dame University Press, 1984], pp. 46-62), I critique further the odd a priori apologetic assumption that one's own group's language is necessarily inaccessible to others.

3. "In a pluralistic society it is both a tactical mistake and an error of principle to attempt to base controversial public policies on purely religious grounds." John Langan, S.J., criticizing a statement of Bishop Thomas Gumbleton about SALT II; *Commonweal*, 29 February 1980, p. 98.

4. I will return later to the difference of agenda which this difference between "common" and "public" may signal.

5. Ronald F. Thiemann, *Constructing a Public Theology* (Louisville: Westminster/Knox, 1991).

6. Robin Lovin, *Religion in American Public Life* (New York: Paulist, 1986); the difference between Lovin and Thiemann serves well to demonstrate how inadequately the adjective serves to define a distinct territory.

which would reward careful critique. I have myself spoken and written in the field, and respect it. Yet *for our present purposes* those "definitional" or "foundational" concerns are not as basic, or as helpful, as some would make them. They do not necessarily lead to important differences in the concrete prescriptive values which different parties will advocate in the public arena, nor to different strategies for different kinds of people to make sense to each other. Different academically formulated justifications for *why* we talk together in the common forum do not correlate closely with *what* we argue for.

As I began writing this paragraph in the summer of 1992, presidential candidate Pat Buchanan was speaking, very publicly, to the Republican National Convention in Houston about his neo-Protestant vision for America. His vision was at the same time utterly public and hopelessly narrow.[7] One of the knee-jerk responses of the counterelite, facing that power move, is to lunge the other way toward what some, especially in the universities, are now calling "political correctness." While differing profoundly about many if not all of the substantial ethical issues, these two opposing parties make quite parallel assumptions about how values work in the public arena. Their formal answers to the "methodology" questions cited above would be similar. To juxtapose Buchanan and politically correct academics is a backhanded way to say why I do not propose, in this lecture, to linger further with that set of questions.

Therefore I shall properly proceed, without proposing my own very best formal definition of the adjective "public" or of the substantive "public good," as those terms appear in the name of the agency which has convened us, or in the titles for our talks. I shall not try to be clear about how the "public" does or should differ from the adjective "common" or the substantive "common good," with which my friends "of the Roman obedience" at Notre Dame would address some of the same questions.[8] I shall abandon for present purposes the notion that ques-

---

7. As I prepare this text for the press four years later, the nationwide party conventions are again documenting how hopeless is any project of clarifying the field by imposing one definition of terms.

8. There are differences of nuance, as I already suggested. The Roman usage tends to be more clear than the Ivy League one about the expectation that the well-being of the whole will coincide with the praxis of catholic morality; i.e., that in specifying

tions of substance would be more easily handled if questions of form were resolved first.[9]

If We Do Not Begin from Scratch, Where Then Do We Begin?

The common historical baseline from which we come to this theme is the legacy of "Christendom," according to which the authority to speak of the public good belonged to the king, who had that role by divine right and graciously shared some of it with his noble cousins of the aristocracy, and some of it with his noble cousins in the clergy. That was the prevailing system from the fourth century to the nineteenth, although other perspectives began to break through the crust beginning in the fifteenth.

One other perspective, beginning as "Renaissance" and ripening as "Enlightenment," found a second claimant to the right to set the terms of the debate about the public good. In this setting an intellectual elite claims to have in hand a sure set of criteria of reasonableness, which everyone would recognize, if everyone had the same educational privileges. These enlightened elites sometimes compete with and sometimes share with the clergy in the privilege of being the arbiters of reality accredited by the king. In other, later settings the "enlightened" can even talk back to the king, constructing for that purpose alternative principles of validation whereby "nature" or "the people" can be construed as validating an antiroyal view. This is however still a variant of the "royal" approach, in that the way to obtain the validation awarded by "the people" was to lead them into the streets and seize power.

---

who is the community bearing that wider good, one takes for granted that they are our kind of people. For the catholic usage, "common" is the opposite of "selfish"; when the label "public" is preferred, the opposite is "parochial" or "provincial."

9. Note my critique of what I call "methodologism" in my contribution "Walk and Word: The Alternatives to Methodologism," in *Theology without Foundations*, ed. Stanley Hauerwas, Nancey Murphy, and Mark Nation (Nashville: Abingdon, 1994). One of the most pernicious forms of sophomorism is to think that "method" can be discussed and resolved for its own sake first, and that once you have done that you have the edge on your interlocutors. This is the rhetorical counterpart of grabbing the mike.

More or less parallel to "Renaissance" and then to "Enlightenment" in time, the stream we call "Reformation" and then "Puritanism" raised another set of counterclaims. These differences matter, because they are all part of our American legacy. No less rational than the Enlightenment, appealing no less to "the people" or to "nature," the Puritan critical stream however differed from Enlightenment at three points:

a. Puritan proclamation made a canonical claim. The Word of God, as active in salvation history and attested in the sacred Scriptures, was held by the Puritans to constitute a higher court, whereas Enlightenment expositions of the rational and the natural claimed autonomy on the human level. Whereas the Enlightenment call for intellectual liberty ascribed to every educated mind autonomy and the right to doubt, the Puritan case for the freedoms of speech and assembly appealed to the sovereignty of the Word of God.[10]

b. Puritan proclamation assumed a congregational structure (in both senses of the verb "to assume"). Independently of the king (or, in the most formative British period, of the queen), the freedoms of assembly, preaching, and the press to which Puritans laid claim brought forth an alternative social location and an original social shape for the truth-finding process. The continental Enlightenment had had its local meeting-places too, but those salons were elite. The Puritan public preaching place, which, as A. D. Lindsay and others have argued, prepared the seedbed for decentralizing viable political democracy, was the procedural corollary of the Puritan doctrine of the freedom of the Word of God.

c. Puritan proclamation was ecumenical in the sense of recognizing no provincial boundaries, relativizing the clan and the nation, and thereby the state. Puritan proclamation was evangelical in claiming the right to address its news to everyone, relativizing older established traditions without smashing them.

In almost every sentence of the above three-point characterization of Puritanism I could have added the modifier "public." The organic development from Huldrych Zwingli, Martin Bucer, and John

---

10. Cf. my discussion of the Puritan roots of democracy in "Response of an Amateur Historian and a Religious Citizen," *Journal of Law and Religion* 7, no. 2 (1989): 415-32.

Calvin, through the British Puritans, through Roger Williams and William Penn, all the way to Alexander Campbell had no secrets. It exempted no potential audience and privileged no elites. One of its mature fruits was the so-called Restoration Movement in frontier America, which had more to do than any other single stream of ministerial initiative with planting Christianity from the Alleghenies to the Rockies, and to which we owe the existence of our host institution, Christian Theological Seminary. In the details of their ecumenical, ethical, eschatological, and educational visions Alexander Campbell and his colleagues and successors of over a century ago would not want us to canonize or imitate them, nor would we want to. Yet their story does give the lie to the notion that the goods to which the radical free church tradition attended were anything but public.[11]

Today I propose to extrapolate from that Puritan posture by speaking in public about gospel values, without worrying about those perspectives from which their claims might be challenged.[12] I have chosen these particular specimens or episodes from our recent shared experience because they provoke and stand up to the test of publicity.

The Public Good in the Mind of Jesus

Sixty years ago, Helmut Richard Niebuhr gave a talk on "The Social Gospel and the Mind of Jesus," which has only recently been published. In it he contrasted his own reading of "the mind of Jesus" with that of

11. The radical free church movements from Williams through Penn to Garrison and Campbell contributed more than their share to concern for healthy political life, to the growth of education, and to the end of slavery. This long history refutes the notion that the type of community stance which the sociologist calls "sectarian" is without wider interest or impact.

12. To the John Langan quote above (n. 3) we should add James Gustafson, "The Sectarian Temptation: Reflections on Theology, the Church and the University," *Catholic Theology Society of America Proceedings* 40 (1985): 83-94. Gustafson's approach to ethical controversy is our generation's prime paradigm of methodologism. Once he has provided an overview of how divergent moral stances make sense, each in its own frame, he considers his work to be done. I respect this posture as having a place in the ecumenical arena and as a useful teaching style; I do not seek further to address it in this setting, since its a priori biases place it under different rules.

the Social Gospel of his time. Without sensing any need to document chapter and verse,[13] he confidently unfolded his own superior picture of the Jesus of the Gospel witness.[14] It interests the later ethicist that this "Jesus" is in significant ways different not only from the Jesus of the Social Gospel movement as a whole but also from the "Christ" of Niebuhr's own, later, famous *Christ and Culture*.

This Jesus, according to the Gospel, according to Niebuhr, had a fourfold strategy. He first called for:

a. repentance, which by conceding and anticipating the divine judgment on all human achievements "gives up the attempt to save the dying system." Such resignation is possible only thanks to

b. faith, which sees future deliverance beyond the judgment. This enables in turn

c. forgiveness and nonresistance, without which one self-elected instrument of divine vengeance merely succeeds another with no real change. The only authentically promising tactic, if a social strategy is to break the "ceaseless round of self-interests arousing self-interests,"[15] is

d. innocent suffering.[16]

13. *Journal of Religious Ethics* 16, no. 1 (spring 1988): 109ff. In none of the numerous books interpreting H. Richard Niebuhr's work have I found an assessment of how, in an age when Scripture scholarship was dominated by literary- and historical-critical deconstruction, an Ivy League ethicist could so sovereignly and self-confidently claim to have for the first time got Jesus right. His brother Reinhold had that same confidence. My reading of who Jesus was and what he meant is much like theirs, but I differ from them in assuming that I need to justify it by using the tools of historical reading.

14. Acknowledging that all readings of Jesus are relative and biased, Niebuhr does still argue that there was "an objective event in time, well documented." He adds four reasons to support his claim that his view of Jesus is more accurate than that of the nineteenth century, and four observations to support its current relevance.

15. This image of breaking the cycle of vengeance is much like Tolstoy's argument about resisting evil by evil; quite different from the way Niebuhr uses Tolstoy as a foil in his *Christ and Culture*. I offer a description and critique of *Christ and Culture* in Glen Stassen et al., *Authentic Transformation* (Nashville: Abingdon, 1996).

16. This reading of Jesus is structurally parallel to that of Tolstoy; this observation dramatizes how the Jesus of this paper is different from the "Christ" of his later *Christ and Culture*.

Niebuhr thus strikes at the heart of our ordinary understanding of social process. What matters for our present search is that Niebuhr describes this reading as a "strategy," not only a spirituality or a speculative theology or a theodicy (though it is also all of those), nor as a tactic that might or might not promise to be effective for getting institutionally from here to there.[17] He describes "the way things work" in social-process terms accessible to any observer. Nothing about this "strategy" is private or particular. If you had asked Jesus why this is the right strategy, he would (according to Niebuhr) have said, "acceptance of the kingdom of God." Yet that construal in faith terms is not needed for the strategy to be clear, to be true to the facts of the case, or to work.

Gospel Order as Paradigm

Karl Barth is often cited in this realm because of his whimsical pamphlet *Christian Community and Civil Community*,[18] to which I shall return. His was one of the first efforts, within mainstream European Protestantism, to come to grips with the notion that the civil community, no longer being defined by a shared faith, could not be addressed naively as if citizens were all believers. He was thus raising the question to which our discussion of "public" discourse attends. His first solution to the question thus raised was a notion of "analogy," which readers have uniformly judged to be (as used in this pamphlet) arbitrary and unconvincing. Barth had done better in his *Justification and Justice* (1938),[19] and then came back to the theme once more in *Church Dogmatics*, IV/2, page 719, the text to which I now direct your attention.

---

17. This was near the time when H. Richard Niebuhr got into his only public controversy with his brother Reinhold, about how seeing history from God's perspective makes it sometimes right to "do nothing" (i.e., to acknowledge that it may be all right sometimes to acknowledge that there is nothing one can do to fix the world).

18. Original, 1946; ET in *Against the Stream* (London: SCM Press, 1954), then in Will Herberg, ed., *Community, State, and Church: Three Essays by Karl Barth* (Garden City, N.Y.: Doubleday, Anchor Books, 1960), pp. 149-89.

19. ET under the misleading title *Church and State* (London: SCM Press, 1939), also in Herberg, pp. 110-48.

True Church law is exemplary [order]. . . . it is the pattern for the formation and administration of human law generally, and therefore the law of other political, economic, cultural and other human societies.

This sentence is Barth's title thesis for section 4, "The Order of the Community," under paragraph 67, "The Holy Spirit and the Up-building of the Christian Community."[20]

The calling of the people of God is thus no different from the calling of all humanity. The difference between the human community as a whole (*"Bürgergemeinde"*) and the faith community (*"Christengemeinde"*) is a matter of awareness or knowledge or commitment or celebration, but not of ultimate destiny. What believers are called to is no different from what all humanity is called to.[21] That Jesus Christ is Lord is a statement not about my inner piety or my intellect or ideas but about the cosmos. Thus the fact that the rest of the world does not yet see or know or acknowledge that destiny to which it is called is not a reason for us to posit or to broker some wider or thinner vision, some lower common denominator or halfway meeting point, in order to make the world's divine destination (Barth would say "determination," *Bestimmung*) more acceptable or more accessible. The challenge to the faith community should not be to dilute or filter or translate its witness, so that the "public" community can handle it without believing, but so to purify and clarify and exemplify it that the world can perceive it to be good news[22] without having to learn a foreign language.[23] The faith community

20. The word "law" for *Recht* in the translation by G. Bromiley is very misleading; "order" is usually better, and I shall continue to substitute it where it clarifies. Even worse is Bromiley's use of "canon law" for *Gemeinderecht*.

21. I first presented this description of Karl Barth's thought in a Stone Lecture at the invitation of Princeton Theological Seminary in January 1980. The series title was "New World on the Way." The lecture was unpublished until the appearance of some of it as "Why Ecclesiology Is Social Ethics," in my *The Royal Priesthood: Essays Ecclesiological and Ecumenical*, ed. Michael G. Cartwright (Grand Rapids: Eerdmans, 1994), pp. 103ff.

22. Cf. my article "On Not Being Ashamed of the Gospel" (n. 2 above). "Good news" is a kind of knowledge which is not known until one receives it, but then is received as good. The concept breaks through the ordinary epistemological dilemma between the particular and the general.

23. Jeffrey Stout addresses the problem of pluralism, within the metaphor of "languages," in his *Ethics after Babel* but does not exploit the full potential of the

can and must be to the world of men around it a reminder of the law of the kingdom of God already set up on earth in Jesus Christ, and a promise of its future manifestation. . . . it can and should show them that there is already on earth an order which is based on that great alteration of the human situation and directed toward its manifestation. . . . worldly law [order], in the form in which they regard it as binding, and outside which they believe that they cannot know any other . . . has already ceased to be the last word . . . ; there are other possibilities, not merely in heaven but on earth, not merely one day but already, than those to which [the world] thinks that it must confine itself.

If the community were to imagine that the reach of the sanctification of humanity accomplished in Jesus Christ were restricted to itself and the ingathering of believers, that it did not have corresponding effects *extra muros ecclesiae*, it would be in flat contradiction to its confession of its Lord.

Thus the alternative which Barth posits over against apologetic inverse solipsism is *confession*. To confess that Jesus Christ is Lord makes it inconceivable that there should be any realm where his writ would not run. That authority, however, is not coercive but nonviolent; it cannot be imposed, only offered. It cannot be excluded by being declared to be alien, or "private" or "personal" or "sectarian," but only by not (i.e., not yet) being heard.

Obviously in these paragraphs Barth is making a normative statement, not an empirical one. He does not say that the Reformed Church of the Canton of Basel City (legally a state church then and even today) or that of Basel Land or of Bern or Zürich is a model for the coming transformation of all humanity. He says this about the calling of the church of Jesus Christ. Yet he says it in such a way that the structures of those cantonal state churches are left without excuse for any point at which their actual order falls short of that of the gospel. Since the

---

metaphor. Real people in linguistically divided cultures do in fact communicate good and bad news, imperfectly but adequately, all the time. Cf. my "Meaning after Babble: With Jeffrey Stout beyond Relativism," *Journal of Religious Ethics* 24, no. 1 (spring 1996): 125-39, and "See How They Go with Their Face to the Sun," chapter 3 in the present collection.

(normative) order of the community of faith is by its very nature human, public, political, economic, and cultural, nothing about the empowering imperatives laid on it by the gospel can be declared less than fully relevant to the church of Basel or Bern, *or* to the city-states of Basel or Bern.

In his earlier pamphlet on the two levels of community Barth had proposed a laundry list of good civic ideas:

- Since God is known through incarnation, concrete human beings are more important than abstract causes.
- Since God justifies (i.e., affirms a framework of right), constitutional government is preferable to tyranny.
- Since the Son of Man came for the lost, we side with the weaker members of society.
- Since God's call frees us, the realms of family, education, art, science, religion, and culture should be safeguarded but not regulated by law.
- Since God calls us to solidarity, individual rights do not overrule responsibility for the whole.
- Since the church recognizes a diversity of gifts, government should affirm a separation of powers.
- Since the church lives from revelation, secrecy is to be condemned in politics.
- Since the disciple of Christ is a servant, rulers are bound to legitimacy.
- Since the church is ecumenical (catholic), the civil community should not be provincial.
- Since grace outlasts judgment, political violence must be only a last resort.[24]

Looking over this list as a whole, critics have all commented, often jokingly, on how miscellaneous it is, how little it demonstrates either Barth's wonted architectonic elegance or his prophetic critical edge. It is as if he had first made a list of standard liberal civic virtues (note that in German the same adjective says both "civic" and "bourgeois") and then looked for some theological counterpart for each of the main points.

24. Herberg, pp. 168ff.

Now in volume IV/2 of *Church Dogmatics* that makeshift appearance is gone. The faith community and the human community are connatural; each is human, historical, social. No apologetic bridge needs to be built from one to the other. No deductive derivation of concrete specifications from general theories or metaphors is needed. If and when and to the extent to which women and men order their common life in the light of Christ's lordship, they are already actualizing in, with, and under[25] ordinary human forms the sanctification of creaturely life. That action is public by nature, with no need for it to be translated or buffered or diluted. The *reason* for that action may not be transparent to those uninformed or misinformed about the witness of resurrection, ascension, and Pentecost, but that does not diminish its public accessibility or pertinence.

> The exemplary nature of Church law [order] cannot . . . be understood . . . in the sense of a law which has to be imposed upon the world. . . . But why not in the sense that it has to express the Gospel to the world in the form of its particular law? . . . the decisive contribution which the Christian community can make to the upbuilding and work and maintenance of the civil consists in the witness which it has to give to it and to all human societies in the form of the order of its own upbuilding and constitution. . . . in the form in which it exists among them it can and must be to the world . . . around it a reminder of the law of the kingdom of God already set up on earth in Jesus Christ, and a promise of its future manifestation. . . . it should demonstrate . . . that there are other possibilities, not only on heaven but on earth, not merely one day but already, than those to which [the world] thinks it must confine itself. (p. 721)

This should suffice (though Barth goes on for pages more) to state the confessional and christological logic of the claim that *the order of the faith community constitutes a public offer to the entire society.* As to its quality, Barth in this passage suggests six characteristics of the faith community, six ways in which it may be exemplary. It is not that first we set about being a proper church and then in a later move go about deciding to care prophetically for the rest of the world. To participate

25. This sequence of three prepositions, which many readers think was given currency by Bonhoeffer, goes back in fact to classical Lutheran dogma on the sacraments.

in the transforming process of becoming the faith community *is itself* to speak the prophetic word, *is itself* the beginning of the transformation of the cosmos. Each of these qualities is a public demonstration of the community to which we are all called:

- Being good news, it is not based upon merit and duty; a grace-driven order of servanthood transcends "the hampering dialectic of fulfillment and claim, dignity and responsibility, taking and giving."
- The qualification to be the subject or actor of divine ordering is not a natural entitlement nor a positive legal authority but the grace of Jesus Christ, inexplicable, not subject to the "merry-go-round" of legal validation games.
- Its authority is not coercion but trust, which is "the law within law."
- Its members commit themselves totally, contributing the wholeness of what worldly powers cannot command.
- Every member is seen as a person, a brother or sister, and as equal, regardless of status, capacity, qualification. . . .
- Church law may be a model in that it is "living": flexible and fluid, "continuously flowing from the worse to the better."

The implication of this exemplarity, by contrast with the way the civil order regularly runs, is obvious. These six specimen dimensions of exemplarity are not a template for remaking the world, yet each of them strikes redemptively at one of the perennial, oppressive characteristics of our public life. It becomes evident all along this exposition how little it would help if we were to seek to filter these affirmations through the grid of an a priori distinction between the "public" world and some other world.

The same is true of the previous section where Barth had written that church order is "liturgical," i.e., that it celebrates and remembers the particular history of Jesus Christ. None of the qualities of this order is esoteric or mystical, subjective or arbitrary, private or sectarian. None of them needs to be a priori inhibited or apologetic[26] out of the fear that the

---

26. Obviously those for whom the term "apologetic" can be used only in a favorable sense will not concede the power of the reflexive solipsism to which I here allude. Yet their tendency to speak as if fidelity and relevance were alternatives, in a null-sum trade-off where more of one is assumed to mean less of the other, betrays that that assumption is still latent.

neighbors might not understand or might feel left out. Not whether the message is for all humankind is the question, but what the message is.

It is thus of questionable utility to concentrate on the *formal* question, "How can the church communicate in the world?" When we ask the question that way, we should not be surprised that we are left with an agenda of things to say which will be very broad, and which our listeners already know. Most of the things needing to be said will be ordinary, not very surprising.

Between H. Richard Niebuhr's list of four marks and Karl Barth's of six, let me close with my own list of five. This list differs from the others in that it is derived straightforwardly, inductively, from the experience of the first Christians, and in that it makes still more evident the unity between message and medium. I repeat here, with apologies for not being more original, the gist of a description I shared in *Theology Today* a while back.[27]

a. According to the witness of Galatians and Ephesians, baptism proclaims an order in which Jew and Gentile, male and female, slave and free have been reconciled not by being homogenized but by accepting one another. Founded in a Gospel truth, this message reaches beyond the church. This is the early Christian root of egalitarianism. Contrasted with Jeffersonian deist humanism, which claims (against the evidence) that all men's being created equal is self-evident, the breaking down of the real wall between communities and cultures by virtue of the real death of the cross is a far more powerful ground for relativizing ethnic differences (without denying or abolishing them). This trans-ethnic inclusivism, with its impact on worship forms and dietary disciplines, may well have been more weighty in bringing about the ultimate divergence of the messianic and nonmessianic strands within the Judaism of the second and third centuries than were differences about doctrines like Christology or hope.[28] The equal dignity of both kinds of

---

27. "Sacrament as Social Ethic," *Theology Today* 48 (April 1991): 33-44, since included in my *The Royal Priesthood*, pp. 360ff. I also presented the same themes in a fuller, more popular form in my *Body Politics* (Nashville: Discipleship Resources Press, 1992).

28. Rosemary Radford Reuther has argued that what estranged the nonmessianic Jews was the Christians' Christology; Louis Martyn hypothesizes that the insertion of the *birkat ha-minim* in the daily prayer was a way for Jews to excommunicate Christians from the synagogues already during the first century. Both hypotheses have been widely echoed; neither of these simple answers is historically sustainable.

people, those with and those without the heritage of Torah, was affirmed not on the grounds of the possession by both of certain virtues, but on the grounds of the cross.

Our world still needs to learn that the reason every person and every kind of person must be seen with equal respect is not that their culture is equally healthy, or that they have earned equal treatment, but that equal dignity is ascribed by virtue of a divine bias in favor of the Other.

b. Jesus directed his followers to forgive one another as God had forgiven them. He even told them how to do it, instructing them in procedural detail. Forgiveness was a person-to-person process, not a priestly prerogative. The same procedure was renewed in movements of reform and community over the centuries. In the sixteenth century Martin Luther, Martin Bucer, and the so-called Anabaptists designated this process as "the rule of Christ." Thus it was not peculiar to one stream of the Reformation.[29] What authorizes it in the Gospel account is the presence of the Spirit of Christ; whom the community forgives, God has forgiven.

Although this way of describing and validating forgiveness is from the Gospel, the need is not limited to any faith setting. As Hannah Arendt wrote of *The Human Condition:*

> Without being forgiven, released from the consequences of what we have done, our capacity to act would, as it were, be confined to a single deed from which we could never recover; we would remain the victims of its consequences forever.[30]

Arendt expressly sets aside the rejoinder: "but is this not a particular, religiously founded possibility, untranslatable to the public realm?" She answers:

> The discoverer of the role of forgiveness was Jesus of Nazareth.[31] The fact that he made this discovery in a religious context and articulated

29. Cf. my study guide to the "Rule of Christ," in *The Royal Priesthood*, pp. 323ff., as well as "The Hermeneutics of the Anabaptists," in *Essays on Biblical Interpretation*, ed. Willard Swartley (Elkhart, Ind.: Institute of Mennonite Studies, 1984), pp. 24ff.

30. Hannah Arendt, *The Human Condition* (Chicago: University of Chicago Press, 1958), p. 237.

31. I do not propose to adjudicate the historical accuracy of the claim, which Arendt shares with H. R. Niebuhr (above), that Jesus' message of forgiveness was original.

it in religious language is no reason to take it any less seriously in a strictly secular sense.[32]

Arendt goes on for a page to elucidate how "our tradition of political thought" selects resources from all kinds of settings, "even though they have been neglected because of their allegedly exclusively religious nature."

No economy can survive without Chapter Eleven; no prison system is viable without parole. No moral culture works without making scapegoats and celebrating rituals of exculpation. Social scientists call it conflict management. Yet forgiveness remains costly, since the first reflex of the self-righteous is to fear that to forgive would be to cheapen sin.[33] Four years ago one presidential candidate suggested that the country should become kinder and gentler; yet (the day I first drafted this paragraph candidate Bill Clinton was speaking at Notre Dame) neither party which wants to rule us is making a case for forgiveness as policy.[34]

c. The early Christians ate together. When the practical problems of serving all the members became visible, the Jerusalem church called new leaders from the less-served part of their membership. When the church at Corinth began to segregate two dining groups, the apostle Paul wrote them that for thus failing to "discern the Lord's body" they would be eating condemnation to themselves. Over time, this eucharis-

32. Arendt, p. 238. Arendt thus has paraphrased here the rejection of what philosophers call "the genetic fallacy." The truth of an insight is not dependent on who found it first. Arendt thus sweeps away dozens of pages of apologetic worrying by Christians about how we might have to dilute our message in order to get the "public" world to listen to us. It is fascinating to observe a secular Jewish philosopher thus sweeping away the "sect/world" disjunction from the other side. One could also cite René Girard on the fundamental meaning of forgiveness.

33. Since the present lecture was presented, Donald W. Shriver Jr., *An Ethic for Enemies: Forgiveness in Politics* (Oxford: Oxford University Press, 1995), has drawn additional attention to the topic. Supportive responses to Shriver by Drew Christiansen, S.J., and J. Bryan Hehir appear in the *Woodstock Report* 46 (March 1995): 9ff. Gregory Jones, *Embodying Forgiveness: A Theological Analysis* (Grand Rapids: Eerdmans, 1995), has also enriched the conversation.

34. The United States in recent years is in fact spiraling headlong in a direction opposite from the rest of the developed world, toward punishment, including escalating use of the death penalty, as social panacea.

tic meal evolved into something less like a meal, but originally, formally, it was indistinguishable from the ordinary Jewish household's regularly, prayerfully eating together. That "there should be no poor among them" had already been YHWH's vision for the Hebrews.[35] This is what Luke's account tells us was fulfilled at Jerusalem, as a model to the world.

Eucharist, thus substantially and historically, functionally understood, is the paradigm for every other mode of inviting the outsider and the underdog to the table, whether we call that the epistemological privilege of the oppressed or cooperation or equal opportunity or socialism.[36] To make such sharing seem natural, it helps to have gone through an exodus or a Pentecost together, but neither the substance nor the pertinence of the vision is dependent on a particular faith.

d. As the early Christians met for worship, all of them were free to take the floor. The more talkative were told to listen, and the more timid were encouraged to speak out.[37] The only mandatory guidelines were procedural, so that all might be heard. Though that liberty was understood as the working of the Spirit of Christ, its shape was the same as what a truly open Parliament, therapy community session, committee of the whole, or town meeting attempts to be. From this original Christian vision have come the stronger strands of what we call "democracy," a vision which does not say that "the people" are always right, or that a majority is, but only that decisions will be better and community more whole if all can speak.

The Puritans who first said this about the way the church assembly should work were, as I said, by 1600, saying it as well to the crown, namely, to Queen Elizabeth, or to what we today call "the state." To call for that freedom is not the result of an idealistic vision of every individual's wisdom or creativity, but of a realistic vision of the objec-

35. Deuteronomy 15:3. Andreas Bodenstein von Carlstadt, Martin Luther's teacher, used the phrase "That there should be no beggars," his translation of this text, as title for what might be called the first treatise on social justice of the Reformation (1522). Cf. E. J. Furcha, ed., *The Essential Carlstadt* (Scottdale, Pa.: Herald, 1995), pp. 120ff.

36. More fully described in my *Body Politics*, pp. 20ff. Similar perspectives on the economic dimension of the Eucharist have been expressed by Tissa Balasuriya, Monika Hellwig, and numerous others.

37. 1 Corinthians 14:26-40.

tivity and dignity of the truth, which will best make itself known if no human controls the meeting.

e. The same Spirit which gives every individual the right to the floor also qualifies every individual for his or her own role or service in the body. For the apostle Paul, who compared the faith community to the human body, no individual's role is replaceable, and none is in its own place less worthy than the next. Not only does this vision undercut hierarchy; it calls for compensatory measures to give more honor to the less esteemed members. What the factory system calls "the division of labor" is less than that, though it is a step in the right direction.

In a culture where the star system has been enormously aggravated by the media, as by the Fortune 500, as by civil politics, we need to rediscover the ways in which the individual, the local, the ordinary can be validated. A corporate executive or a television anchorperson, or a widely read author, is not worth more, is not less replaceable, than the man or woman in the street.

Summary

So by my count there are five sample civil imperatives within the vision of the first Christians:

- egalitarianism as implied by baptism into one body,
- socialism as implied in the Eucharist,
- forgiveness,
- the open meeting, and
- the universality of giftedness.

If we were to settle down together to work at the common life of our town or our country, each of my five marks of the healthy corporate life would give us plenty to do, as would the earlier suggestions from Niebuhr and Barth.

If on the other hand our concern is the a priori methodological worry about whether the faith community has anything to say to the wider world, or any right to say it, I trust that the samples should suffice to show that the question was wrongly posed. When Jeremiah told the exiles in Babylonia to "seek the shalom of that city where I have sent you," there was never reason for debate about whether that shalom was knowable to the Babylonians, or about whether it was relevant. The need was for the Jewish exiles themselves to believe that that was their mission. When Jonah was told to go to Nineveh, his reason for going the other way was not the fear that his particular Hebraic worldview would seem sectarian or esoteric to the Ninevites, but rather the fear that they might hear and be saved, which is what we are told did happen.[38]

After having accentuated the breadth of applicability of the faith community's being connatural with the wider society, as a result of which the church's clearest word to the world is inseparable from the church's own integrity, we do well to take account of the challenge of one point at which it has been held that this claim is the least credible, namely, "the word of the cross." I hardly need to educate this audience concerning the place of the cross in Christian testimony, especially in settings of renewal and judgment, from Paul through the mystics to Luther to Kierkegaard to Jürgen Moltmann,[39] to Arthur MacGill[40] and Douglas John Hall.[41] Is this not one point, you will ask, where the *specifically* Christian message is opaque to the outsider? Does not our culture's univocal commitment to power as the essence of human dignity, and to empowerment as the cure for indignity, set aside the possibility that a statement like the one Paul said he had heard from God, "my power is made perfect in weakness" (2 Cor. 12:9, RSV), could ever be even understood, to say nothing of being accepted?

I shall make no attempt in the last few lines of this presentation to *argue* the point. Yet I can at least, and must, affirm it. The notion that "power" is univocal and unilinear is one of the mythical dimensions of modernity. That myth has served us (or we have served it) for some generations, but it is increasingly refuting itself as our economy bumps

38. The above sentence is not about the historicity of the events in the Jonah account, but about the worldview the narrative assumes. There was no doubt about whether the Gentiles could understand what the prophet would say.

39. *The Crucified God* (New York: Harper, 1974).

40. *Suffering: A Test of Theological Method* (Philadelphia: Geneva Press, 1968; Philadelphia: Westminster, 1982).

41. *Lighten Our Darkness: Toward an Indigenous Theology of the Cross* (Philadelphia: Westminster, 1976); *God and Human Suffering: An Exercise in the Theology of the Cross* (Minneapolis: Augsburg, 1986).

up against the ceiling of our physically finite globe, and as our most powerful weapons become radioactive junk. The very notion of the modern nation is falling apart from Azerbaijan to Mogadishu to Sarajevo to Rostock to Cuzco. The Pauline vision according to which the "powers" which frame our lives are at one and the same time *both* creatures of God for our good *and* oppressors is increasingly seen to describe reality more adequately than the univocality myth, as we are being told by the likes of William Stringfellow and Jacques Ellul.[42]

That power is weak and weakness strong is no poetic paradox; it is a fact of life. What recent ecumenical thought calls "the epistemological privilege of the poor," what comparable Roman Catholic texts call God's "preferential option for the poor," what Tolstoy meant much earlier when he said that the oppressed are the bearers of the meaning of history, is not poetry but serious social science.

When Paul wrote that the word of the cross is weak to those who look for signs, but God's saving power to those who believe, he was promoting not otherworldly mysticism but the kind of political reality which brought down Bull Connor in 1963, Ferdinand Marcos in 1986, and Erich Honecker in 1989. I don't know what particular regime Arthur Cleveland Coxe was thinking about when in a hymn he penned the question, "O where are kings and empires now of old that went and came?" That question was part of the Pauline/Lutheran point. The rest of the hymn was less fitting, as Coxe went on to describe the church as unshaken and immovable. The point is rather that the church's being shaken and moved, being vulnerable, defines or constitutes its participation in the travail of the Lamb who was slain and is therefore worthy to receive power and wealth and wisdom and might and honor and glory and blessing. That suffering is powerful, and that weakness wins, is true not only in heaven but on earth. That is a statement about the destiny not only of the faith community but also of all creation.

Perceptive listeners already well oriented in the "standard" debate whose terms I am challenging here may have noted that in this lecture I have not made an issue for its own sake of the ethics of violence, a theme I have written about elsewhere. The omission is intentional. The

---

42. Hendrik Berkhof, *Christ and the Powers,* summarized in my *The Politics of Jesus,* 2d ed. (Grand Rapids: Eerdmans, 1994), pp. 134ff., further elaborated in several volumes by Walter Wink.

notion that the *focal* or *primary* reason for tensions between the faith community and other communities is a difference between "radicals" and "establishment" in their views about the moral legitimacy of state violence is a widespread assumption in theological ethics, but it is also deeply misleading. Most of what a public order does is not violent. Most of the ways an unbeliever will reject the values which the Christian espouses are not ways to kill. The readiness of our civil societies to kill is not the worst characteristic of unbelief, nor the most definitional one. Most of the reasons for Christians not to feel free to behave in the world according to its own rules are not the fear of shedding blood. Rather than elaborate in this chapter the argument against making the "sword" the essential definition of the public order,[43] I have preferred to let the demonstration be tacit.

Thus it is that to participate in the work of Christ can be described in the first vision of John not only as "serving God (what priests do)" but also as "ruling the world (what kings do)."[44] Described indifferently as "royal priesthood" and as "priestly kingdom," believers together are not called out of but sent into the real (public) world where sacrifice and sovereignty happen.

43. I have made that point more than once elsewhere, especially in challenging the widespread use of the Reformed/Anabaptist polar typology: "Reformed versus Anabaptist Strategies," *TSF (Theological Students' Fellowship) News and Reviews* 3 (February 1980): 4-7. See also *Authentic Transformation*, pp. 55ff., where I demonstrate the confusion resulting from its misuse by H. Richard Niebuhr.

44. Cf. my lecture "To Serve Our God and Rule the World," presented to the Society of Christian Ethics in 1988, reprinted in my *The Royal Priesthood*, pp. 127-40. This stance is powerfully communicated by the last book of our Bible, but it should not be thought that Christians came only late in the first century to seeing things that way. It had been the normative Jewish world vision since Jeremiah; cf. below pp. 41-42 and 55-60.

CHAPTER 2

The New Humanity
as Pulpit and Paradigm

Our theme this evening[1] lies at a point where at least three different fields of interest overlap.

The first area, the one signaled by the name of our host institution, is what in recent decades has come to be called "ecumenism." Instead of simply going about the rest of our mission as Christians, and doing as much of it as possible together with fellow Christians, we have learned to ask more pointedly about the dividedness of the churches and their reconciliation, as a topic for its own sake. What should be our understanding, theologically and practically, of our institutional dividedness, and what should be our vision for the unity of the church?

The second theme area is a favorite topic of debate in our day. How can or should the integrity of the faith community, as a body with its own mission, be related to the concerns and needs of the rest of society? Depending on the subtopic, this may be called "mission" or "prophecy" or "social ethics." For some, the only task of Christian faithfulness is to make "public" sense. For others that should be the last

1. Presented as the annual Dunning Memorial Lecture of the Ecumenical Institute, St. Mary's Seminary and University, Baltimore, 14 November 1994. Although the supporting agency is completely Roman Catholic, the program of the Ecumenical Institute is thoroughly ecumenical. Its dean who invited me, Dr. Michael Gorman, is a United Methodist minister.

of our worries. We are at best pilgrims and strangers, they protest, tolerated aliens in a world that does not listen to us. We have learned that the worst moral sellout is to enter an alliance with the dominant political and economic powers of the world, as Christians have been doing ever since the fourth century. This debate has to do not only with ethics but also with what we call epistemology, namely, the problem of knowledge; is the "truth" of what we say about God and the world supposed to be comprehensible to our non-Christian neighbors? convincing to them? Should the stances Christians take in public be run through the grid of whether average people outside the churches will respect them?

Moving now to the content of ethics, there is yet a third standard, formal question. Are there any normative guides, identifiable as Christian, for the shape of our faithfulness, or do we only do the best we can with the same insights everyone else has access to? Books and papers proliferate arguing that the Catholic position, or the only position which is credible on this subject in our contemporary pluralistic culture, is that there is no specific Christian ethic. Some even argue that that conviction — namely, that there is no specifically Christian ethic — is a specifically Christian (or specifically Catholic) truth.

This third question can be tested by opening a fourth; namely, by asking about the *substance* of moral discernment. Is there any moral imperative which belongs to the Christian gospel in a constitutive way? Is there any imperative which is "more than moral" because it has to do not merely with right and wrong behavior, or not merely with right and wrong reasons for behavior's being right or wrong, but with being Christian?

Each of these four questions has been become quasi-classical; the opposing views are standardized. Each is made narrower by the focus on the other. Each figures in a standard course on ethical method. For each of these four themes we could proceed, as a graduate seminar would, by a survey of the literature or the major writers, and an analysis of the several contesting arguments, which most of you would recognize. But don't worry; I don't propose to give you that course. I think I have said enough to show the pertinence and the familiarity of the issues. For this evening, however, I propose to begin from the other end, namely, at the beginning, with a simple reading of a few representative apostolic texts, and then to ask how their vision might free us from some of the above dilemmas.

The first is from the second letter to the Corinthians:[2]

Ethnic standards have ceased to count in my estimate of a person; even though I once regarded Christ "according to the flesh," I regard him thus no longer. If one is "in Christ," there is a new world. The old order has gone and a new world has begun.[3]

What the New English Bible rightly translates as "a new world," meaning a new stream of history under newly defined conditions, whereby ethnicity is no longer important, has for centuries been wrongly read as "he is a new creature," taken as meaning a renewed individual. The evangelical paraphrase *The Living Bible* accentuates the subjectivity even more. It renders: "When someone becomes a Christian he becomes a brand new person *inside*."

There is in the Greek no grounds for rendering the original term *ktisis* "creation," as meaning an individual, to say nothing of adding the subjectifying adverb "inside." Paul's argument is about why the congregations he founded and guided were bicultural.

The term "new humanity" in my title comes from our second text, in Ephesians:

He is himself our peace. Gentiles and Jews, he has made the two one, and in his own body of flesh and blood has broken down the enmity which stood like a dividing wall between them . . . so as to create out of the two a single new humanity in himself, thereby making peace.[4]

The Greek is translated as "one new man" in the older English versions, but even with that the allusions of the rest of the text to the reconciling of two streams of history and culture do not permit the individualistic distortion which the Corinthians passage has suffered. "One new humanity" is the right translation. There were two histories,

---

2. I have offered a thorough exposition of the literary, grammatical basis for the following understanding and its moral impact, in my "The Apostle's Apology Revisited," in *The New Way of Jesus*, ed. William Klassen (Newton, Kans.: Faith and Life Press, 1980), pp. 115-34.

3. 2 Corinthians 5:16-17.

4. Ephesians 2:14f., NEB.

two cultures, one with law and one without, one with promises and one without. Now the death of Christ has torn down the wall between them, creating a new bicultural history. A few verses later Paul calls this event "my mystery." He claims revelatory authority for the event in church-planting history into which he had been drawn without his intending it.

The third brief apostolic anchor for my commentary is from Peter's first letter:

> You are a chosen race, a royal priesthood, a holy nation, God's own people, that you may declare the wonderful deeds of him who called you out of darkness into his marvelous light. Once you were no people but now you are God's people; once you had not received mercy but now you have received mercy.[5]

The "exiles in the dispersion" to whom this letter was addressed will have recognized in these words a midrash on Hosea. "Not my people" and "no mercy" were the names Hosea gave to the children born to his unfaithful wife. Hosea's fractured marriage was an enacted prophetic parable, dramatizing the lostness of God's disloyal people and the promise of restoration. The phrases "royal priesthood" and "holy nation" are drawn from God's speech to Moses in Exodus 19. Each of the four nouns designates a collectivity: chosen *race,* royal *priesthood,* holy *nation,* God's own *people,* while each of the adjectives denotes distinctiveness. This distinctiveness is not something that the addressees have merited, but a gift of grace. It is a privilege, but its purpose is not that its beneficiaries should enjoy it for themselves, but rather that, by the very fact of being what they are, they should *"declare the wonderful deeds of him who called you."* This is quite similar to the way the prologue to the Sermon on the Mount had introduced its radicalizing the obedience of the law by saying that it would proclaim something: "Let your light shine in the sight of [everyone] so that, seeing your good works, they may give glory to your Father in heaven."[6]

---

5. 1 Peter 2:9f., RSV.

6. Matthew 5:16, RSV. I exposit further the meaning of ethics as proclamation in "The Political Axioms of the Sermon on the Mount," in my *The Original Revolution* (Scottdale, Pa.: Herald, 1971), especially pp. 41f., and in *Nevertheless: The Varieties of Religious Pacifism,* 2d ed. (Scottdale, Pa.: Herald, 1992), pp. 62ff.

To summarize: without our needing to read any of these texts closely, their common testimony, from several strands of the apostolic canon, is very clear. Ethics is more than ethics. Actions proclaim. The new peoplehood constituted by the grace to which the readers of these texts had responded is *by its very existence* a message to the surrounding world. The medium and the message are inseparable. *What* God is doing is bringing into existence a new historic reality, a community constituted by the flowing together of two histories, one with the law and one without. *How* God is doing it is not distinguishable from *what* God is doing, and *how the world can know* about it is again the same thing.

That is what my announced title means by saying that the "new humanity" is a "pulpit." Just being, just being there as an unprecedented social phenomenon in which persons from two contrasting, even conflicting histories rejoice in their being reconciled, is the necessary but also sufficient condition of being able to invite the rest of the world into the new history.

Our primary concern this evening is not for the philosophical presuppositions of moral discourse, but if we do not attend at least briefly to some such matters, they can trip us up later. Let me then remind you that for many academics there is still a wall of separation between the particular meanings of a faith stance, which they call "sectarian," and the "public" accountability which respects the values of other communities.

All of these texts demonstrate that that classic dilemma is a wrongly posed question. One can only put the question that way *if* one has already chosen a particular stance based on denying the message of these texts. Ever since YHWH of Hosts, God of Israel, spoke through Jeremiah to the people in the dispersion at Babylon, instructing them to "seek the peace of the city where I have scattered you," it has been the wrong question. Having a particular identity and making sense to one's neighbors, serving their well-being, are not disjunctive alternatives. In fact there is no reason to want to make sense to your neighbors if you have no identity worth sharing with them. And for monotheists, vice versa is also true; there is no reason to have a particular identity if it is not to be shared with others. The life of diaspora Jewry from Jeremiah to the time of Jesus (and since) was characterized more than we usually remember by its public visibility; synagogue life was observable. In contrast to the Eastern temple cults and mystery religions,

Jewish life had no secrets. God-fearing Gentiles could observe and understand what was going on when Jews gathered around their Torah, and many Gentiles were in fact attracted by it. Jews earned their livings providing services to the Gentile economies, sometimes to landlords and rulers. Their cosmopolitan connections made them the best cross-cultural translators, scribes, accountants, educators, and compilers of proverbs. Far from being self-contained, they were at home in a world wider than the provincial cultures of Egypt, Mesopotamia, Greece, or Rome.[7]

Most of our contemporary epistemologically preoccupied thinkers, who worry about making reasonable sense to their unbelieving or otherwise-believing neighbors, would certainly deny that they hold any anti-Judaic bias. Yet it is clear that in setting up their sense of what would count as cross-cultural sense making, they are quite un-Jewish. Their grid cannot do justice to the way in which a particular faith-defined community (or, if you wish, a particular community-defined faith) has across the centuries been demonstrably larger and not smaller than the local "publics" among which it was dispersed, whether that be the Jews in Babylon in the age of Jeremiah and Ezekiel, or in Rome or Spain or Asia Minor in the age of Paul, or in Alexandria or Marseille in the age of Constantine, or in Moscow in the age of Lenin, or in New York or Los Angeles today.

What two and a half millennia of Jewish history have demonstrated prototypically, shorter stretches of experience have exemplified again in the history of the several particular faith communities in America, be they Roman Catholic or Quaker or secularist. Only a believing community with a "thick" particular identity has something to say to whatever "public" is "out there" to address. And to repeat the vice versa from before, only the community which welcomes the challenge of public witness can justify (not merely to outsiders but also to its own children) its distinctive existence.

My metaphor of "pulpit" or "pedestal" expresses the functional necessity of just being there with a particular identity. If there had not been a critical mass of Quakers in early Pennsylvania, living out a nonviolent, dialogical lifestyle, the uniqueness of that colony in contrast

---

7. This theme is developed much more fully in the next chapter, "See How They Go with Their Face to the Sun."

to the others, with regard to religious liberty, democracy, respect for the Indians, and early challenging of slavery, could not have happened. Something similar would be true of the place of Roman Catholics in early Maryland. Had there not been Catholic Worker houses since the 1930s, there could not have been a Catholic peace witness in the 1970s. Had there not been solid black Baptist and Methodist churches and colleges in the South for generations, there would not have been an effective civil rights movement beginning in the 1950s. The faith community whose vision of what they stand for is strong enough that whether they stand by it does not depend on short-range applause or success is the necessary condition for the wider witness. A moral insight which cannot survive when held to *against the stream* by tolerated but disadvantaged aliens is not worthy to be proclaimed to the public.

The second metaphor in my title is "paradigm." This points to the awareness that the way most communication works is not by projecting and then reassembling a maximum number of atoms of information, nor of axioms and maxims, but by pattern recognition. This is prototypically illustrated by five parallel phenomena which are all part of our common apostolic heritage. I last gathered them in my pamphlet *Body Politics,*[8] but none of them is my discovery. I begin by itemizing all five without much detail. They could be listed in any order, and there could very well be a sixth or seventh.

1. The Jesus of Matthew's account twice uses the verbs "to bind" and "to loose" to denote a function which he wanted his followers to discharge in his name. It means both to forgive (or to withhold forgiveness) and to make moral decisions. It is to be done by means of person-to-person encounter, with a reconciling intention, and with Christ's own authority behind it. This model has been taken seriously in the Rule of Benedict, and in the reformations called Anabaptist[9] and Quaker and Methodist. If decision making

8. I should perhaps apologize for citing myself at this point, but there is nothing idiosyncratic about the classical themes I selected. *Body Politics* (Nashville: Discipleship Resources Press, 1992).

9. Although the so-called Anabaptists of the sixteenth century made much of what they called "the rule of Christ," they had not invented either the term or the idea. They shared the idea, and the actual word usage, with Martin Luther and with Martin Bucer, Calvin's teacher.

through reconciling dialogue is the way for the people of God to define the ongoing meaning of their peoplehood, it is also the model for the ways a wider society should make decisions and resolve conflict. In our time "conflict resolution" and "mediation" have become a part of the disciplines of sociology and psychology for interpersonal and intergroup relations; the rules are the same.

2. Jesus' disciples formed a small commune around him during his lifetime, and when after his ascension they solidified that pattern of eating together, they considered it the right way both to *remember* his death and his resurrection appearances and to *affirm their hope* of his return. Our history of centuries of speculation and controversy about what happens to bread and wine when a certain special person speaks certain special Latin words over them obscured from our memory for a long time the fact that the *primary* meaning of the eucharistic gathering in the Gospels and Acts is economic. It was the fulfillment of the promise of the Magnificat that the rich would give up their advantages and the poor would be well fed. Luke's report probably is intended to signal the fulfillment of the mandate of Deuteronomy (15:4) that "there should be no poor among you" (NIV).

   It was in order to manage this primeval socialism that the Jerusalem church first expanded its leadership to include non-Palestinian leaders, the first step (according to Acts) toward the opening to the Gentiles. In recent years various theologians have set about retrieving the paradigmatic power of the Eucharist as the grounds for the preferential option for the poor. At the Lord's Table, those who have bread bring it, and all are fed; that is the model for the Christian social vision in all times and places.

3. The term "new humanity" with which we began, or the phrase "new creation" which has the same meaning in other epistles, means as we saw that Jewishness and Gentileness have flowed together in one new cultural history of salvation. But when we began I did not point out that the literary and liturgical settings in which we find these terms embedded have to do with baptism. To be "in Christ" through baptism means to have entered this new history. Interethnic reconciliation is a part of redemption. It is not a social idealism supported by an appeal to creation or reason. It is the result of the cross.

Enlightenment humanism tells a different story. According to an ancient American document, as you well know, we are supposed to hold it to be a self-evident truth that all "men" are equal by creation. We could of course dwell on more than one shortcoming of that revolutionary vision. "All men," when that declaration was trumpeted across the Atlantic in 1776, did not include women or black or red men or poor men. Nor is the *notion* of creation endowing creatures with rights self-evident. But the more fundamental error is that people are *in fact* not equal by creation. Every well-established understanding of creation in the roots of our culture has seen it as explaining not how we are the same but how we are different. Slaveholders in the antebellum South of this country, Afrikaners in the Republic of South Africa, and Ian Paisley in Belfast have all rooted their ethnic separatism in a doctrine of creation. A psychologist and a social theorist have just in recent weeks sparked a new firestorm by saying it again about IQ and earning power.[10]

According to the apostolic witness, interethnic harmony is a work not of creation but of redemption. To make anyone believe in the equal *dignity* of all humans God must intervene. It took the cross to break down the wall. In the movements of Gandhi and King it took freely chosen, innocent suffering to renew in our century the possibility of reconciliation between peoples.

4. The "Paul" of Ephesians used the term "fullness of Christ" to describe the unique social pattern which he called his readers to actualize in their common life. The earlier Paul of Romans 12 and 1 Corinthians 12 had made the same point with other language. Every person in the community has been given by the Spirit a distinctive portion of grace which consists in a role in the community. That role can and should be named, so that the individual can be challenged to fulfill it well, and so that the community can rejoice in it and monitor its functioning. Every member of the body has a role; no role is more central than any other, and the least-honored roles should be most affirmed.[11] The relapse of early

10. Charles Murray and Richard Herrnstein, *The Bell Curve: Intelligence and Class Structure in American Life* (New York: Free Press, 1995).

11. Cf. my *The Fullness of Christ* (Elgin, Ill.: Brethren Press, 1987).

Christianity into sacerdotal patriarchy led to the loss of this vision as a way of realistically sharing the roles of members in a community, but it has occasionally resurfaced in visions of shared ministry. Today in fact this vision is more widely operative in the rest of society than in the traditional churches, as the division of labor has enabled the culture of the university or the factory or the city.

5. The guidance Paul sent to the Corinthians about how to hold a meeting in the power of the Spirit prescribed that all present should be free to take the floor. The only authority role in the meeting would be a moderator to make sure that all get that opportunity, that they speak in turn, and that anyone speaking in another tongue be translated. In radical Protestantism, especially in Quakerism, this vision was retrieved and implemented with great creativity and thoroughness. Especially since the Puritan reformation it has reached out powerfully into the wider society in the form of town meeting democracy and the imperative of the freedoms of assembly, speech, and the press. As I needed to say before concerning interethnic reconciliation, the basis for this freedom is not in the nature of things as they already are by nature or by creation, but in the divine intervention which we call the work of reconciliation, which ascribes status to the underdog and the outsider, loosens tongues and opens ears. That everyone who has something to say gets a hearing is not a "given," the way things are; it is a gift which the community is enabled by the power of the Spirit to impart.

There you have before you the fivefold pattern. In each case the shape of grace is described and prescribed *and practiced* in the early church as a social process pattern, *enabled* and *mandated* as a part of the good news of redemption. Yet in each case that way of interacting in the faith community is so concrete, so accessible, so "lay," that it is also a model for how any society, not excluding the surrounding "public" society, can also form its common life more humanely. The church is called to live, and is beginning to live (to the extent to which we get the point), in the way to which the whole world is called.

Before we open the meeting for your critical response, one more theme needs to be touched. There are components of what I have said thus far whose congeniality in the wider society, whose aptness as paradigms, at least in our world, would seem to be widely understandable and acceptable. Yet there are also dimensions of the apostolic witness, especially if we let the apostles remind us of the centrality of the cross, which are less attractive. I ought to name three of those "scandal" factors; they overlap.

1. In words which all three Synoptic Gospels report (each in a different setting), Jesus called his followers to follow him in renouncing dominion in favor of servanthood. In our own culture, as in most others, self-esteem is linked with "empowerment" and dignity with "leadership" or "autonomy." Some argue that the servant is the best leader, or even the most powerful leader, even in government or industry, but it is a paradoxical point and most of us do not believe it, including those of us who are presently servants.

2. The point at which the Sermon on the Mount focused most clearly the intensification of the law, which the heralding of the coming kingdom enables, is that, like our heavenly Father and like Jesus himself (although our imitating Jesus is not the theme of the sermon), we are not to answer evil with evil but to love our enemies. Ever since Augustine, theologians have invested great ingenuity in dulling the edge of that call. Ever since Tolstoy at the beginnings of modernity, honest readers have had to admit that that is what Jesus meant, even when they do not intend to follow it. Loving the enemy is one good candidate for the status of a moral imperative specific to Christianity, or to Jesus, which I was asking about at the outset, if there is such a phenomenon within ethics (although, for reasons I alluded to earlier, I am not preoccupied with disengaging the distinctiveness of Christianity).

3. One simple yet central component of viable community is forgiveness. Forgiving frees all the parties to the social nexus from the retaliatory mechanisms which lie at the bottom of cultural evolution. Forgiveness is a part of the process of "binding and loosing" described above. It is the only social process which is referred to in the prayer Jesus taught us. As independent a social philosopher as Hannah Arendt has identified it as the necessary condition for a society's ability to survive.[12]

12. Note the fuller attention to this theme above, pp. 30-31.

The retaliatory imperative is at the heart of numerous of our society's current debates, as (alone among the industrialized nations) we in the United States escalate the punitiveness of our criminal justice system. Civil justice as well is increasingly punitive, as we have recently seen in judgments against McDonald's when spilled coffee is too hot and against Exxon when spilled oil is too dirty. From Cain and Lamech in Genesis 4 to the sociologist Durkheim to the cultural philosopher René Girard to the fifty new capital offenses in President Clinton's new federal crime bill, the theme of tit-for-tat punishment is the key to understanding the pathology of how we live together. Killing the killer is the standard response. Killing a scapegoat instead of the killer is, according to René Girard,[13] the improved response which makes viable civilization possible. Forgiveness is one way to connect the death of the scapegoat to the offenses which keep being committed, but as our national experience demonstrates, most of us consider it unacceptable.

These three strands join in one holistic, christological, paradigmatic proclamation: servanthood, enemy love, forgiveness. If we are interested in making sense to our unbelieving or otherwise-believing neighbors, let this threefold cord be the test case.

Let those who fear sectarian self-sufficiency and seek "public" relevance show us how they can articulate, in reasonable discourse describing the nature of things so that all our neighbors will come along, the relevance and the realism of servanthood, enemy love, and forgiveness. This, and not domination, ethnocentricity, and punishment, is the divinely given nature of things that we are called to show the world.

Let those on the other hand who fear selling out, whether to the liberal or the conservative versions of establishment, those who prefer to locate the community's dissenting integrity only internally, show us how their tactical distancing from mainstream conformities heightens the clarity with which these three strands of fidelity are manifested to the watching and waiting world.

Most of the time when the apostle Paul was writing about Jews

13. One effort to interpret the thought of Girard is James G. Williams, *The Bible, Violence, and the Sacred* (San Francisco: HarperCollins, 1991).

and Greeks, his concern was with their reconciliation. Yet we do have one weighty passage where they are named as characterizing two kinds of unbelief; namely, near the beginning of his first letter to the Corinthians.[14] Jews, Paul tells us, are concerned for self-authenticating signs, and the cross in its apparent weakness causes them to stumble. Greeks are concerned for wisdom, and to them the cross looks foolish. I suggest that to juxtapose this passage with our present theme may be illuminating.

The "communitarians" of our time, for whom all meaning is internally self-authenticating, may be taken to stand for the people whom Paul in this passage calls "Jews." They will not risk the challenge of telling the world that servanthood, enemy love, and forgiveness would be a better way to run a university, a town, or a factory. They pull back on the grounds that only they have already experienced the power and novelty of that threefold evangelical cord in the worship and ministry of the church. They affirm integrity but at the cost of witness.

The "public catholics"[15] on the other hand are like Paul's "Greeks." They are concerned not to look foolish to their sophisticated neighbors by making any claims or promises linked to the particularity of the Jew Jesus (or of their own denominational past). By dropping the particular baggage of normative servanthood, enemy love, and forgiveness, they think they might make it easy to get across Lessing's ditch and to talk their neighbors' language, but they do so at the cost of having nothing to say that the neighbors do not already know.

Paul's stance in the face of this bifocal challenge is not so much "neither of the above" as "both." Being himself eminently both "Jew" and "Greek," he affirms both identity and intelligibility not as poles of a zero-sum trade-off, so that more of one means less of the other, but as each being the necessary condition of the other, each being pointless without the other.

To my five paradigmatic organic functions, or to my threefold cord of christological specificity, other elements could be added. I make no brief for the exhaustiveness of these listings. I do make a brief for the

14. 1 Corinthians 1:22.

15. The adjective "catholic" here refers to a style, and to the fact that *some* advocates of this view claim it is specifically congenial with a Thomistic theology; yet it is a view held by most liberal Protestants as well, and not by the pope.

aptness of the shape of my synthesis. Because the risen Messiah is at once head of the church and *kyrios* of the *kosmos*, sovereign of the universe, what is given to the church through him is in substance no different from what is offered to the world. The believing community is the new world on the way.

CHAPTER 3

"See How They Go with Their Face to the Sun"

I. Prologue and Prototype: *Galuth* as Calling

The vision of things I have been invited to present in this special setting[1] calls for several prefaces by way of orientation. It is at home in no one semantic world, in no one social world. My topic itself thereby fits our conference, in that it instantiates the cosmopolitan homelessness it describes.

I have drawn my title from a corpus of literature which fits our theme only in some ways, not in others. Stephan Zweig wrote his poem-drama *Jeremiah* during World War I, during his military service as a journalist and archivist in Vienna. While working on it he thought it was his most important work. It represents the last pre-Holocaust generation of the German-speaking Jewish cultural elite, affirming both identities simultaneously, in the confidence that they could be reconciled. Zweig's own reaffirmation of his Jewishness took place in that setting. Zweig first made a confessional statement in a letter of October 1916 to Martin Buber; *Jeremiah* was finished the next spring. The ways

---

1. First presented at Loyola Marymount University, Los Angeles, 23 September 1995, as the opening address of a colloquium on "Communities in Exile" convened by the university's Institute on Faith, Culture and the Arts. Printed here by permission. It is possible that the colloquium papers may not be published.

in which that ambitious synthetic vision, as represented in the 1920s by Buber and his friends and the journal *Der Jude,* is irretrievably lost need not be itemized here.[2] What does interest us here, and relates to our study, is that despite being obsolete in those ways, the dramatic poem *Jeremiah* affirmed the vision of *galuth* or diaspora identity which accepted as normative God's negative judgment on the Davidic project, after the failures of four centuries.[3]

I am not concerned here to study where Zweig got the numerous new elements of the story of Jeremiah, which go beyond what we find in the canonical prophetic book of Jeremiah or the last pages of 2 Kings and 2 Chronicles, in order to make a dramatic plot for a play that could be staged. Did he find some of that in rabbinic legend sources? Did he invent it from whole cloth as any playwright has the right to do?

Nor do I assume that the original Jeremiah, in any of the ways historical research or imagination can reconstruct, was as clearly a pacifist of the generation of *All Quiet on the Western Front* as Zweig makes him.[4] Settling those details is not necessary to enable us to see how Zweig's conclusion to the work affirms that dispersion is mission.

To be scattered is not an hiatus, after which normalcy will resume. From Jeremiah's time on, rather, according to the message of the play, dispersion shall be the calling of the Jewish faith community. That is our present concern. Zweig describes the procession of expellees from Judaea in a way which fully fits with the message of Jeremiah's later letter (chapter

2. This short-lived but enormously creative world is evoked well by the introductory materials in Arthur A. Cohen's *The Jew: Essays from Martin Buber's Journal "Der Jude"* (Tuscaloosa: University of Alabama Press, 1980). It is also well characterized by Leon Botstein's introduction to the 1987 edition of Zweig's *Jewish Legends* (New York: Markus Wiener).

3. Zweig himself wrote: "It is the tragedy and the hymn of the Jewish people, of the elect; yet not in the sense of prosperity, but of endless suffering, endless collapse, endless rising again, and the power unfolded through that destiny. The conclusion proclaims simultaneously the exodus from Jerusalem to the endlessly rebuilt Jerusalem. The war opened this tragedy up to me, who love suffering as power, yet feel it with chills as fact. Should my intent ever be efficacious, this will be the time." Zweig to Martin Buber, 8 May 1916, *Gesammelte Werke,* vol. 4 (Frankfurt: S. Fischer, 1982), pp. 347f.

4. Nor do I need for present purposes to unravel the small differences between the German version in the 1982 *Gesammelte Werke* and the 1922 English translation by Eden and Cedar Paul "from the Author's revised German text." I shall take the liberty of citing either version.

29 in the prophetic book) to the people in Babylon, although he does not cite that letter. In that letter God instructed the people in Babylon to stay there, to renounce notions of an early return to Judaea, to settle in, to buy land and plant gardens and vineyards, to marry off their children and enjoy their grandchildren, and (especially) to

> seek the welfare of the city where I have sent you into exile, and pray to the LORD on its behalf, for in its welfare you will find your welfare. (Jer. 29:7, RSV)

Zweig sees the scattering of the Jews, in other words, not as a detour for only the next seventy years after 586, but as the beginning of the mission of the next millennium and a half.[5] That is my present point. The move to Babylon was not a two-generation parenthesis, after which the Davidic or Solomonic project was supposed to take up again where it had left off. It was rather the beginning, under a firm, fresh prophetic mandate, of a new phase of the Mosaic project.[6]

Zweig's vision, like Jeremiah's letter, makes the hope of a return to Jerusalem functional *as postponed*. The notion of return has its meaning not as something the people in Babylon or elsewhere should be bringing about by their own strength, or waiting around to see happen, or planning for. It is functional as metaphor for God's renewing the life of faith anywhere. I shall cite only a few snatches from the play:[7]

---

5. "I love the diaspora, and affirm it as the meaning of [Judaism's] idealism, as its cosmopolitan general human vocation. I would wish for no other union than in the Spirit, in our own only real element, never in one language, one people. . . . I find the present condition the most magnificent in humanity; to be unified without a language, without obligation, without homeland, only through the fluidity of being. . . . Every narrower, more real togetherness would appear to me as a diminution of this incomparable condition. All we need to strengthen is to appreciate this condition, as I do, not [see it] as humiliation." Zweig to Martin Buber, 24 January 1917, *Gesammelte Werke*, vol. 4, pp. 349f.

6. I don't think that a careful reading of Ezra and Nehemiah denies this, but that argument is not my present concern. That is a subject concerning which Daniel Smith of this university knows more than I ever intend to. Jeremiah, Ezekiel, the prophet of the Servant Songs, Ezra, and Nehemiah all have distinctive slants. I am not convinced that "Second Isaiah" is an exception to this, as was suggested by someone at the LMU event.

7. *Gesammelte Werke*, vol. 4 (Frankfurt: S. Fischer, 1982); English translation by Eden and Cedar Paul (New York: Seltzer, 1922).

PEOPLE: Schauen wir wieder Jerusalem?
Shall we ever see Jerusalem again?

JEREMIAS: Wo immer ihr euch in euch selber aufrichtet
und feurig von Furcht und Fremdnis erhebt
Da ist es aus Wunsch in die Welt gedichtet,
Da ist der Traum unseres Heimwehs erlebt,
an jedem Orte, wo euch Glaube inwohnet,
Ueberwölbt euch hell seine mauernes Krone:
Wer glüht, sieht ewig Jerusalem!

Wanderers, sufferers, march in the name
of Jacob your father, who erstwhile with God,
Having wrestled the livelong night,
Strove till dawn for a blessing. . . .
Wander your wanderings, watered with tears.
O people of God, for wherever ye roam,
Your road leads through the world to eternity, home.

Zweig's poem-drama culminates in five "choruses of wanderers," which articulate the Jewish sense of mission. The first three of these "choruses" conclude with the vision of an ultimate return to geographic Jerusalem; the last two do not. Here a few lines from the fourth:

(IV) Wir wandern durch Völker,
wir wandern durch Zeiten,
unendliche Strassen des Leidens entlang

The tale of our suffering ever renewed;
Aeon after aeon eternally vanquished . . .
But the cities wither, and the nations
shoot into darkness like wandering stars.
The oppressors who scourged us with many whips
have become a hissing and byword among the generations
Whereas we march onward, march onward, march onward,
drawing strength from within, eternity from earth,
and God from pains and tribulations.

The prose which frames these concluding poems is a kind of chorus of men called "Chaldaeans," i.e., the foot troops of the conquering empire. The Chaldaeans marvel at how the emigrants do not look defeated:

> We are the victors, they the defeated . . .
> an invisible force must sustain them . . .
> What sustains them is their faith in the invisible God

> Siehe, siehe wie sie in die Sonne schreiten!
> Es ist ein Glanz auf diesem Volke.

> See how they are walking to meet the sun.
> His light shines on their foreheads,
> and they themselves
> shine with the strength of the sun.
> Mighty must their God be!

II. Diaspora as Normal Jewish Existence

The first way I sought to locate my point was in the poetic words of Stephan Zweig. The second will be to review the notion of what scholars call "canonization," i.e., the process whereby a body of people come, over time, usually over a long time, to regard a particular body, not an unmanageably large body of literature, as the literature the reading of which defines who they are.

This phenomenon is misunderstood when it is taken, as it has been by the Protestant scholasticism of recent centuries, as calling for a debate about the miraculous way in which that literature came into being, or about the inerrant authority of its contents. It is also misunderstood when Catholics, responding to that Protestant critique, claim that it was the hierarchy which gave the canon that status.

What matters more is that we take stock of the setting in which that selection took place. The action of selecting is itself a testimony to the normative self-understanding of the community which did it.[8] The He-

8. It is important to say that at bottom the selecting was done by the com-

brew scriptural canon was selected in the dispersion, and it is best understood as throwing light on the diaspora identity into which God's people have been sent.

Life in *galuth*, or diaspora,[9] is not without its dimensions of profound and painful alienation. Psalm 137 has become for us the prototypical expression of that suffering:

> How can we sing the Lord's songs
> in a foreign land?

Yet, painful as the question is, that is what the Jews learned to do, and do well. It may well have been in this age of *galuth* that the Psalter began to form as a central identity resource, part of the canon, beside the Torah. The very possibility of the mocking challenge "Sing us one of the songs of Zion!" (137:3, RSV) presupposes the awareness on the part of the "captors" that, despite having no temple, the Jews had an important worship life of their own.[10] Even that experience reinforces their identity.

Within this missionary vision, the role of "seeking the welfare of that city" becomes quite concrete, both in real experience and in legends which reflect, interpret, and in turn further foster that experience. What we might call the "Joseph paradigm" became a standard type.[11] In three different ages and places, the same experiences recur

---

munity. More often people will credit "the rabbis" or "the priests," but there were also scribes and sages, each with necessary roles. Yet the role of each made sense only thanks to the viability and the integrity of the community as a whole.

9. Etymologically these terms, one Hebrew and one Greek, both mean simply "scattering." Those with a view of the past Davidic establishment as ideal will give them the negative overtones of "exile" or "banishment." For Jeremiah it is mission. (The Greek form includes the sense of broadcasting seed.) The Jews were sent there to identify their own welfare with that of that place, to bloom where they were sown.

10. We might compare this to the way in which white Americans' awareness of the power of the spirituals and of blues has contributed to both the viability and the self-respect of African Americans.

11. Cf. Lance M. Wills, *The Jew in the Court of the Pagan King: Ancient Jewish Court Legends* (Minneapolis: Fortress, 1990). Wills unfortunately limits his analysis to the literary level. He does not ask what community life these legends testify to or contributed to, what concept of God or of history, and so forth.

in the Hebrew story.[12] Joseph, Daniel and his three friends, and Esther all found themselves involuntarily at the heart of the idolatrous empire. Each ran the risk of faithfulness to their people and to the revealed will of the one true God, when their civil disobedience could have cost them their lives. Each was saved by divine intervention, with the result that the pagan tyrant was converted to the recognition of the one true God, vindicating them against their enemies and giving Jews a role in running the empire.

Periodical pilgrimages back to Jerusalem were a part of diaspora identity. The pilgrim psalter, Psalms 120–134, one of the nuclei for the formation of our Psalter, begins with the singer living "among those who hate peace" (120:5f., RSV). The places named, Meshech and Kedar, are neither in Mesopotamia nor in Palestine. One is in Arabia and the other in Anatolia; they testify to the resilience of Jewish identity all across the ancient Near East. They remind us that although it was the deportation of 586 which became prototypical, and although with time Babylonian Jewry became culturally central, the phenomenon of dispersion always was much wider.

More than Christians are aware, Babylon itself very soon became the cultural center of world Jewry, from the age of Jeremiah until the time we in the West call the Middle Ages. The people who recolonized the "Land of Israel," repeatedly, from the age of Jeremiah to that of Johanan ben Zakkai, and again still later, were supported financially and educationally from Babylon, and in lesser ways from the rest of the diaspora. Our Palestinocentric reading of the story is a mistake, though a very understandable one. It was imposed not only on Christians but also on many Jews because of the way the first-century events became legend.

What it meant to be Jewish on a world scale, from the age of Jeremiah to that of Theodore Hertzl, depended more on the leadership in Babylon, where living without a temple was possible and was accepted

---

12. As with the Babel story itself, my present interest is not in testing the historicity of these accounts. My concern is their portrayal of the stance of fidelity under pressure, as it contributes to a community's self-understanding. The less these stories of Hebrew heroes in pagan courts are "historical" in the modern sense of attestation in the face of doubt as having "really happened," the more valid they are as testimonies to the worldview and lived experience of the people of the Jeremianic mission. Part of the Tobit story fits the same pattern.

as permanent, than on the Palestinian institutions, distracted as they were by the agenda of Maccabean rebellion and Herodian negotiation, and then by Roman destruction. In all the different ways represented by Sadducees, Pharisees, Maccabeans, and Essenes, Jews in Palestine had no choice but to define their identity over against the dominant Gentiles, and to be divided from one another by their conflicting responses to that challenge. On the other hand, the synagogues and the rabbis in Babylon, and in the rest of the world where the Babylonian model was followed and the Babylonian teachers were consulted, were spared that self-defeating distraction, so as to enter creatively into the Jeremianic phase of creating something qualitatively new in the history of religions.

I leave to the experts in the history of religions to determine which component of this innovation was the most original, which was more central or definitional than the others, and how to label them with the special kind of vocabulary of the guild.[13] In lay terms, living without a temple, while yet retaining the mythic memory of the temple and the hope of the return in the messianic age, enabled the creation of a faith community with a globally new gestalt, marked especially by the following:

- The primary vehicle of identity definition is a text which can be copied and read anywhere. Decentralization and fidelity are therefore not alternatives, as they are with any religious forms which need a priesthood in a temple.
- The ground floor of "worship" (if that is the word for it) is reading and singing the texts.
- A valid local cell of the world Jewish community, qualified to be *in that place* the concretion of the people of God, can exist wherever there are ten households. No priesthood, no hierarchy is needed. If they can afford a rabbi, his role is that of a scribe, rather than that of prophet, priest, or prince.

---

13. Jonathan Z. Smith uses the conceptual grid of "local/alocal"; see Smith, *Map Is Not Territory: Studies in the History of Religions* (Leiden: Brill, 1978). Other religions, whether tribal and traditional or imperial, locate God. Jews can serve their Lord anywhere. We might debate what is cause and what is effect about that observation; there can be no debate about the shift's being definitional.

- The international unity of the people is sustained by intervisitation, by intermarriage, by commerce, and by rabbinic consultation, needing no high priest or pope or king to hang together. When, some time later, a central senior Jewish spokesman, the *resh galuth,* "ethnarch" or "exilarch," was called forth by the Babylonian power structure, he was intermediary, coordinator, culture broker between the community and the Gentiles. He was not a Jewish emperor.[14]
- Although there is plenty of material and plenty of freedom with which thinkers over the centuries can develop Jewish philosophical systems (cosmological, mystical, linguistic, scientific), the ground floor of identity is the common life itself, the walk, halakah, and the shared remembering of the story behind it.
- Nothing about the self-esteem of the bearers of this new lifestyle is dependent upon or drives toward cultural homogeneity, political control, or autarchy. Jewish culture is comfortable and creative in dialogue with whatever Gentile world it lands in, as long as it is tolerated. The foundational narrative from the Davidic age and institutions is now placed in a wider frame where Abraham, then Joseph, then Shiphrah and Puah, then Moses, then Daniel and his three friends, then Esther and Mordecai live among the nations, confounding the Gentile seers and emperors with the superior wisdom and power of the one authentic God.[15]

This cultural *novum*[16] was capable of enormous flexibility, planting colonies of similar shape from Spain to China, from the North Sea to

14. The same is true of the central role of the *Gaon,* a sort of senior rabbi. His authority was great but it was earned, in a setting devoid of central sacral authority or imperial appointment.

15. Cf. above notes 11ff. The "historicity" question we need to pursue in these stories is not about whether there ever was really an Esther, or when was Daniel, but about the life setting in which rereading these stories in the synagogues made sense of peoples' lives in the diaspora. Nor were such experiences limited to the courts of kings; there were also Tobit and Susanna.

16. Jacob Neusner, in *Method and Meaning in Ancient Judaism* (Missoula: Scholars Press, 1979), p. 151, cites Jonathan Smith in describing this "atopical" quality as the inner mental structure of the Mishnah. It would however be an historical error to think that it first arose in the second and third centuries of our era. It arose in the age of Jeremiah. What happened after Bar Kokhba was that the alternatives fell away, and the Jeremian vision expanded to fill the available space.

the upper Nile. Wherever they went they created new trades, new arts, new literatures, even new languages, without losing their connections to Moses or one another, or their hope of return.

III. The Ambivalence of the Davidic Project

It is of great significance that, however the traditions now grouped in the Hebrew canon were remembered and then redacted, these texts kept alive the memory of how the rise of the Davidic dynasty had been a disappointment not only to Samuel but to God. As we read the narrative of the book of Judges (9:7ff.), the oppressive nature of kingship "like the other nations" was already discerned in Jotham's fable, in the face of Abimelech's false start. That awareness was still there when God and Samuel gave in to the demand of the elders in 1 Samuel 8, saying in effect to those who wanted a king like those of the Gentiles, "You'll be sorry."

The northern kingdom, subject to recurrent "charismatic" usurpations resembling the rise and fall of the "judges" from Joshua to Samuel, and David's own takeover from Saul, fell first. Judah was dynastically stable and lasted longer, but God finally gave up on both of them. The historiography which scholars call "deuteronomic" and "deuteronomistic" retold the history, correlating the ups and downs of the royal houses with their rising and falling faithfulness to the law, but when we remember that that retelling was done and committed to writing in the setting of diaspora, it constitutes a document of the acceptance of the Jeremianic turn; there is in the multiple strata and versions of the entire narrative no irridentism.

The story goes on from there in the same key. In what the books of Ezra and Nehemiah recount, whatever be their historicity and their relation to each other, all that happens stays well within the constraints of submission to the Gentile empire. Nothing like "kingship" or "statehood" is advocated by any party as desirable for the honor of God or the dignity of the people. Thus the reorientation of identity by the Jeremianic shift even comes back to give a new quality to the part of the story which returns to Eretz Israel.

IV. Retrieving the Genesis Legend

Both by its argument and by its snappy title, Jeffrey Stout's *Ethics after Babel*[17] has become a landmark around which the discussion of the social setting of values is organized. His theme is a very contemporary, very methodologically sophisticated analysis of what it does to ethical discourse to have to be carried on in a setting of pluralism. Yet Stout claims depth (and attracts attention) for his topic by juxtaposing it to the ancient Hebrew legend.

In the following paragraphs I shall, like Stout, converse in an interlocking way both with the modern methodological challenge of how to converse about morals and how to converse with our Hebrew backgrounds. Yet it is not primarily with Stout that I seek to converse. I propose to reach beyond what Stout intended to do with those resources, to retrieve the heritage of the centuries during which the people of God discharged their mission without being in charge of the world.[18]

A. *"Babel" the Primeval Symbol*

"Babel" in Stout's use, as in much of our literate culture, is the code word for the recognition, which Stout's generation of moral philosophers cannot overlook, in the "postmodern" late twentieth century, that meaningful moral discourse is always located within a given community, so that there can never be just one right way to talk morally. Therefore we must face the fact of the multiplicity of communities of moral discourse. For Stout, "Babel" stands for that multiplicity.[19]

17. Boston: Beacon Press, 1988. Cf. the "Review Symposium," *Theology Today* 46, no. 1 (April 1990): 55-73.

18. Cf. my essay "On Not Being in Charge" (below, n. 34). Cf. also another aspect of the conversation with Jeffrey Stout in my "Beyond Babble" in the April 1996 *Journal of Religious Ethics*.

19. It is never quite clear whether for Stout the challenge he intends "Babel" to symbolize is the *modern* loss of a common discourse or a trait of the human condition ever since prehistory. Most of the time the former seems to be intended, but Stout is not interested in analyzing whether community-dependent pluralism was a problem before modernity.

This way of putting the question of validity would seem to assume the structural a priori of establishment. It posits as a desideratum, the loss of which has now put us at a disadvantage, a setting where there could be, would be (and by implication once was) only one community whose shared meanings defined value language. The little word "after" in Stout's title does make it seem that there was some earlier time, maybe not too awfully long ago since we in modern times are just now struggling with its loss, some pre-Babel state of things, when this confusing pluralism did not bother people as it does us. "Babel" before the divine intervention then becomes the mythic metaphor for that lost unity.

Yet as we shall soon see, what Stout "after Babel" regrets losing is what YHWH in the Genesis story said his creatures should not have been trying to protect (and did not yet possess) in the first place. The first meaning of Babel in the Genesis legend is the effort of a human community to absolutize itself. The canonical setting[20] is the story of the spreading out of the immediate descendants of Noah around the narrator's entire known world.[21] Babel in the myth of Genesis places the multiplicity of cultures under the sign of the divine will. It was rebellious humankind, proud and perhaps fearful, who wanted to live all in one place and thereby replace their dependence on divine benevolence by reaching heaven on their own. The intention of the people at Babel was to resist the diversification which God had long before ordained and initiated, and to maintain a common discourse by

20. "Canonical" as a method code term means that if we want to know what a term means over the long run, we do best to read first the text as received by those who preserved it. This involves no disrespect for the several other hermeneutic or historical subdisciplines which seek to discern or project more detailed understandings of how the text came to have its present form, or of "what really happened" behind the legends.

21. Although chapter 10 lays out a confusing spread of names and places, it accounts for only three generations. Verses 5, 20, and 31 had anticipated the Babel account by already describing a multiplicity of languages and nations. Claus Westermann (*Genesis 1–11* [Minneapolis: Augsburg, 1984], pp. 531ff.) catalogs how all of the components of the Babel account are prefigured by other legendary material in ancient Asia; etiology for the name "Babel," etiology for the diversity of languages, etiology for the placing of the nations, etiology for the ruins of a tower. Brueggemann (*Genesis* [Atlanta: John Knox, 1982], pp. 97ff.) agrees that adding up such components does not exhaust the text's message.

building their own unprecedentedly centralized city.[22] They were the first foundationalists, seeking by purposive focusing of their own cultural power to overcome historically developing diversity.[23]

B. Dispersion as Grace

The second level of meaning of Babel is that God responded graciously to that defensive effort, namely, by the divinely driven dispersal of the peoples, restoring the centripetal motion. It was YHWH who scattered them, for their own good. This scattering is still seen as benevolence in the missionary preaching of the Paul of Acts (14:16f.; 17:26f.). It is "confusion" only when measured against the simplicity of imperially enforced uniformity. It is narrated as a gracious and creative intervention of God, reinforcing the process of dispersion and diversification which had already begun[24] and which God intended as a good thing. Thus the "confusion of tongues" is not a punishment or a tragedy but the gift of new beginnings, liberation from a blind alley.

Later readings, in ways which reach all the way down to the

22. Later interpreters and archaeologists, taking the *ziggurat* to be a kind of temple, have seen here an account of the origins of some specifically pagan cult. The story does not say that. That the building was supposed to reach the sky is compatible with the vision of the one true God as ruling from heaven which prevailed in the previous ten chapters and which was present in the ancient Near Eastern legends. The metaphor is monotheistic. Some readers make the point that while bricks and bitumen are fine for ordinary buildings, you need stone for skyscrapers. I doubt that the ancient bards also wanted to make that point.

23. The Akkadian/Babylonian root *babili* is taken to mean "Gate of God," although linguists can doubt that. In any case the Hebrew etymology assumed in Genesis 11:9 from *balal* (to confuse) misleads the reader. What the tower builders wanted was unity. Diversity, which is only "confusion" if you posit uniformity as desideratum, was God's prior purpose and was the product of God's corrective intervention.

24. In the light of the dispersion already mandated and completed in chapter 10, the Babel project is explicitly narrated as conservative, defensive, restoring God's original intention. The people who had gone to Shinar were the children of Nimrod (the first "mighty man," whatever that means), son of Cush (whose other descendants went mostly to Africa), son of Ham. This passage, 11:1ff., relates to chapter 10 as 2:4ff. relates to 1:1–2:3; it reaches back into the earlier broader narrative to retell one fragment of the story.

present,[25] have considered that first dispersion to have been a wrathful act of an offended God, punitive or defensive in intent and destructive in its effect.[26] That is not in the text.[27] The more we understand the general vision of God as creator and sovereign, the less reason there is to see this intervention as in any way petulant or punitive. Diversity was the original divine intent; if God is good and diversity is good, then each of the many diverse identities which resulted from the multiplying of languages and the resultant scattering is also good.[28]

C. Galuth *as Vocation*

The third meaning of Babel is not just a metaphor or a legend. Here we begin to move beyond the purview of Stout's modern methodological agenda, rejoining the theme with which we began. Babylon was the

25. William Schweiker's use of Babel in his paper "Power and the Agency of God" (*Theology Today* 52, no. 2 [July 1995]: 215) exemplifies the temptation of American intellectuals to appeal to biblical material as prototypical for whatever one is interested in, leapfrogging over the historical and linguistic disciplines.

> Several of the features of the text stand out for the purpose of our present inquiry. . . . The parallel between Genesis 11 and the contemporary world-view as I have specified it is perhaps too obvious to elaborate.

Yet very little of what Schweiker finds "standing out" or "obvious" needs the Babel story to make sense, or relates to scattering. In his confidence that the Bible is a mine of symbolic connections for anyone to exposit, Schweiker is typical of our age's confidence that antiquity is an open book. Another specimen of this confidence is Reinhold Niebuhr, *Beyond Tragedy* (New York: Scribners, 1937), pp. 27-46.

26. Some of this notion of petty punitive anger on God's part is affirmed in Westermann's account. One of the places where this tilt surfaces most easily is in Christian interpretations read into the Lucan account of Pentecost. But its omnipresence in history is also represented by Stephan Zweig's 1916 essay on the Babel story ("Der Turm zu Babel," *Gesammelte Werke; Die schlaflose Welt* [1983], pp. 68ff.).

27. The later dispersion *to* Babylon (in the age of Jeremiah) may have been seen as a punishment by some Hebrew historians, but nothing in the text says this about the first dispersion *from* Babel.

28. Cf. Bernard Anderson, "The Babel Story: Paradigm of Human Unity and Diversity," in *Ethnicity, Concilium,* ed. Andrew Greeley and Gregory Baum (New York: Seabury/Crossroad, 1977). One set of thinkers of the last generation who have had a stake in retrieving this affirmative vision of multicultural diversity was the conservative Protestant theorists of "church growth." Brueggemann's commentary supports this view.

actual imperial capital of the ancient Near East when Jerusalem was captured in 587 and Jews were taken there as captives.[29] That transfer is of course understood as in some sense the earned chastisement for the sins of the people (or more properly of their ruling elites),[30] but that is not the primary point made by Jeremiah when he interprets the event in the light of God's gracious sovereignty. It is the false prophets who promise that the captivity will soon be over, a mere detour along the triumphal path of the house of David.[31] The real mission of the scattered Jews, according to Jeremiah's message, we already saw, is to settle into Babylon, to make themselves at home (marry their children, buy land and eat its produce, build houses), and to

> seek the welfare of the city where I have sent you into exile, and pray to the LORD on its behalf, for in its welfare you will find your welfare.[32]

Seldom does one see it pointed out that the development of the Genesis story as we have it constitutes a piece of evidence on what I was saying before about the age of canonization. It was the generations of Jewry living around Babylon who told the Babel story as the immediate background to the call of Abraham.

29. There is room for considerable historical refinement and debate concerning how many of the inhabitants of the then territory of Judah were in fact carried off, and what kind of vestigial Jewish life remained possible in the land of Israel. What matters for our purposes is that the story line moves to Babylon, even though not all of the people did.

30. The general understanding, held by scholars today, of the editorial slant of the "deuteronomic historian(s)" is that those narrators' reason for retelling the whole history of royal Israel was to show who was to blame for the exile. But the fact that there was unfaithfulness along the way does not make the mission to Babylon any less a mission. It merely intensifies what we have already seen about the moral ambivalence of kingship.

31. The false prophets are Hananiah in chapter 28; Ahab and Zedekiah in 29:15 and 21; Shemaiah in 29:24f., 31ff. Shemaiah is described as rejecting Jeremiah's message after it had been delivered.

32. Jeremiah 29:7. Cf. my earlier description of this vision in my essay "Exodus and Exile: Two Faces of Liberation," *Crosscurrents* (fall 1973): 297-309. Recently it has been creatively restated in the work of Daniel Boyarin.

V. How the Jeremianic Model Prefigured
the Christian Attitude to the Gentile World

Thus far I have been recounting the Jewish experience, as it were, for its own sake. Yet an important benefit of seeing this story more clearly, and the reason I do it now, is the way it illuminates Christian origins. I illustrate it here by lifting out only one representative dimension. There is a standard debate among the historians of Christian ethics concerning whether (or rather how or why) Christians before Constantine were pacifists. People like Tolstoy said they were, on the basis of a simply rigorous reading of a few words of Jesus. Others said they were not, on the basis that Tertullian, by arguing a century and a half after Jesus that those of his fellow Christians who served in Caesar's armies should not be doing so, proved that it was happening.

What has been completely absent in this scholarly debate[33] has been any recognition that Christian moral standards may have been largely derived from, and therefore could be fruitfully illuminated by, older Jewish models of how to relate to this world's powers.[34] The historians on both sides have quibbled about this or that legalistic reading of a few words of Jesus, ignoring both the sociological and the theological contexts within which first-century believers sustained their view of history under God.[35]

---

33. Recent summaries confirm no real change in the field for a century. David G. Hunter's "The Christian Church and the Roman Army in the First Three Centuries," in *The Church's Peace Witness*, ed. Marlin E. Miller and Barbara Nelson Gingerich (Grand Rapids: Eerdmans, 1994), pp. 161-81, reviewed the literature, as he had done before in "A Decade of Research . . . ," *Religious Studies Review* 18, no. 2 (1992): 87-94. That title wrongly suggests that there has been scholarly progress. Even if Hunter had drawn on the fuller bibliographies of Peter Brock (*The Military Question in the Early Church: A Selected Bibliography of a Century's Scholarship: 1888-1987*, copyright P. Brock [Toronto, 1988]) and David Scholer (*Early Christian Attitudes to War and Military Service: A Selective Bibliography*, Theological Students' Fellowship *Bulletin* [September/October 1984]: 23f.), there would have been no new wisdom to report. Since Thomas Clarkson published *An Essay on the Doctrines and Practice of the Early Christians as They Relate to War* (London: Hamilton, Adams and Co., 1832), no new sources have been found.

34. The next few paragraphs parallel a paper entitled "On Not Being in Charge," in *War and Its Discontents: Pacifism and Quietism in the Abrahamic Traditions*, ed. J. Patout Burns (Washington, D.C.: Georgetown University Press, 1996), pp. 74-90.

35. Cf. note 41 below.

I first defined this "Jewish quietism since Jeremiah"[36] in sociological terms; it is marked by the synagogue, the Torah, and the rabbinate. Of course I could have added kashrut and circumcision. Yet if you had asked those Jews (including the first Christians) to explain themselves and their attitude toward pagan empires, whether the Mesopotamian ones before or Rome in the first century, their answers would have been theological.[37]

a. They would have said that since God is sovereign over history, there is no need for them to seize (or subvert) political sovereignty in order for God's will to be done.[38] God's capacity to bring about the fulfillment of his righteous goals is not dependent upon us, and certainly not dependent on our needing to make exceptions to his Law in order to make events come out the way he wills them.

b. They would have said that establishing the ultimate righteous social order among nations will be the mission of the *meshiach* and should be left to him; to do his work for him would be presumptuous if not blasphemous. This is what the mainstream critics of Zionism said a century ago, and what the *neturei karta* community says of the State of Israel even today.

c. They would have said that the efforts of the Maccabees, the Zealots, and Bar Kokhba to restore a national kingship had not been blessed by God, and that three failures should have been enough to teach us that lesson.[39] The Maccabees and the Zealots have a larger

36. The term "quietism" was inserted in the St. Louis study by the conference planning process at Washington University. I accepted the term then as aptly pointing toward an issue, but I continue to challenge the adequacy of this characterization. It is not the case that the only alternative to violently taking charge of society as a whole is to be "quiet," any more than it is the case that nonviolence is a priori weak.

37. This adjective is not the one either the Jews or the Christians of the first century would have used. Yet something like it is needed to undercut the claim, made (about Jews) in a paper by M. Broyde in the St. Louis symposium, and (about Christians) by numerous historians (cf. above the listings of Scholer, Hunter), that the early Christian renunciation of violence was *merely* tactical, a pragmatic survival technique, with no roots in spirituality or in an understanding of how God works in history.

38. This is the obverse of the Constantinian assumption, which would have been unthinkable in the first century, that only the Christian king can move history as God wants.

39. It is not only that the Maccabees and the Zealots did not ultimately triumph. Their first successes led them to become oppressive and to fall out among themselves. Not because they were weak but because they were strong and "succeeded," they fell prey to what they claimed to defeat.

place in the Christian memories of those centuries than they do in the thought of the rabbis.[40]

d. They would have said that if an all-righteous God wanted to chastise us for our sins, which (at the very least) some prophets have said may sometimes be God's purpose, our self-defense would interfere with that purpose. The notion that God's own people are especially subject to having their sins punished, by virtue of the special privileges of their election, may have become more weighty in the Jewish thought of a later age than it was in the canonical period, but it is already present in the prophets. As soon as that attitude toward one's own sufferings is possible, the injustices suffered by God's people take on a different meaning and seeking to prevent them becomes impious.

e. They would have said that the death of the righteous "sanctifies the Name"; i.e., it makes a doxological contribution on the moral scales of history, which our avoidance of suffering (even if unjust) would obviate. We cannot be clear that "Your name be sanctified" in the "Our Father" already meant that then, but clearly that phrase soon became the technical label for martyrdom as a positive human contribution to the achievement of God's purposes.

Each of these five explanatory sentences ought to be a chapter; yet even in this brevity the Jewishness of the case against "taking charge" of the course of history is evident. From Jeremiah until Theodore Hertzl this was the dominant Jewish vision.

There is wide recognition that the Christians of the first two centuries were pacifist, or at least that their most articulate teachers of whom we have record were. The historians debate whether this was univocally the case, and ethicists debate whether, if it was, it should be normative for later Christians. Yet in all of that voluminous debate, neither party takes account of the fact that the ethos of the early Christians was a direct prolongation and fulfillment of the ethos of Jewry.[41]

---

40. One need only note that the Maccabees are not in the Hebrew canon, a point first made to me by Rabbi Stephen Schwarzschild.

41. This neglect of attention to the Jewishness of Christianity is no less striking in the pacifist-leaning works of Cadoux, Hornus, Bainton, and Brock than it is in the nonpacifist readings of Helgeland, Cunningham, Ryan, Swift, Johnson, etc. Cf. note 33 above. David Hunter's term "research" in the title cited above is something of a

Both sides of the debate as to whether the early Christians were pacifist have, as I said above,[42] tended to proceed legalistically, as if the Christian movement had taken off from scratch with only a few words of Jesus to guide it, so that a fine-grained debate about whether those few words had to mean just this or just that would have been the primary tool of moral discernment.

It is rather the case that Jesus' impact in the first century added more and deeper authentically Jewish reasons, and reinforced and further validated the already expressed Jewish reasons,[43] for the already well established ethos of not being in charge and not considering any local state structure to be the primary bearer of the movement of history. To this same stance the second generation of witnesses after Jesus, the "apostles," added another layer of further reasons, still utterly Jewish in form and substance, having to do with the messiahship of Jesus, his lordship, and the presence of the Spirit.[44] Much later, some nonmessianic Jews formally rejected these ideas about Jesus and about the Spirit; nonetheless they were at the time unimpeachably Jewish ideas, and they made clear why a "quietist" stance in the Roman/Mediterranean world made good sense. Until the mes-

---

misnomer. Most of what Hunter reviews is old and much-reread material. Christians who are interested in learning from the dialogue with Judaism, and the historians who follow the contested history of thought on the morality of war, seem not to be doing their research in the same world.

42. Cf above note 33. My 1991 statement of the same point has just been published in "War as a Moral Problem in the Early Church," in *The Pacifist Impulse in Historical Perspective*, ed. Harvey Dyck (Toronto: University of Toronto Press, 1996), pp. 90-110.

43. Cf. my chapter "The Moral Axioms of the Sermon on the Mount," in *The Original Revolution* (Scottdale, Pa.: Herald, 1972), as well as my earlier summary of this part of the present paper's theme in the paper cited in note 42.

44. Cf. my chapter "If Christ Is Truly Lord," in *The Original Revolution*, pp. 52ff., now retitled as "Peace without Eschatology?" in my *The Royal Priesthood: Essays Ecclesiological and Ecumenical*, ed. Michael G. Cartwright (Grand Rapids: Eerdmans, 1994), pp. 143ff. Some interpreters make much of the delay of the parousia as forcing on the Christians of the second or third generation a revision of their worldview. There is no evidence that such a change made any difference for their attitude toward violence. The Jewishness of their pacifism was not contingent on a particular apocalyptic perspective; and in any case an apocalyptic perspective is not contingent on confirmation or falsification through events.

sianity of Jesus was replaced by that of Constantine,[45] it was the only ethos that made sense.[46]

VI. How the Jeremianic Model Is Bigger than Stout's *Fragestellung*

Leaping from the grand lines of the Hebrew story, here narrated from the record, to the postmodern agenda as named and epitomized by Stout, with which we began to describe the contemporary encounter with relativity, we may now be able to note the ways in which the Jeremianic missionary vision, presupposing and moving beyond the world-historical vision of Genesis 11, transcends as well our modern problematic, stated prototypically by Stout, in ways that might have something to tell us. They might have something to tell both the dispersion communities[47] and those who would want to be the cultural establishment.

There is in the Jeremiah vision no counterpart for our regretting the loss of the univocality of the age, which in Christendom stretched roughly from Eusebius to Hegel (but lingers on in philosophical foundationalism), when European intellectual elites could claim to prescribe one unified meaning system for the world. Stout

45. By the fourth century *christos* had become a proper name. Thus neither Constantine nor his biographer Eusebius would literally have used that title for him; yet functionally "messianity" describes Eusebius's view of Constantine's place in salvation history. The *meshiach*, the "Anointed," is the man who by special divine intervention ("unction") has been empowered to inaugurate the next phase of God's saving history. That is what Eusebius said about Constantine and his age.

46. When not long after the middle of the second century some Christians did in some way participate in the Roman army, as some clearly did (although we know about it only from the words of those who thought they should not, and there is no way to know how many there were, or what their roles were), it was not because they had any responsible theocratic visions of taking charge of history, or controlling the destiny of the empire. They probably did it because (in peacetime, which prevailed in most of the empire most of the time) the work was easy and the rewards generous, without troubling themselves with much moral analysis.

47. That the faith community should properly be expected to be a minority in a wider world is said in very diverse ways by Karl Rahner, Juan Luis Segundo, George Lindbeck, Stanley Hauerwas, and others.

does not say he bemoans the loss, yet the way he shapes the story signals a kind of wistfulness, as if the exercise of his profession had been more rewarding, or at least simpler, before somebody moved the landmarks.

Jeremiah does not tell his refugee brothers and sisters to try to teach the Babylonians Hebrew. The concern to learn goes in the other direction. Jews will not only learn the local languages; they will in a few generations (and for a millennium and a half) be serving the entire ancient Near Eastern world as expert translators, scribes, diplomats, sages, merchants, astronomers. They will make a virtue and a cultural advantage of their being resident aliens, not spending their substance in fighting over civil sovereignty. Their conviction that there is but one God — creator, sovereign, anikonic, historically active, able to speak — enhances their cultural creativity over against the polytheistic, super-stitious, tribally structured, fertility-focused popular religions of their neighbors.

Somewhere, some time, in the Jeremianic setting, there arose what I claimed above was the most fundamental sociological innova-tion in the history of religions, namely, the culture of the synagogue.[48] There is here no priest accredited by his qualification to administer cultic ceremonies. There is no high priest mandated by the emperor. Precisely because the Jerusalem temple is not portable and its functions not replaceable, what Jews gather around elsewhere will be not an altar but a scroll. The legitimacy of the local gathering depends on no central hierarchy, although its fidelity to the message of the scroll may be served by a rabbi trained in a school.[49] Any ten households qualify

48. "Synagogue" is here a code word for the set of social changes already described formally above. Messianic Judaism in the first century, which we now call "Christianity," went on from here with no basic change as far as social structure and worldview are concerned. "Christians" (most accurately described for the first generations as "messi-anic Jews") modified the synagogue pattern only slightly by their openness to non-Jews, and by their love feasts; the lay, book-centered, locally managed format of the synagogue remained. When the synagogue polity came later to be overshadowed among Christians by sacerdotalism and episcopacy, that represented a fall back into the pre-Jeremian patterns of Hellenistic paganism.

49. The intellectual capital of world Jewry remained in Babylon for a millen-nium, despite the recurrent efforts to reconstitute a center in Judaea or (later) in Galilee. Rabbis, including the great Hillel, were sent from Babylon to set up schools there.

as a local cell of the worldwide people of God. Since what they do when they gather is to read together, a canon of Scriptures must develop.[50] There will be no orally transmitted mysteries reserved to the initiated.[51]

When Jews in Babylon participated creatively, reliably, but not coercively in the welfare of that host culture, their contribution was more serious than "bricolage."[52] There was no problem of shared meanings, since they had accepted their host culture and become fluent in it. Their own loyalty to their own culture (kashrut, anikonic monotheism, honoring parents, truth telling, work ethic, circumcision) was not dependent on whether the Babylonians accepted it, yet much of it was not only transparent but even attractive to Gentiles. Living in Babylon, then, amidst the cultural phenomenon which Stout now calls "Babel," namely, the absence of univocality, was not a problem for

50. The very notion of canon is/was one component of the originality of the synagogue. All major religions have scriptures; but something more is going on when the set of texts which are worthy of being copied, read ceremonially, and exposited reverently is limited by a decision which one records, and is thereby made usable for the community as identity marker. It is fascinating that in the recent renewal (in academic scholarly milieux) of the notion of "canon," there is more attention given to the importance of reading the scriptural texts side by side than to the diaspora situation in which they came to be chosen for canonical status. The notion of "canon" is not itself present in the texts which are in the canon. That notion is defined by the social setting in which those texts begin to function to formulate identity. In other words: the meaning of "canon" is not in how the texts came to be (so as to make us study authorship and accuracy) but in how (and in what setting) the disciples came to be guided by them (so we should study the diaspora). This insight is assumed but not exploited in Joseph Blenkinsopp, *Prophecy and Canon* (Notre Dame, Ind.: University of Notre Dame Press, 1977).

51. Later the notion of a second, privileged oral tradition, beside and besides the written text, was to surface both in rabbinic Judaism and in Roman Catholicism. When it does arise, its role is paradoxical; although it claims orality as a further mode of revelation (to bypass the fact that it is not authorized by the first text), that claim serves to validate a second body of writings, called (in the Jewish case) "the oral Torah" but in fact also written down, and (in the Roman case) "oral tradition." This "other canon" must validate as well an institutional magisterium claiming the monopoly of interpreting (in writing) what (it claims but need not — and of course in fact cannot — prove) had been handed down orally.

52. This was the term Stout pressed into service (borrowed from Lévi Strauss) to signal his modesty about the scale and strength of transcommunity conversation. I shall make more of it later.

them.[53] The surrounding Gentile culture had become their element. The polyglot Jews were more at home in any imperial capital, more creative and more needed, than were the monolingual native peasants and proletarians (and priests and princes) in that same city.

The one thing that never would have occurred to the Jews in Babylon was to try to bridge the distance between their language world and that of their hosts by a foundationalist mental or linguistic move, trying to rise to a higher level or dig to a deeper one, so that the difference could be engulfed in some *tertium quid,* which would convince the Babylonians of moral monotheism without making them Jews, and to which the Jews could yield without sacrificing their local color. They did not look for or seek to construct common ground. Jews knew that there was no larger world than the one their Lord had made and their prophets knew the most about. Its compatibility with kinds of "wisdom" that the Gentiles could understand[54] seemed to them to validate their holy history rather than to relativize it. When Hellenism penetrated their world, they did not hesitate to affirm that whatever truth there was in Plato or Aristotle was derived from Moses.

53. Jews in fact enjoy linguistic diversity so much that they keep on developing their own further variants. The Ashkenazim of Eastern Europe used, and carried with them to America and Israel, their own form of German. The Sephardim scattered around the Mediterranean world carried with them their own variant of early Spanish. But Yiddish and Ladino/Judesmo are only the best-known examples of a large variety. The many ways and places in which Jews interacted with host culture languages are reviewed in Herbert H. Paper, ed., *Jewish Languages: Themes and Variations* (Cambridge: Association for Jewish Studies, 1978) (brought to my attention by colleague Michael Signer). Like the hermit crab, Jewish culture positively enjoys being at home carrying around someone else's shell.

54. "Wisdom" is the literary critics' term for a kind of literature which is cross-culturally understandable and does not refer much to holy history. For some moderns, the existence of "Wisdom" material in the Hebrew canon is taken as relativizing the particular identity of the YHWH, the "God who acts," of the stories of Abraham and Moses. For the Jews living the experience, however, the opposite was the case. They made Gentile proverbs their own. It was they who brought Egyptian and Mesopotamian proverbs to Asia Minor and to Rome.

VII. Further Testing

To take thus seriously the Babylonian basis of continuing Jewish identity would call for further discussions, not provided in this text as of now, at some of the points where it goes beyond the limits of the standard account:

a. The standard account sees the course of history moving back from Babylon to Jerusalem with Sheshbazzar and Zerubbabel, Ezra and Nehemiah, and the construction of the second temple.[55] The Maccabees are part of that story, i.e., of the effort to reinstate Palestinian kingship as the normative posture, and they too failed. A more consistently Jeremianic account will need to retell that story of the too-early returns to the land, attending both to the events and to their theological interpretation by prophets and by the several "priestly" historians and redactors.

According to one way of disentangling the sources,[56] the books of Ezra and Nehemiah are not two faces of the same story, but alternatives. To take Jeremiah seriously, it would seem to me as a lay reader not versed in historic de- and reconstruction that both of them need to be seen as inappropriate deviations from the Jeremiah line, since each reconstituted a cult and a-polity as a branch of the pagan imperial government.[57] Of course the Maccabees were even more a mistake, as

55. Sheshbazzar is mentioned only in Ezra 1 and 5; Zerubbabel is in Ezra, Nehemiah, Haggai, and Zechariah. James D. Newsome Jr., *By the Waters of Babylon* (Atlanta: John Knox, 1979), is one of several attempts to construct a continuous story around these four names. Yet his conclusion is that there is no story to tell; there is no narrative that goes on from there. Newsome's mistake is thinking that "the History and Theology of the Exile" should conclude in three generations with the return to Judaea, rather than recognizing that the dispersion has continued, properly, faithfully, for two and a half millennia. Similarly Ralph Klein, *Israel in Exile* (Philadelphia: Fortress, 1979), while very creative in reading some of the texts written (or redacted) after 587, is completely blind to the way those texts gave a long-term identity to the permanent diaspora. Klein reads the material, oddly, counterfactually, as if the "exile" was supposed actually to end in three generations, and did.

56. Scholars have always had trouble connecting these two accounts. They tell significantly different stories about more or less the same time, places, issues, and people. The perspective cited here is that of Prof. Daniel Smith Christopher, one of the planners of the conference at Loyola Marymount and a student of the literature of the "exile."

57. Most of the text of Ezra is about the politicking for imperial authorization to rebuild the temple. In 7:12 Ezra is called "the scribe of the law of the God of heaven." To Artaxerexes these words meant "secretary for Jewish affairs." It was the title for a cabinet role in the pagan empire.

was the Sadducean collaboration with the Roman Empire, in order to maintain the cult, the system which was in charge in Jesus' time.

b. A more adequate account would need to make more of the antiroyal strand of the earlier history, only briefly noted above — Judges 9, 1 Samuel 8, Deuteronomy 17:14ff. The later redactors of the historical books who left stand those antiroyal accounts at the front of their narrative certainly counted on their readers' memories to see later events in their light.

c. The prophesied hope of return to Jerusalem, which would ultimately be implemented not by politicking elders but by messianic miracle, needs to be further interpreted. Whether that mythic return be "next year" as in the Seder ritual[58] or "seventy years" as in Jeremiah's message, it is clear by now (whether "now" be the first century of our era or the twentieth) that the adequate fulfillment of that promise was not in Ezra or Nehemiah, or in the Maccabees or Bar Kokhba.[59] Most Christians do not say either that it was fulfilled without remainder in Jesus.

d. If the Babel event of Genesis does not denote a divine judgment but a positive mission, what then becomes of the standard Christian vision of Pentecost as the miracle of interlinguistic reconciliation? I am confident that a fair reading of the account of Luke in Acts 2 will be compatible with the best reading of Genesis, but I shall not argue that now.

VIII. The Polyglot Advantage in Matters of Language; the Limits of a Metaphor

I already noted that there is something odd, perhaps paradigmatically odd, about Jeffrey Stout's use of the French term *bricolage* to describe how one goes on working toward cross-community communication after

---

58. That phrase "next year in Jerusalem" has been in the Seder a long time (in Gentile terms), but not more than a thousand years according to L. Hoffman. For the first millennium of the diaspora Jews did not conclude their Passover with those words. But with or without the words, the worshipers did not expect literal fulfillment.

59. Jews whom I respect have the right to say, and some do say, that it was not fulfilled either in David Ben-Gurion, Golda Meir, or Menachem Begin.

abandoning hope for univocality. The overtones of the verb *bricoler* in ordinary colloquial French include:

a. that one is amateur, not expert, not credentialed, and not needing to be;
b. that there is no reason to have to do it right, perhaps no firm definition of what it would mean to do it right;
c. that one does it irregularly rather than routinely and reliably;
d. that every trial is tentative, "trying this on for size," with no great stake in any one effort; flippant self-spoofing and mockery of others protect against too much investment. There is nothing in *bricolage* worth dying for.

When we hold this list of overtones up against the life of Jews in Babylon from 580 B.C.E. for a millennium (or for that matter the life of Jews in Spain before 1492, or Jews in Vienna or Vilna until this century), watching how they talked Babylonian well enough to be scribes, translators, diplomats, and merchants, we would have to say that "none of the above" characteristics of *bricolage* apply, except for the wholesome presence of a little Jewish humor (d. above) around the edges. They not only kept their subculture alive; Jews in fact contributed mightily to making the Gentile world viable.[60]

This enormous flexibility and creativity force us to return to the question, Is there is anything nonnegotiable in the dispersed minority's witness? Anything untranslatable? Of course there is; it is that there is no other God. The rejection not only of pagan cult but also of every way of putting their own YHWH/LORD in the same frame of reference with pagan deities, even not speaking the divine NAME as others would, was tied for the Jews in Babylon with the proclamation of his sovereignty

---

60. "Seek the peace of the city" is too weak a translation for Jeremiah's command. It should be translated "seek the salvation of the culture to which God has sent you." Joseph's answer to Egypt's famine problem, or Daniel's role in Darius's reorganizing the Persian empire into manageable satrapies, represents prototypically a Jewish role in contributing to secular well-being which is far more than mere minority survival. As a twentieth-century observer, I have the impression that Jews are too hesitant to avow the importance of their contribution to the viability and the quality of many societies, perhaps out of fear of provoking more anti-Semitic mythmaking.

over creation and history. There is no setting into which that deconstructing, disenchanting proclamation cannot be translated, none which can encompass it.

That anti-idolatry message is not bad but good news. It can free its hearers from slavery to the powers that crush their lives.[61] Many Gentiles watching the Jewish culture saw it that way, so that *long* before Christian beginnings, standard ways had been found to welcome "godfearers" on the edge or even in the middle of the synagogue.

IX. The Setting of Suffering

Beyond the above three meanings of Babel there is another, less clearly located than those three in time and place and less broadly present in the record. In Scripture and tradition, the name "Babylon" came to be used as metaphor for any and every great idolatrous and oppressive empire. Christians recognize this usage, perhaps even give it priority, because the Apocalypse of John used the name "Babylon" (although not very often) as a cipher for Rome (whereas the rabbis had used an earlier metaphor, calling the Romans "Hittites"). Assyria in the age of Isaiah, Babylon in that of Jeremiah, Nineveh in that of Jonah, and then Rome in that of the New Testament Apocalypse are in one sense all the same thing: the great world city, oppressive, drunk on power, worshiping idols, claiming to be the center of the world, persecuting the saints, and doomed to destruction.

Yet it will not be the saints who will destroy Babylon. Their suffering at its hand is part of "sanctifying the name of YHWH." There is no thought (when this meaning of "Babylon" is used) of the saints escaping that fate by emigrating to the earthly land of Israel, any more than by assassinating the tyrant.

---

61. This is the parcel of truth in the movement which a generation ago characterized biblical faith as "secular"; cf. Harvey Cox, Ronald Gregor Smyth, and a few lines from Dietrich Bonhoeffer. Authentic monotheism disenchants an otherwise spooky and ironclad cosmos.

X. Is This a Way Other Subject Peoples Might See Themselves?

I close by declaring my complete lack of authority to answer this next question. Is there something about this Jewish vision of the dignity and ministry of the scattered people of God which might be echoed or replicated by other migrant peoples, like the expatriate Chinese around the edge of Asia or the Indians in East and South Africa? Might it give hope to other refugees, like the Armenians who were scattered in the 1920s? To other victims of imperial displacement, like African Americans?[62] To the victims of the most recent horrors of Rwanda or the Balkans?

Might there even be something helpful in this memory which would speak by a more distant analogy to the condition of peoples overwhelmed by imperial immigration, like the original Americans or Australians, or the Ainu or the Maori? At *least* this juxtaposition may serve to challenge the assumption of the imperial immigrants that they ought to interpret their racist triumphalism (as we know some of their predecessors did) as analogous to the conquest of Canaan.

---

62. We have long been aware of how the ancient Hebrew message was preached and sung by African slaves in America and their descendants. Other forms of the question, as experience by other peoples, were part of the conference at Loyola Marymount for which this paper was commissioned.

CHAPTER 4

Is Not His Word Like a Fire?[1]
The Bible and Civil Turmoil

For present purposes we may open our study of the working of the Scriptures as a cultural power with the Renaissance and the Reformation, when the culture-shaking force of the appeal to Scripture over the heads of the doctors, the bishops, and the fathers entered a new phase.[2] There had been Bible teaching and preaching before, among the Franciscans and the Waldenses, the Lollards and Hussites, but it crossed a quantum threshold of intensity with Gutenberg and Erasmus, and the

---

1. This text has been substantially rewritten from materials presented to a seminar session in a Conference on Biblical Studies convened by the Divinity School of the University of Chicago in honor of William Rainey Harper, 3-5 October 1979. The plenary papers were published in Hans Dieter Betz, ed., *The Bible as a Document of the University* (Chico, Calif.: Scholars Press, 1981). The assigned theme of the subseminar was "The Bible and Civil Ordering and Reordering." My assignment was "The Bible and Civil Reordering," by which the planners probably meant to invite me to treat "liberation." The phrase "civil ordering and reordering" seems to have been intended by the conference planners as a circumlocution for "politics." My rewriting soon after the event was greatly helped by the contribution of critics at the seminar; but it would be unfair after all these years to name all the people I need to thank.

2. See the chapter on Scripture and tradition, pp. 63ff., in my *The Priestly Kingdom* (Notre Dame, Ind.: Notre Dame University Press, 1985), or my treatment of "The Authority of the Canon," in *Essays on Biblical Interpretation*, ed. Willard M. Swartley (Elkhart, Ind.: Institute of Menonnite Studies, 1994), pp. 265-90.

numberless colporteurs and tract writers without whom what we usually call the Reformation[3] would not have been thinkable.

Did Erasmus edit the New Testament or was there a deeper sense in which the New Testament edited Erasmus? Did Gutenberg print the Bible or did the Bible in some sense call Gutenberg's press into being? Did movable type explode the Bible's availability, or is there a prior sense in which the expansion of literacy and the development of print media were themselves the products of a changed concept of canon and community?[4]

It is important to note that this vision of the canonical Scriptures as critical fulcrum arose well before any of the major movers of the sixteenth century; before Luther and Zwingli, Carlstadt and Luther, the spiritualizers or the Anabaptists had given their answers. The notion of the Bible as critical power should thus not be correlated too closely (as we have tended to do it for a long time) with only one set of the changes in piety and polity which in the 1520s resulted from one form of biblicism.

Nonetheless the Protestant Reformation, and later evangelicalism as an intensification thereof, does exemplify the notion of the Bible as a power for civil change in a way we may take as representative. The elements of this structure of critical appeal are numerous and well known. They are not all of the same age nor of the same profundity:

a. There is the protoreformed or neoprophetic vision of "the Word" as a divine agent in its own right. That "Word" as preached is not quite identified with, but neither is it separable from, the biblical text. During their early years the Reformers had this vision of "the Word" as a power, quite unrelated to the building of doctrinal systems.

b. There is the doctrine of perspicuity, which without deprecating literary scholarship empowers or even imposes a laicizing and popularizing of the hermeneutical process.

c. There is the "inward testimony of the Holy Spirit," which assures

3. My own field of doctoral research was the early years of the Protestant Reformation in the upper Rhine basin, where the preeminent reformer was Huldrych Zwingli, in his turn a disciple of Erasmus.

4. The themes of the Chicago seminar reflected the influence at Chicago of Paul Ricoeur, who has renewed in a new key the Reformation vision of how a text can have a life of its own, not reducible to the way the university dissects the story of its redaction, nor to the way "theology" reorganizes its propositional content.

the reader that she or he understands the text aright, thereby reinforcing the laicizing move with a higher level of mandate. It was to make its own later history, what historians call "spiritualism."

d. There is the doctrine of the later Protestant Scholasticism, affirming the inspiredness of Holy Writ as a corpus of uniquely revelatory propositions, best served by organizing and teaching them in a logically structured compendium.

e. There is the development, not much later, of Pietist and Puritan patterns of conversion and subjective renewal, so understood, practiced, and taught as to be subject to replication. These experiences could be generalized as models for the faith life of ordinary people, as the contemplative inwardness of pre-Reformation mystics had not been.

I have named five factors; there may well be more. Each had its own independent pre-Reformation roots and was to have its own further cultural history, with its excesses and embarrassments.[5] Yet working as an ensemble, a set or a structure of mutually interreinforcing rules, they constituted a global redefinition of the relation of original Christianity to what the evolution of Christendom over centuries had done with it. The Bible thus understood *both* demands and enables change *both* in the heart and in polity. Western Christian history has since then been the history of those changes.

The other component of post-Renaissance modernity, beside Reformation biblicism, is the Enlightenment, with its hermeneutic of objectivity and generalizability, its skepticism about privileged information and provincial perspectives. For any orthodoxy, enlightenment is corrosive. But Reformation biblicism was not an orthodoxy. If the appeal to Scripture were civilly conservative, it would also be (as many much later had reason to think) philosophically conservative. But if biblicism is a critique of culture, as it certainly was in the 1520s, then enlightenment is its ally.[6]

It was only when the reading of the Bible was freed by enlightenment's methodical doubt from the assumed orthodox identity between

5. The later developments, listed here as d. and e., are the ones from which the most embarrassment has come.

6. I shall return to the appropriateness of linguistic and literary studies of the Bible in the Baptist origins of our host institution.

what it says and what we believe,[7] that the readers could discover its internal diversity, its ancient Near Eastern specificity, first of all within its own environment but then also over against our later theological systems and our present preaching patterns. Enlightenment enhances the objectivity of the Bible over against our previous appropriation of it. Combining evangelical biblicism and the sobering discipline of enlightenment objectivity locates the structural meaning of a scriptural canon operating in a community confessing an historically rooted faith. "Scripture" is now operationally defined as witness from/to a norming past, of such quality that the voices from that thus-recognized past can stand in judgment upon later betrayals of their story.

That canonical-critical thrust is narrowed when, as we have done it in the West from Augustine through Luther and Pietism to Kierkegaard, Bultmann, and Billy Graham, its focus is upon a righteousness which is *coram Deo,* in "the heart," and not "merely" civil. That narrowing is however potentially, if not necessarily, a betrayal. When systematized, it sets up as a screen between us and the text the Neoplatonic scheme according to which the opposite of the City of God is the earthly city; i.e., God is located and works in an *other* world.

To this challenge the canonical answer is clear, against all apoliticisms. From Abraham to the Apocalypse, the city God builds is on earth. The narrowing to the Augustinian agenda may be of some use, transitionally and pastorally, for some corrective purposes. It may be needed to warn against self-righteousness and to enable us to converse in our neighbors' idiom of humanistic individualism. It may refine in a salutary way our expectations of direct relevance. Yet it becomes a betrayal when it denies that the newness of the gospel can take on flesh.

---

7. Much conversation has been stirred in the guild by an oversimple contrast between what the text "meant" and what it "means." Like any blunt instrument, this distinction can be destructive or even silly when used roughly. Yet it makes a necessary point, which is at the base of the original notion of canonical critique. We shall best understand what a text intended if we free it from the assumption that we already agree with it. Krister Stendahl is usually cited as the popularizer of this insight, in his article "Biblical Theology," in the *Interpreter's Dictionary.* Ben C. Ollenburger has laid out broadly the limitations of the simple dichotomy in his paper "What Krister Stendahl 'Meant' — a Normative Critique of 'Descriptive Biblical Theology,'" *Horizons in Biblical Theology: An International Dialogue* 8, no. 1 (June 1986): 61-98.

It has been a broadening of the canonical-critical thrust when from William of Orange through Cromwell, through William Penn and Abraham Lincoln to Gustavo Gutiérrez, the distinctiveness of the Word's civil reordering has been risked in the common coinage of effective government. That broadening can also be, but also need not necessarily be, a betrayal. The besetting temptation is the Solomonic or Constantinian one, when it reduces the *reordering* the prophetic Word demands and enables to the hallowing or the reforming of the present order. Some Solomonism may be fitting, when in a particularly favored circumstance the road is open for creative social construction, but such circumstances are not only not the norm, they are practically impossible.[8] It becomes betrayal when any power structure is identified as the order God desires.

The Neoplatonic narrowing and the Solomonic broadening just described are not opposite poles of a scale, with the faithful, biblically driven reordering claiming the happy middle ground. They are rather allies. The Neoplatonic dualism between inner and outer or between spirit and matter usually serves to defend religious establishment against this-worldly criticism. The Neoplatonic temptation limits us to something very distilled and general, a single slogan; to a mood like "trust" or a motive like "love," "empowerment," or "humanization," leaving the rest to be played by ear. The slogan derives its concrete moral content from sources not subject to criticism. To "play by ear" is to accompany a new melody according to previously learned habits of harmony. In the social realm those "habits" are Solomonic at bottom. Playing by ear is also an elitism; it claims for oneself a level of virtuosity which most others do not have. The "Solomonic" temptation reaches for a system of rules foreseeing all possible challenges. The two are more alike than they are different; they inform each other. Both lack a particular peoplehood distinguishable from both the individual and the empire.

A standard mental strategy whereby Neoplatonic language supports the Solomonic structure is what Gustavo Gutiérrez calls "the distinction of planes." To contrast the inward with the outward life, justification *coram Deo* with human righteousness, the individual with

---

8. The story of William Penn's becoming a ruler demonstrates how rare such a possibility has to be, but also that it cannot be declared a priori impossible.

the social, the "existential" with the institutional are not all the same argument, but they can all be used for the same purpose. By relegating the canonical appeal to one of those other levels, the civil realm is kept free to follow its own rules.

The response of the canonical critique to this defense is not one formal principle or hermeneutical clue but the irreducible narrative substance of the old story of Abraham, Moses, Jeremiah, and Jesus. The anchor foot which keeps flexibility from becoming betrayal, keeps "discernment" from becoming arbitrary, is the story itself, not some mental "truth" above or behind it.

The Bible does not speak into the civil order without being read by a believing community. It is not only a story *about* a community, as I shall be demonstrating further below; it is read in a community which owns it as their shared story.

That story is about a people, a civil reordering in their very existence, not only potentially or by implication. No "bridge" or "translation" is needed to make the Bible a book about politics. The new order, the new humanity, does not replace or destroy the old, but that does not make the new order apolitical. Its very existence is subversive at the points where the old order is repressive, and creative where the old is without vision. The transcendence of the new consists not in its escaping the realm where the old order rules, but in its subverting and transforming that realm. It does that by virtue of its being an alternative story. The effect of the Bible in human history is to order and to reorder because that is its theme. What it recounts is what it does. Violence and suffering, offense and reconciliation, coercion and liberation are its proper substance in the ancient Near Eastern story itself, before they are the effect of its proclamation in other times and places.

Civil ordering and reordering is the proper subject matter of biblical narrative, poetry, prophecy, and wisdom;[9] it was far more central to the texts as we have them, when they were written, than was any

---

9. Biblical poetry and wisdom are no less "narrative" than are the chronicles and parables; our concern is not with literary genre but with substance. The way in which the scholarly accent has moved in recent decades from "the mighty acts of YHWH" to Wisdom has been a significant corrective, but it makes no difference to this present point.

concern for the ontology of divinity, the correctness of ritual, or the authenticity of inwardness.[10]

It befits the particularity of this story that I should illustrate it not with generalities about the Bible's orientation but with a few concrete samples. What the culture-critiquing and culture-creating power of the Bible demonstrates, not between the paired temptations described above but instead of that dialectic, is a long and rich story, a generous but finite number of tested paradigms. These may with sensitive analogical reasoning be transposed to other times, other places, even other issues.

How God Orders and Reorders; Specimens

1. YHWH War

The wars of YHWH are an alternative model of peoplehood. Israel came on the scene as a political *novum* around the specific institution of the wars of YHWH, which constituted an alternative both to sacral kingship of either the Canaanite or the Babylonian type and to particularist tribal separation. YHWH's militant presence provided a power for defense without a standing army, a legendarium filled with almighty deliverances where the Hebrews' weapons had usually been of secondary significance and were sometimes not even used.[11]

---

10. At this point in the Chicago text I alluded to, and set aside for attention elsewhere, the notion that the civil impact of the Bible might be the result of a distinctive Hebraic Weltanschauung, which could be held to be normative because in choosing the Jews God ruled that Hebrew is the best language for theology. Cf. the theses of Boman, Cherbonnier, Tresmontant.

11. On the significance of YHWH war, cf. my texts: " 'To Your Tents, O Israel': The Legacy of Israel's Experience with Holy War," *Studies in Religion* 18, no. 9 (1989): 345-62; "If Abraham Is Our Father," in *The Original Revolution* (Scottdale, Pa.: Herald, 1971), pp. 85-104; "God Will Fight for Us," in *The Politics of Jesus*, 2d ed. (Grand Rapids: Eerdmans, 1994), pp. 78-89. Far from constituting an embarrassment for those who follow Jesus' nonviolence, Hebrew holy war is the historical foundation of the same. Cf. Gerhard von Rad, *Holy War in Ancient Israel*, ed. Marva Dawn (Grand Rapids: Eerdmans, 1991).

A colleague at the Chicago seminar pointed to the obvious fact that there are other ways to understand Israel's wars. Of course; yet for that to be an interesting argument, the thrust of the present paper must be accepted. For that interesting

Israel's very existence as nation is not a self-guaranteeing institution but a recurrent gift of grace. The battle call is not "to the barricades!" but "stand still and see the salvation of YHWH!" Despite the ethnic givenness of the Hebrew confederacy's core, probably far less defined by consanguinity than the later accounts let us believe, the nation's identity is prototypically enacted in Joshua's call to a choice. Peoplehood is a gift, not a given, in the former covenant no less than in the latter. That nation's survival is not assured (to use Isaiah's vocabulary) by horses and chariots but by faith.

The same nationhood may and in fact does move forward through the abandonment of kingship or what we later would call statehood (in the terms of Jeremiah's message). This truth about peoplehood was true then and is still true now. Christians have been backing away from the reordering impact of that message since the fourth century.

2. YHWH's Servant

What is said of the people and its survival is no less true of the sovereign. The Anointed is neither a zealot nor an emperor but the Servant of YHWH. The heir of David, to whom it was said,

> It is not enough that you should be my Servant [only] to raise up the tribes of Jacob. . . . I will give you as a light to the nations,[12]

is not the victor over Cyrus but his victim. That lordship is servanthood, that he who empties himself unto death is elevated to the right hand of the Father, is not a gnostic redemption cult historicized; it is the career of YHWH's Servant doxologized. It constitutes within real human history a concrete (civil!) alternative both to the world-dominating claims of Cyrus (or Caesar) and to the righteous zeal of the Maccabees. This is not political language being used metaphorically to describe spiritual transcendence or quietism. It is a concretely alternative way to be God's Servant, in both corporate and individual personhood.

---

argument to be pursued, the critic would need to take the literature and the ancient culture seriously, as most of the persons wanting to challenge (or simply to jettison) the YHWH war tradition do not bother to do.

12. Isaiah 49:6, RSV.

3. Christ and the Powers

The new order established by the Servant is not limited to the life of inward faith. Christ is not only head of the church but *kyrios* over the powers. His sway is not limited to the civil/corporate life of the believing people. When the apostle Paul speaks of "principalities and powers, thrones, . . . dominions . . . ," it is to claim that even the cosmos is shaken by the cross. There is a patiently growing scholarly consensus to the effect that in Paul's "exousiology" we have to do with an alternative political cosmology or philosophy of history, neither sacral imperial order nor "national liberation," but a universe being reordered by the Word of the resurrection.[13]

4. Paul's Secret

According to Ephesians 3, the "mystery" made manifest through the Pauline mission is that Jewishness and Gentileness are joined in one new humanity. This "mystery" is neither a ritual nor a gnostic insight but a political fact. The fact is to be "proclaimed to the principalities and powers"; again this is a public and political event, not a ritual innovation or a gnostic illumination. Neither ethnic isolation nor cosmopolitan chaos, neither melting pot nor confederation, the new humanity is called elsewhere a citizenship, a city, a new creation. Jew remains Jew, Gentile remains Gentile, but they eat at the same table (which blows the Jews' rules) and they pray to the same God of Abraham, father of them both (which blows the Gentiles' minds).[14]

---

13. Since I reviewed the work of MacGregor, Caird, Berkhof, and Rupp in my *The Politics of Jesus,* pp. 134-58, the theme of the "powers" has enjoyed considerable and growing scholarly support; there are interpreters who consider it odd but none who have offered serious grounds for ignoring these texts nor for understanding them otherwise. Cf. most recently Walter Wink, *Naming the Powers* (Philadelphia: Fortress, 1984); *Unmasking the Powers* (1986); *Engaging the Powers* (1992). Similar, very creative though less academically careful use has been made of the same concepts by William Stringfellow and Jacques Ellul.

14. This is not a mere ritual innovation; it is a sociopolitical shock to the existing culture. Cf. the chapters "Disciples Break Bread Together" and "Baptism and the New Humanity," in my *Body Politics* (Nashville: Discipleship Resources Press, 1992), pp. 14-46.

5. John's Bellyache

The key to the story in the Apocalypse is a scroll whose being sealed
in chapter 5 is grounds for weeping and whose being unsealed in chapters 6–8 outlines the script for salvation. Then in chapter 10 John is
commanded to eat a "little open scroll."

> I took the open scroll and ate it.
> It was sweet in my mouth and made my belly bitter.
> I was told, "You must again prophesy
> about many peoples and nations and tongues and kings." (10:10f.)

A Word written, unsealed, pleasant to receive, painful to digest,
makes of the seer/eater a prophet to the nations.[15] In the irreducible
objectivity of its writtenness, troubling the prophet's viscera but not
coming from there (as some pagan oracles did, and as some modern
psycho-humanism claims to), obliging him willy-nilly to be a proclaimer,
this vision prefigures the political potential of canonicity for culture
criticism and re-creation. That the book is not to be added to (22:18f.)
is the condition of its power to keep on speaking afresh.

To quote the much-abused 1620 sermon which sent the Plymouth
"pilgrims" off to America, "The Lord has yet more light and truth to
break forth from his holy Word."[16] That this renewed breaking forth of
light and truth goes on, and on, as much in the world as in the church,
is both our history and our hope.

6. Other Biblical Paradigms

These specimens lifted up from within the Bible are only an illustrative
beginning of the gathering of resources. They are themes generously

---

15. We need not decide whether the "small scroll" of chapter 10 is the same as
the "scroll written on both sides," whose being sealed in chapter 5 and then being
unsealed by the Lamb from there to 6:1 was the plot of the drama. The reconciling of
all "tribes, tongues, peoples, and nations" was the theme of the first vision, so that the
two visions might overlap and the scroll might be the same.

16. This phrase from Puritan John Robinson's farewell sermon to the Mayflower
company is carved into a cornerstone at Chicago Theological Seminary, just a block
east from Swift Hall where the 1979 seminar was held.

dealt with in the literature, and their pertinence to the civil agenda is quite apparent. There must of course be reference to the theme of exodus, which has become the dominant motto of an entire contemporary school of theology.[17] There would be the moral vision of the so-called deuteronomistic historian, interlocking in his patterned narrative the disobedience which causes decay and the repentance which enables renewal. There would be the way the man Jesus incarnated and thereby redefined the divine purpose.[18] There would be the way the celebrative practices of the apostolic communities modeled a new society.[19] There would be the set of apostolic teachings gathered under the title *Haustafeln,* usually interpreted as support for conservative politics but in reality revolutionary.[20]

It is important that there be in this way a broad array of paradigms; to use only one, as some crazies use the Apocalypse or as some conservatives use the Davidic kingship or the Mosaic death penalty, is a serious mistake. The importance of a faith community's having a canonical corpus rather than a mere charter is that it offers a near-endless source of additional resources, of different genres and themes.[21]

Contextual Modesty

Having set forth these specimen paradigms, rough but numerous, it is fitting that we return to the challenge from those who assume that any

17. The exodus theme is cheapened and overdone in much "liberation" literature recently, but it is nonetheless valid. Cf. my "Exodus and Exile: Two Faces of Liberation," *Crosscurrents* (fall 1974): 297-309, and my "The Wider Setting of Liberation Theology," *Review of Politics* 52 (spring 1990): 285-96.

18. This was of course the point of my *The Politics of Jesus*.

19. Cf. my "Sacrament as Social Ethics," *Theology Today* (April 1990), reprinted in *The Royal Priesthood: Essays Ecclesiological and Ecumenical,* ed. Michael G. Cartwright (Grand Rapids: Eerdmans, 1994), pp. 359ff., and my *Body Politics*.

20. Criticism of the social strategy of the early Christians as "passive," or as submitting to the patriarchal structure of the time, has been mightily overdone in New Treatment scholarship. When read with correct respect for the setting, the impact of the early Christian messages was the contrary; cf. "Revolutionary Subordination," in my *The Politics of Jesus*, pp. 163-92.

21. Cf. in my "The Hermeneutics of Peoplehood," p. 30 in *The Priestly Kingdom*, the image of the "scribe" selecting "treasures old and new" from his storehouse.

moral vision for society must take the form of a global, systemic, pre-scriptive scheme, speaking normatively to each possible question.[22] The need is not for a beautiful vision to impose from above by authority; it is for critical resources to apply from below. The vision of righteousness imposed from above is not wrong only because it usually calls for coercive violence, or because it is often given wrong content by its most ambitious advocates.[23] It is also wrong because any set of specifications that would fit one setting would be wrong elsewhere.

Canon as Critical Tool

Thus it is historically true, at least since the Renaissance and Reformation, that the way Scripture works to order and to reorder is not that Scripture lays from scratch a foundation on which we then build with integrity. It is not that, according to either the Puritan vision or the Catholic one, the Bible provides a changeless charter. It is rather the case that Scriptures are appealed to as a critical instance in the controversies about reformation and change. The church is not built upon a canon. Scripture comes into being with status as "canon" in midstream, as a believing community needs to illuminate and adjudicate choices among alternative futures in order to be true to the common past. It is then that Scriptures are called upon; only when they are thus called upon does a second order ruling become necessary ("canon" in the

22. A Lutheran critic at the Chicago seminar asked for a full systemic specification of the world I would want. Yet if I had described it, he would, as Lutheran, have rejected it as formally improper, since the newness of the gospel cannot be realized in history. For the Lutheran critique, the reason "civil ordering and reordering" is problematic is the systematic dualism of the two kingdoms. My reason for not accepting the challenge of laying out a sweeping prescription for him to test was not the fear of being entrapped by the Lutheran dualism, but (a) the awareness that we are in a realm under someone else's lordship, joined to (b) the practical confidence that there are other ways to test a moral witness than by asking hypothetically in a divinity school lounge how it would manage the world.

23. Dominant models of the above, easily exploited by critics of the canonical appeal, are the claims to biblical warrants made in favor of apartheid, monarchy, slavery, patriarchy, or the persecution of homosexuals. This is hardly an argument against the canonical appeal; "nature," "reason," "conscience," and "tradition" have regularly been used just as destructively in favor of the same mistakes.

narrower sense) as to which witnesses we agree we can all appeal to. The creation of "Scripture" is thus a critical event and not a conservative phenomenon.[24]

I just alluded to the Catholic and the Puritan types as the dominant ways, in our recent Western cultural history, to understand imposing a normative vision, in God's name, on society as a whole. The two visions differ as to where they *claim* to get the standards they apply; the "Puritans" claim a warrant in biblical revelation, whereas the Catholics argue more from nature and reason.[25] This makes little actual difference in the structure of the issue, or in their social guidance. Both make the state, in its national form, the primary instrument of governing the implementation of divinely mandated righteousness. Both envisage the problem of constructing a social ethic as if it were to be applied from scratch, or from above; that is why their call for a generalized systemic blueprint comes at the outset. Both justify war if necessary. Both are very selective in their use of biblical perspectives. For both, "the church" relates to the realm of justice through the privileged instrument of the clergy structure speaking to rulers.[26]

I have just alluded to the Lutheran critique, which undercuts the "Catholic" and the "Puritan" visions on the grounds of a systematic theological commitment to a dualism committed to keeping "law" and "gospel" apart. I agree tactically with the Lutherans, i.e., in challenging the very notion of a systemic vision, but for other reasons. The assumption that we need to start with a prescriptive model for governing a society is questionable not because of a distinction of planes but because

24. This was shown long ago by Oscar Cullmann in his article "Tradition," in *The Early Church* (London: SCM; Philadelphia: Westminster, 1956).

25. This is the way the difference is characterized by James T. Gustafson, in his *Protestant and Roman Catholic Ethics* (Chicago: University of Chicago Press, 1978). Gustafson describes the methodological self-consciousness of contemporary ethicists far more than he does their earlier history. The scale Gustafson has set up makes no place for the alternative I suggest here, since in categorizing modes of reasoning he leaves out of his typology the difference in concepts of the people of God and thereby has no place for a community hermeneutic.

26. For the prototypical sixteenth century where these "types" came into being, this description of clergy authority is literally accurate. In our age there are other clerical elites — theologians, social agency staff, lobbies, university faculties — but it remains the case that the normal path from theological insight to public policy decisions is not thought of as through the open conversation of the entire believing community.

of a difference of communities. The Bible makes much of the difference between belief and unbelief, and raises special doubts about the appropriateness of state violence as an instrument of righteousness. The Bible speaks of the people of God as an instrument of God's justice not to be telescoped into the role of civil government. In all of these ways, what the "Catholic" and "Puritan" visions have in common is more important for our purposes than their differences.[27] Both undervalue the importance of the contemporary faith community *as gathered, worshiping, dialoguing body* in making the bridge between the collection of biblical paradigms and our present. Both are inadequately respectful of the flexibility and plurality of cultures; they thereby hamper rather than encourage the community's capacity to carry the biblical paradigms creatively from one culture to another.

Thus the question, "How does Scripture work to order and reorder?" is transmuted into the question, "What shape ought the believing community to have, in order for the Word thus to work?" It would need to be a community that disavowed the Solomonic or Constantinian vision of giving the civil community no choice. It would need to be a community whose very self-definition is its corporate aptness for the hermeneutic task.[28] It would need to be a community committed to the ministry of "firstfruits," prefiguring in its own life the kingdom reality to which the whole world is called. This is the type of community sociologically characterized as "baptist."[29]

If Scripture were a systematized compendium of final answers, to be applied with compelling deductive logic to all future settings, then the person to do it would be the most learned master of the texts, or of deductive logic. If however our guide is a repertory of more or less pertinent paradigms, needing to be selected and transformed transculturally in ever new settings, no one person can monopolize that process. It must be carried by the entire believing community, joining complementarily those who are most authentically part of the local

27. Cf. "The Constantinian Sources of Western Social Ethics," in my *The Priestly Kingdom*, pp. 135-47.

28. Cf. my "Hermeneutics of Peoplehood," in *The Priestly Kingdom*, pp. 15-45.

29. There is a more than poetic aptness to the fact that William Rainey Harper, founder-dean of the divinity school which convened this anniversary event in his honor, was both a Baptist and a Scripture scholar.

setting with those who best represent the worldwide community and the canonical memories.[30]

This hermeneutic role of the community is thus primordial; i.e., we have to talk about it first. It is however by no means an exclusive possession, especially not in the post-Christian global culture. The question, "Is this something only Christians can say?" is pointless in this setting. When the empirical community becomes disobedient, other people can hear the Bible's witness too. It is after all a public document. Loners and outsiders can hear it speaking, especially if the insiders have ceased to listen. It was thanks to the loner Tolstoy and the outsider Gandhi that the churchman Martin Luther King Jr. with his Boston personalist education was able to bring Jesus' word on violence back into the churches. It was partly the outsider Marx who has enabled liberation theologians to restate what the Law and the Prophets had been saying for centuries, largely unheard, about God's partisanship for the poor.

30. I detailed something of the indispensable plurality of functions in my "Hermeneutics of Peoplehood." Its critical implications for the "high" conceptions of ministerial authority are detailed in my *Fullness of Christ* (Elgin, Ill.: Brethren Press, 1987).

PART 2

Presence and Power
in the Revolution

CHAPTER 5

The Racial Revolution
in Theological Perspective

Preface

The Church Peace Mission (CPM) was one of the most undersung intellectual forces at work behind the American religious and social scene during the troubled 1960s. Founded in 1950 with the vision of rooting Christian concern about the remilitarization of America more deeply in the several churches than had been achieved thus far by the less ecclesiastical Fellowship of Reconciliation, CPM sought a dialogical and ecumenical handle on moral thinking about war and violence.[1] It convened large public conferences (Detroit, 1950; Evanston, 1959), but most of its work was done in small meetings and by circulating pamphlets and a newsletter.[2]

One of the significant small meetings convened by the CPM was a study event at the Episcopalian center "In the Oaks" at Black

1. The institutional base of the Church Peace Mission was the three historic peace churches and the several denominational peace fellowships within the nonpacifist communions (Episcopalian, Presbyterian, Baptist, etc.), working in loose liaison with the Fellowship of Reconciliation. During this period John Heidbrink served as the Fellowship of Reconciliation staff liason to the denominational fellowships. Paul Peachey, Mennonite sociologist, former relief worker, served as CPM staff during its later years.

2. Its archives are conserved in the Friends Peace Archive at Swarthmore, Pennsylvania.

Mountain, North Carolina, 9-12 December 1963 on "Revolution, Nonviolence, and the Church." It brought together several of the leaders of the Southern Christian Leadership Conference[3] and the Student Nonviolent Coordinating Committee with persons from the peace churches. Another fruitful initiative was a conversation at Gethsemani, the Trappist monastery, where Thomas Merton first engaged representatives of the non-Roman pacifist movement.[4] Yet another was a study conference of Scripture scholars which issued in the book *Biblical Realism Challenges the Nation*.[5] CPM continued to foster dialogue by means of its pamphlet series[6] and by maintaining one ongoing study group which continued for over a decade and later wrapped up their common visions in *Peace, Politics, and the People of God*.[7] The following text was presented at Black Mountain, near Asheville, North Carolina, and never published.[8] The text itself is presented as an archival text from generations ago. Occasional updating explanatory footnotes are added.

3. The better-known black leaders present included Andrew Young, James Bevel, Vincent Harding, James Lawson, C. T. Vivian, and Charles Sherrod of the SNCC. Among supportive whites from the same movement I remember only Will Campbell.

4. Cf. the brief outline entitled "Retreat, November 1964; Spiritual Roots of Protest," in *Thomas Merton: The Nonviolent Alternative*, ed. Gordon Zahn (New York: Farrar, Straus & Giroux, 1980), pp. 259f. My fuller notes from this event are in the Merton archive at Bellarmine College, Louisville, KY 40205-0671. The meeting had been planned by Merton in consultation with Heidbrink and Peachey, although neither of them was then able to attend, Heidbrink being hospitalized and Peachey in Europe.

5. Paul Peachey, ed. (Scottdale, Pa.: Fellowship Publications and Herald Press, 1963).

6. Among the most substantial of the score or so of pamphlets were *The Christian Conscience and War*, a forty-seven-page statement by thirty-two theologians and church leaders, and *Your Church and Your Nation: An Appeal to American Churchmen*, by Paul Peachey. The series also reprinted responses I had written to the views of Reinhold Niebuhr and of Karl Barth on war.

7. Paul Peachey, ed. (Philadelphia: Fortress, 1986).

8. It was once circulated in mimeograph form at the request of Mennonite Graduate Fellowship, as background material for a conference in December 1967 on "The Christian and the World Revolution."

The Racial Revolution in Theological Perspective

1. *The Ready-Made Questions*

A fleeting and distant acquaintance with the current civil rights movement suffices to provide one with a full agenda of academically challenging problems. The movement seems, especially to those not deeply
involved in it, to be made to order as a test case for theories of social
ethics. The public statements of its leaders, though guided by quite
different concerns, are stretched and twisted to fit existing frames of
thought. The result is a set of classic polarities, drawn largely from the
long history of ethical theory and laid over the movement to see how
they fit. The presence of these conventional analyses in the minds of
critics, supporters, and leaders of the movement obliges us to note them
at the outset, even though we do so in the conviction that they fail
both to do justice to what is really going on and to provide any further
guidance. Our proceeding first to name them, if only to set them aside,
will be necessary if we are to avoid misunderstanding of what must be
said later.

a. *Law and Order or Revolution?*

Most of the adversaries, and also some uneasy friends of "the movement" (for brevity's sake I shall use this generally accepted but vague
shorthand label), admonish, "Your cause is just, but you must further
it only by legal means. If you just disobey local laws, then you must do
so only when federal law is on your side. Otherwise, in the interest of
combating a specific evil you undermine society itself." This chiding is
not always believable when it comes from those whose "deliberate haste"
had made so little progress in the last decade. Yet the argument has a
point.

The revolutionary will tend to answer, "You don't negotiate for
inalienable rights; the moral law takes precedence over civil law. No
social system may be tolerated if it is immoral." Yet no one would carry
such a thesis to its ultimately anarchic conclusions. Movement leaders
have demonstrated too much finesse, patience, and timing in their
negotiating detailed improvements to be thought of as espousing any
vision of disincarnate moral absolutes ready and waiting to be translated
tomorrow into political systems, or into heroic stances of moral disobe-

dience, with no ragged edges. Movement leaders recognize that one segregationist governor might be worse than another. They are willing to accept a federal civil rights law as representing some progress, even if it does not provide all they wanted and even though they know it will not be applied immediately everywhere. Yet the debate often goes on in "absolutist" terms, with legality on one side and, on the other, the kind of appeal to absolute morality, above all human law, which the mainstream of theological thought in recent generations has clearly abandoned.

b. Love or Justice?

More theological importance for the theorists hangs on the interpretation of the movement's demand for "justice." The sit-ins and marches can be spoken of as a "war without violence,"[9] as the only kind of coercive weapon the underdog has, as new revolutionary forms of social power arrayed against an "enemy" to force institutional realignment in favor of the oppressed. This conflict remains nonviolent because only thus is it effective; violent means would be necessary and therefore right. The adversary's will must be brought to submission. He must be crushed — not physically but in his will and in his social posture, in his "personality" in this deepest social sense — by pushing him into a corner where he has no recourse but to grant to the mass of nonviolent underdogs what they demand. Although the justice thus obtained is the indispensable precondition of loving social relations, the movement itself is less than loving and no less intrinsically sinful than another kind of warfare.[10] It wields power; and power is always selfish and proud. Its immediate goal of tolerable justice must be realized before men will have the liberty to love.

9. The phrase was given currency as a book title by Krishnalal Shridharani in 1939 (Harcourt Brace); cf. my paper "The 'Power' of 'Nonviolence,'" Joan B. Kroc Institute for International Peace Studies working paper 6:WP:2, Notre Dame, IN 46556. Shridharani was one of the first interpreters to America of the witness of Gandhi and one of the influences on Bayard Rustin, who was in turn one of the influences behind the SCLC.

10. Reinhold Niebuhr made much of the argument that Gandhi was not pacifist, because nonviolent action is "coercive." For that criterion to be both clear and decisive it would have to be assumed that the loving alternative is to have no concrete influence upon others.

For others the only strength of the movement is in its moral integrity. Its nonviolence is not interchangeable with other methods, for it is an expression of genuine love. The purpose of the sit-in is not to coerce the "adversary" but to communicate to him, to "get through to him," to bring to his attention moral dimensions of his behavior which he had not recognized. In line with this end, care is taken to leave him a respectable way out without loss of face. The boycott is not a weapon but a refusal to cooperate with wrong practices. The "demonstrations" are just that: efforts to *point* people's awareness to moral issues. Only for a good cause could such a method work, since it derives the strength of its protest from the wrongness of that protested against. The transformed institutions are an ultimately certain but not an immediately calculable outcome; the method is justified not by its success but by its integrity. In South Africa, for instance, nonviolence would hardly "work" in any foreseeable way; yet violence would not therefore be justified.

c. Church or World?

The movement was born in churches and continues to find there a major portion of its strength. It can be argued that even those of its branches whose leadership is less "clerical" are taking an essentially Christian position; that only the New Testament can explain the trust they place in suffering love, their hope against hope and their patience before defeat and delay. Only for Christian disciples is such a posture intellectually coherent and psychically possible, some would argue.[11] To propose it as a strategy for the whole human race would at once puritanically ask too much of persons who cannot draw upon the moral resources for heroism and weakly ask too little of Christians (in that it gives apparent, clear, religious sanction to the self-interest of a class and race).

"But the black churches are not merely churches," comes the rejoinder. By virtue of segregation, they are the nerve centers of African American society, maintaining a unity of church and society such as

11. Such an argument might be self-righteous. One who holds it might be simply ignorant of the moral resources of other worldviews. That fact does not keep it from being the case that there is a special connaturality between nonviolence and the posture of Jesus, which many other ethical perspectives do not seek to parallel.

the rest of Christendom has long since lost. Nonviolence is, at least in our civilization, a general human possibility, an accessible ideal, a moral way for a people to deal with conflict.

d. The American Dream or the Fourth International?

Many spokesmen for the movement testify to a deep confidence in American institutions: the passage of a civil rights law, successful voter registration, the intervention of federal troops, or "an appeal to the conscience of the nation" can be trusted to move things forward. "Just let democracy work; all we want is our constitutional rights." It seems that for these African Americans America is all right, except for the one injustice of having kept one race out of the melting pot.

Yet for others "the whole system is rotten." Democratic forms and the good offices of the Justice Department can be used if they are available, but they are neither fair enough nor fast enough. More must change than the election laws; the "right to work" is a farce as a profit-oriented economy produces too few jobs. The militant minority of the hitherto oppressed should keep its identity, not enter the melting pot. This identity will serve not only to obtain preferential compensation for past discrimination, but to carry the revolution far beyond segregation into the very underpinnings of the economy.

e. Conquering Hero or Suffering Servant?

"The Negro is winning and knows it," summarizes one observer. Ever since the "high law" of the U.S. Supreme Court and the "higher law" of absolute morality came into conjuncture in 1954, victory for righteousness has been assured. The moral victories of the Montgomery bus boycott, the student sit-ins, the Birmingham demonstrations, and the march on Washington have made the flood invincible. Just as it did in the labor movement, success around the corner raises new issues: that of self-confidence, that of disappointment when the goals first fixed, when once achieved, disappoint. "Fewer martyr songs and more phone calls to the attorney general" may already be a sign of the exultation of victory in view.

But does this mean the movement is after all above martyrdom? Would the same policies and programs have been wrong, or impossible, or unwise, if there had been no 1954 Supreme Court ruling? Would its methods be wrong in Angola or the Union of South Africa? Would

Montgomery have been equally a moral victory if the outlawing of the car pool had preceded by six months the Supreme Court's sanctioning of the boycott?

2. The Promising Questions

Not only the interpretation of the movement to its supporters and to public opinion, but policy making and interagency relations as well, suffer from the absence of a common self-understanding within the movement to which these unresolved polarities point. Nor are these challenges all subforms of just one question. For those who are in agreement on one question find themselves lining up differently on the next. Yet to argue away at them would waste our time, for the questions themselves testify to a way of thinking which has not been helpful. Each so outlines a general problem of moral analysis that there can be no solution; for neither extreme position seems adequate, yet a halfway compromise or mixture would have neither integrity nor direction. I propose therefore, having recognized the indecision to which they testify, to cast about for the missing dimensions which could replace dilemmas with directions. I propose to do this with a special concern for those insights of biblical and historical theology which are less often drawn into ethical debate.

The first of these perspectives is the new form taken in our age by Christians' concern for the identity of the Christian community in its relationship to the "world." Debate on "church and state" or "the church and secular vocations" has gone on for ages, as if the issue were the relationship between two administrative hierarchies or between two segments of a person's life; yet under it all nothing had shaken the assumption that all of society could and should be spoken to in Christian terms, and that the Christian community can well afford to sacrifice its specific identity in the creation of a wider Judeo-Christian civilization.

Historians of many traditions have identified the "fall of the church" in that very marriage of Christianity with the power structures of Roman and then Germanic Europe which had for long been thought of as a great victory. For some the great tragedy was the support, and therefore the control, of the organs of the church by the heads of state. For others it was the horrors of the Inquisition or the Crusades which mark the nadir of infidelity. For still others the growth of the papacy, the incorporation of pre- and sub-Christian religious attitudes and practices, or the uncritical acceptance of feudal social patterns counts as the central offense.[12] While each of these traits is in its way a touchstone, the deeper shift behind it all *was the loss of the identity of the Christian community*, as visible over against the world, replaced by the effort to "Christianize" (thinly) the entire society. Once the premise that Europe is "Christendom" has been granted, the rest follows. The church-state tie and even the Crusades can make sense (as they still do in our day, in modern forms, to a host of Americans) once the first assumption, namely, that everyone is "in," is made.

Our concern in this study will be partly with the fact that even those who most clearly disavow the Constantinian epoch in the church's history — pacifists, church-state separatists, humanistic integrationists — can still be captive to the same patterns of thought about morality in society.[13] Ethics can continue to be seen as social engineering.

Most obvious of the results of this mental shift is that *ethics is for everybody*. Thinking about right and wrong must now be tailored to fit everyone, singly and collectively, as the actors for whom we think ethically. For the individual, this means that the heroic dimension of Christian obedience, the self-abandon and the witness of nonconformity are necessarily gone; this can't be asked of everyone. Those who persist in asking it of themselves must be relegated to the honorific irrelevance of the "monastics," the "vocational" prophets and gadflies; even they are not evaluated by the rightness of their own position but by how they contribute to the whole.

But our present concern is not personal ethics but the collective "tailoring" of morality. Morality is now thought of as what you run a society by; what I have called a kind of social engineering. The "right"

---

12. For a fuller review of the notion of "the fall of the church" and the metaphorical meaning of "Constantine" as standing for a transformed church/world relationship, cf. my *The Priestly Kingdom* (Notre Dame, Ind.: Notre Dame University Press, 1985), pp. 72ff., and "Primitivism in the Radical Reformation," my contribution to Richard T. Hughes, ed., *The Primitive Church in the Modern World* (Chicago: University of Illinois Press, 1995), pp. 82ff.

13. Cf. the notion of several strata of "neo-Constantinian" attitudes as described in my *The Original Revolution* (Scottdale, Pa.: Herald, 1971), pp. 141ff. Or in *The Royal Priesthood: Essays Ecclesiological and Ecumenical*, ed. Michael G. Cartwright (Grand Rapids: Eerdmans, 1994), pp. 198ff.

is not what everyone could do if he wished (whereby we close our eyes to the fully obvious fact that most don't care to). More important, the right is what, if everyone would do it (though we know they won't), would *work.* "What would happen if everybody did it that way?" is the standard ethical yardstick, the rejoinder to every new imperative.[14] Or "Can you expect everyone to be willing to do that?" If it does not promise somehow to be possible, effective, a way of acting can hardly be right. This yardstick is universally used in Christian thought, even though we are quite aware at the same time that most of the people in the world will not be acting according to the standards which we propose for Christian obedience.

It further follows from this orientation that *a moral choice is basically a choice of institutions.* Institutions are the way in which love is organized to become relevant to human needs. We therefore do not begin with the person-to-person dimensions of human relationships, but with structures. An ethical choice is right if it can effectively be translated into organizations and thus make over society according to its preferences. It further is assumed in this connection that getting power over the institutions and finding the way to change them is prior to discussion of what to do with them. Only when you are in the driver's seat can you ask where to take the vehicle. So first get there, at whatever cost. Thus it is that the Middle Ages were able to think of the prince as the first Christian of the realm. In the Reformation a Luther could call the princes "emergency bishops." The reforming preachers Huldrych Zwingli at Zürich or Martin Bucer at Strasbourg could equate the civil authorities as "principal members" with the "elders" in New Testament church government. Today it is agencies like Moral Rearmament which beam their appeal to men in high places. Seeking and wielding political influence is the noblest kind of public service. Even when the church accepts working on moral issues with ordinary people like us, it is often with the rationale that public opinion is after all the strongest weapon. Or when nonviolence is preferred as means of social struggle, it is because this is the most effective weapon in certain situations.

We have been attending to the logical implications of the Con-

---

14. I review several dimensions of this shift from the moral logic of the gospel to that of Christendom in "The Constantinian Sources of Western Social Ethics," in my *The Priestly Kingdom,* pp. 135ff.

stantinian synthesis for the structure of Christian moral thinking. It has other effects as well, especially in the sociological realms. The "church" is no longer predominantly a body of people and secondarily the things they do together and the facilities they use to do them together; it is rather the institution which services the entire population with a certain category of "religious" resources. The church is the service station for "crisis experiences" and for "the depth dimension." Except in emergencies it should stay out of economic and political concerns and deal with the needs of the soul.

A further development from this fallen condition of the church is that the local selfish concerns which it has found necessary to "baptize" in order to keep in touch with people, and keep them available for Christianization, become smaller and smaller. First it was the whole Roman Empire which became a Christian civilization; then it was a fraction thereof; then it was a "Holy Roman Empire" which excluded most of Europe; and finally it has become the nation or even the class within the nation, in the name of which it is proper to wage a holy conflict against the rest of the world. Thus our "baptized group egoisms" not only become smaller; they also become less self-critical and more brutally egoistic.

Yet another sociological outworking of the merging of church and society is that the basic moral and social decisions are made by those in charge, namely, the rulers, and are therefore always socially conservative. The function of social creativity is left to rebels who, since they rebel against the system of which religion has become an integral part, are often also rebelling against religion. Instead of being driven by faith into ever new and higher forms of creativity, the new and creative people are obliged to think of themselves as being "opposed to religion"; at the same time any newly creative impulses which do nevertheless arise out of the central experiences of the church are partitioned out of the political order, since the body of Christianized society has other organs for dealing with political concerns and politics is not the place of the church.

It would be possible to debate in an abstract way whether in principle the effort to make the vision of a Christianized civilization operate is desirable or not. Christians of the "mainstream" traditions would tend to respond in the affirmative; those of the free church traditions would have their doubts. But such a debate is useless and unnecessary at this point, since the lesson of history is clearly that, *even if* such an aim were desirable in the abstract, it is not now an available option. Even if it were a good thing, the time is past when it could be attempted with any hope of success.

Our continuing attention to the racial revolution shall therefore first of all be illuminated by the awareness that *the vision* of creating, through a merging or fusion of the structures of church and society, *a truly human* and thereby truly Christian *total society needs to be abandoned.* This by no means is a position of resignation or of conservatism; it simply places in a more biblical, more realistic, and more eschatological framework the abiding Christian claims, demands, and hopes for the social order.

One of the most regrettable outworkings of the Constantinian vision is its success in "brainwashing" its adversaries, so that even when they react against it they do so in the same terms. One enormously regrettable secularized form of this phenomenon is the way in which the young nations of Africa and southern Asia react to European colonizing nationalism with a "nationalism" which is an almost perfect reflection of what it rebels against; namely, that naive glorification of a local political entity which modern Western peoples, having tried it for centuries, are attempting to overcome. The same is true of the most legalistic way in which the rebels against Puritanism react to their Puritan heritage. Their response to their own moral education is either in a systematic and in fact rigid "relativizing" or in commitment, equally rigid, to some new humanistic or pragmatic set of obligations.

Something comparable must be observed in the extent to which the church has remained the center of African American society, far more extensively than is the case for the rest of American Christianity. In spite of generally rising membership figures, the Caucasian churches speak with some authority only to a minority of the concerns of a minority of the population. Even those whose general attitude toward the churches is sincerely positive make many of their decisions in other communities than the church, and along the lines dictated by other power structures, most of them segregated and all of them under white control. It is only in the churches that African Americans have been permitted full self-determination; thus the churches have continued to provide a rallying point, a source of ideas and of hymnology, even though much leadership in the contemporary movement comes from persons who place little trust in the Christian community as either the earnest of a new kind of society or as an agency for social change. This continuing close relationship of the churches to even non-Christian African American society and the continuing capacity of the churches to provide ideas for broader social movements seem at first to be a source of promise and hope, just as the same kind of identification appeared promising in the ages of Charlemagne or of Miles Standish; yet it may also reflect in ominous ways the identification of the church with one society and its centers of leadership which not only has already generally failed in the Western world but has also been recognized to have been one of the initial sources not only of racism but of the general moral weakness of the churches.[15] Thus, though recognizing gratefully the hearing which church leaders continue to have within African American society, I shall need to attempt in the following meditation to break through the "Constantinian" assumptions and to seek for a more careful vision of the function of the church in a world which has come out from under her guardianship. My attention must therefore be given to the redefinition of the mutual interrelations between the church and movements of social renewal which must of necessity and most properly be somewhat independent of her leadership. In seeking thus to bring to focus the distinction between the movement and the churches, I by no means intend to reject the movement; though points may need to be made which in another context might have that meaning.

The Criterion of Christian Ethics Is Not Effectiveness but Incarnation

Christians are not the propagators of a set of abstract and impersonal principles received "by revelation" and needing to be passed on in a purely verbal form to all who will listen and even hurled at those who do not. Our testimony is not ready-packaged phrases like "Thou shalt love" or "The body is the temple of the Holy Spirit" or "Discrimination is sin." Christians are rather witnesses to a person; to God who in Jesus Christ has become our neighbor and teacher and servant; a person

---

15. This lecture predated the rise of black Islam, which since the '60s has changed strongly the sense in which "the movement" could be at home with Christian rhetoric, but did not change at all the deep unity between religiosity and black identity.

whom we must in every act either confess or disavow; a person from whose full humanity must be derived and by whose own personal obedience must be tested every effort to state Christian ethical guidance in terms of "norms" and "principles." Only as descriptions of who he was do our phrases have any substance or any authority.

Jesus Christ is proclaimed by the church as Lord. This is her way of saying that loyalty to him is ultimately effective. And yet it is not within our power to "sight down the line" and to justify the good action we are called to carry out today in terms of the good results we are sure to be able to promise.

The standard by which we measure our obedience is therefore Jesus Christ himself; from him we learn that brokenness, not success, is the normal path of faithfulness to the servanthood of God. This is not to glorify failure or some sort of heroic uselessness, but to claim, as a confession that can be only made in faith, that true "success" in Christian obedience is not to be measured by changing the world in a given direction within a given length of time, but by the congruence between our path and the triumph of Christ.

Every kind of brutal pragmatism down through the centuries has justified itself by the good results; so has every idealistic glorification of whatever anyone is currently doing to save the world. We must relearn the humility of measuring our obedience not by our claims to get something done, which really does not lie in our hands, but rather by its faithfulness to the word which God has spoken to man in the Man of his choice.

This insistence upon the moral priority of the incarnation must be guarded against at least two serious misunderstandings.

a. One traditional way of looking at this problem is the rhetorical contrast between pragmatism and idealism. This assumes that we have a standard of what it means for something to "work," which is itself not subject to moral evaluation, and that on the other hand the "higher" standards being held forth by the "idealist" cannot fully be related to real experience. The meaning of the incarnation is precisely that this dichotomy is not only illogical but that it has been given the lie by the ministry of Jesus. The paratroopers in Little Rock or the federal marshals in Oxford[16] were meant to be "effective"; yet they froze a conflict

---

16. These references are both to then-recent federal armed intervention in Southern cities to enforce desegregation orders.

situation rather than freeing it. The choice is now between "effective as we now figure it out for ourselves" and "effective after the measure of revelation in Christ."

The same would have to be said about such rhetorical polarizations as "love versus justice," or about the way some clothe self-defense or self-affirmation under the label of "love for neighbor" by preferring the interest of the "neighbors" of one's own class or nation to that of "foreign" and "enemy" neighbors. When we insist that Jesus Christ alone is the standard, we are not preferring love to justice or idealism to pragmatism. We are rather confessing Christ as Lord. It is ultimately only the presence of God among men and women which is practical, and it is only love which is really just.

b. The same thing needs to be said about the caricature of Christian discipleship as a search for "purity," as if the most devoted Christians, the strongest critics of violence, or the sharpest adversaries of social injustice were people unwilling to get themselves involved in the dirt and the confusion of everyday reality. Certainly there has been, far too often in Christian history, a Christian search for moral impeccability, but it has not based its claim on an appeal to the example and the experience of Christ, nor is it presently the motor of any social movement, and especially not of nonviolent social action, which is a most involved and confusing way to contribute to social change. The integrity with which Christian ethics is concerned is not the perfection or the innocence of the individual Christian but the welfare of the neighbor. The concern is not for keeping oneself unspotted so much as it is for rigorously refusing to be the cause of the neighbor's suffering.

Identifying with the incarnation as not only the standard but also the motivation and the power for Christian obedience will mean that when exercising a social critique, the Christian will identify himself with the "other," the enemy. To the extent to which there is any point in passing out grades of right or wrong, it is evident that the powerful persons in any society are more guilty of injustice. This however does not mean that the Christian is able to bless indiscriminately anything done in the interests of redressing the balance between the dominant and the exploited elements in society. When conflict arises, the prime obligation of Christian love is to the enemy. In the present case, considering the vision of "the movement" as we enter the 1960s, the "enemy," insofar as it is a person as distinguished from institutions, is quite evidently the frightened Caucasian who hides behind unjust institutions because of his apprehension of what will happen when he loses his privileges. The Christian's concern is not only to identify but to help change unjust social structures. Yet he is committed to changing them *in the way of Christ*. This kind of love is more costly in its relation to the agents of evil than in its obvious agreements with those who suffer unjustly. The most costly dimension of the love of Jesus was not his agreement with the justified complaints of his oppressed brethren but his willingness to suffer at the hands of the Romans.

The identification of Christ with the poor, the constant theme of Old and New Testament prophetic proclamation, is not understood if we see in it simply a call to upset society and make the poor rich and let the rich take their turn to suffer. The identification of God's suffering servanthood is with men *in their suffering;* it does not concentrate *first* upon an illusory vision of ending all suffering by a simple shift in the social order, and that is precisely why the change it brings about is real and durable.

It would seem clearly to follow from some of what has been said above that the theological basis for involvement in the nonviolent racial revolution, although clear and unambiguous, is not to be too easily identified with the practical and psychological considerations which have driven many others to support the same undertaking.

Christian Obedience Is for a Minority

One of the most widespread intellectual instincts of our civilization is the assumption that a moral teaching can be tested by its "generalizability." Any suggestion, any expression of conviction about moral behavior immediately calls forth the test question: What would happen if everybody did it? The critics of violent solutions to social problems are assumed to be advocating anarchy at home and submission to enemies abroad, since this, it is assumed, would necessarily be the inevitable results of everyone's practicing nonviolence. We need to learn to challenge the logic of this question. It is not legitimate to limit the discussion of right behavior to a calculation in the terms of social engineering of how things would work if everyone were to take this line. For the very fundamental fact of social behavior, in the light of which we must make all our decisions, is that not everyone else will be doing the same thing. Ethics is then the study of how to behave when others don't.

Most evidently, Christian discipleship is for a minority in that it presupposes the resources of faith: the assurance of forgiveness, the counseling and accepting fellowship of the Christian brotherhood, the presence of the Holy Spirit as source of insight and motivation, a changed attitude of the regenerate will. It is the puritan misunderstanding of Christian obedience to feel that there is any value in imposing on others who do not claim to dispose of these resources the kind of external behavior patterns which, for committed Christians, are the normal expression of an attitude of faith. A hypothetical world where it could be presupposed that everyone else would operate on the basis of Christian assumptions, where we could generalize our Christian standards, would be precisely a world in which Christian behavior would not be much needed.

The difficulty of applying Christian ethical standards to social problems as if they were to be followed by everyone is not only that *Christian behavior presupposes the resources of faith;* a further and still less debatable reason is the simple fact that committed Christians do not have control of most of the organs of society. This observation is of course dulled in its self-evidence in North America by the way in which Christianity has become the general label for anyone's good intentions. To speak therefore more carefully, most of the organs of social decision and control in our society are not at the disposal of persons whose prime purpose in life is to love their neighbors as disciples of Jesus Christ. Christian ethics must therefore be tailored to face a situation in which, just as clearly as was the case in the time of the apostle Paul, society is in the control of men who have no intention of letting servanthood be the standard of their decisions. We thus stand before the choice:

a. We may share with the present rulers of society the assumption that we must first grasp the tools of social control and then use them for our purposes. If this is our decision, then by the very determination to get power first we have lost the message we had to speak to the world of power. Or else,

b. We must learn to reject, not only in its fascist outworkings but already in its initial expression, the idea that one must first obtain power and then use it for good. Christian ethics is precisely a way of behaving in a world where the good are weak — or to say the same thing in other words, where the only power of the gospel is the power of God.

Does this recognition of the minority position of the church mean that we have nothing to say to the rest of society, to those whose motivation we recognize to be less than committed Christian faithfulness? By no means. There is no theology according to which this conclusion would follow, although the various traditions are fond of accusing one another of this kind of conclusion. Traditional theology has often spoken of "natural law" as a basis of a word to the larger society. The present leaders of the movement tend more often to speak of a "higher morality" by which all human moralities and all legislation must be judged.[17] Though we might have some doubts about the language and the traditional outworkings of this approach, there is no reason for not sharing the conviction that there are grounds for speaking to all men of right and wrong. We can and must speak not only to "men of good will" in high offices but also to tyrants and cowards, communists and segregationists of what righteousness would mean. But while so speaking we should not assume that these grounds are the same as those that apply to Christian obedience, nor should we trim the standards of Christian obedience down to the level of what can be asked of everyone else as well.

The Church Is a Visible Group of People Relating to One Another in the Name of Jesus Christ

Much theological discussion of the church's responsibility in society is carried on at the level of abstraction, describing a solid doctrinal base for the church's being concerned for society; yet when the question comes back, "Who is going to do this?" it is not immediately clear that a better doctrinal understanding of the church's responsibility issues in a better way of dealing with contemporary ecclesiastical reality.

This is not only the case for traditional orthodoxies; it is also true of much very recent thinking about the church's "servanthood" and "secular" responsibilities. The inadequacy of contemporary ecclesiasti-

17. The most widely noticed instance of this kind of claim is of course its use when the case is made for disobeying the demands of the present unjust legal system.

cal organization leads people to resignation rather than to creatively discovering new structures of Christian fidelity. The combination of the newly perceived rationale for involvement in the world with continuing doubts about the usability of existing church structures issues paradoxically in a renewed Constantinian approach, in which it is the entire society and its present "nonecclesiastical" structure in which we hope to see the transformation of man and of society worked out. The church is then thought of as taking on a specific nonconformed and suffering identity over against the structures of this world only at those most extreme and very rare cases where "this world" is particularly recalcitrant and impossible to work with. Thus it strangely works out that a brand-new kind of argument for Christian social responsibility issues in very traditional patterns for the implementation of this obligation.

With the abandon of a vision of a visibly identifiable Christian fellowship, we have no longer a "church" seeking to relate itself to the world, but rather an aggregation of loose individuals each trying by himself to be Christian in his place. The "church" thus redefined still stands apart from the general mass of individuals, some of them trying to be Christians more seriously than others, but not as a visible fellowship. The church continues rather, even in the newer ways of thinking of the ministry of the laity, to be sociologically identifiable only in the structure of the preaching ministry, since the only specifically Christian contribution being made to the renewal of secular society is a message. It is quite true, in this context, if we are to continue to think of the "church" as that administrative structure which arranges to fill pulpits, that then any vision of "imposing Christian standards on society" is suspect, because it means clericalism. Then the accent immediately falls not upon the principles to be implemented but upon the political claims of the body claiming to represent them, namely, the clergy. However, in suggesting here that the overcoming of Constantinianism will mean a rediscovery of the church *as congregation*, we are protected against the special distortions of seeking authority for a clerical elite.

Since in the Constantinian picture the Christian congregation is thought of as a preaching post and not as a distinguishable fellowship in society, the premium concern of those interested in social movements must always be for the strength of an individual in his relation to the mass. This is the situation in which the demagogue is indispensable. He must be a strong man to speak to the masses; concomitantly, he who can claim to speak for the mass is thereby strong.

It is over against the sanctification of the existing structures of society and the glorification of Christian individualism, both taking place at the cost of the believing community, that we affirm with the New Testament and with the free church tradition through the ages that the church as a new kind of social structure, a new kind of human community, is a third option. Whereas other social groupings (the state, the trade union, the corporation) are by definition established around a shared (legitimate) selfish interest, so that their very structure causes them to be more self-seeking than an individual might be,[18] the church is the one society in which the terms of membership — namely, the confession of faith and cross-bearing obedience to Jesus Christ — would, to the extent to which it is honored, make people less rather than more selfish. By no means is this to say that the church is exempt from temptation, especially to the sins of pride and self-satisfaction. This is however not because of the confession of commitment to Jesus Christ but in spite of it.

Also on the simple level of personality resources, the church, seen as a fellowship of people with varying gifts and responsibilities, provides the kind of mutual acceptance and support and criticism which makes of each individual a more complete person and of the total body an organism considerably more effective than would be the sum of its parts.

If the church is in this sense the body of persons gathered around the name of Jesus Christ, certain limits must be set to the availability of her sanction for and support of causes within the larger society, even where those causes are recognized by her to be essentially just. Whether or not a church building can be used by the Student Nonviolent Coordinating Committee as a locale for mass meetings or whether the church can be a source of leadership resources such as those provided by the Southern Christian Leadership Conference is a question whose answer can be spelled out only after it has first been settled that the church is not *primarily* an instrument to speak to or for the masses about how those masses might transform the social and political structures to which they are subject. Her pulpit is no podium and her preacher should be no demagogue.

18. This is the point Reinhold Niebuhr intentionally overstated in the title to his *Moral Man and Immoral Society* (1932).

The Church Accepts Living under an Unjust Social Order

The most marked social trait of the church in the early centuries and in many crucial decades since then has been the way in which she, often alone among subject people, accepted without surprise the suffering inherent in confessing the name of Christ as Lord in the midst of a society rebelling against him. This readiness to suffer under unjust rulers has been accepted by Christians in the past as a part of the way of the cross to which they have been called. The ultimate hope for the transformation of their social relationships was placed not in an immediate upsetting of tyrannical rulers but in the total transformation of human relationships through the hidden lordship of Christ.

The reader will respond impatiently, "This is just what we have had too much of already! Such subjection is just what the oppressors have been calling us to over the centuries; and the great injustice has been compounded by the fact that the oppressed have wrongly thought it their duty to accept oppression. Is it not immoral to live under an immoral social order?"

Let us not be too hasty to discard the message of the New Testament at this point. First of all, the hasty response suggested above misinterprets the actual facts.[19] Those who have oppressed others of their brothers, be they the white oppressors of the American or South African blacks or the industrialist oppressors of child laborers in the early decades of the Industrial Revolution, have not been saying it is the Christian duty of the poor to accept an unjust social order. They have rather said that an order in which the poor have to suffer is a just order. This is quite a different point. The same has been the case in those points where the subject peoples have abjectly bowed to things as they were. This resignation has not been Christian submission to a fate one no longer had the courage to denounce. Thus the identification of Christian patience with the lassitude currently being (unfairly) attributed to "Uncle Tom" betrays a serious misunderstanding.

A second objection of many to the thesis stated above arises from the assumption we have already challenged that a Christian teaching

---

19. A decade later I returned to this NT theme in the chapter on "Revolutionary Subordination," in my *The Politics of Jesus*, 2d ed. (Grand Rapids: Eerdmans, 1994).

would need to be measured by whether everyone can apply it. All that I am currently saying is that *the Christian church,* according to the testimony of the New Testament, accepts living under an unjust social order. Anyone who is not committed to Jesus Christ in such a way as to be led to such a position and who thinks himself capable of some better solution is fully at liberty to respond to injustice in another way. What we need to study in a theological interpretation of "the racial revolution" is not whether the New Testament condemns our modern standards of effectiveness but rather what light the New Testament throws upon the contemporary faithfulness of those who are committed to the lordship of Christ. That some think his lordship is unacceptable because it seems to be costly, or to be ineffective, has been a permanent part of the picture since well before the crucifixion of him who through all time will be "a stumbling block to the Jews and folly to the Greeks."

One way to test the rationale we are attempting to work out for social change in North America is to ask how much of what we say could be applied today in East Germany or South Africa or China; i.e., in countries where the cause of social justice and the cause of the church are both currently not favored by those in political power. Much of the interpretation and strategy of the contemporary civil rights movement is derived from the 1954 U.S. Supreme Court decision and from the assumption that the standards of democratic justice to which the movement appeals are not only technically but really guaranteed by the American Constitution and by the present intentions of the federal government. Whether this assumption holds even in North America is of course questionable, since the powers which really make decisions about what will ultimately happen are not this simply to be identified with the federal administration or with the Constitution or the Supreme Court's decisions. The real process of government is to a considerable extent underground, with more basic decisions often being made in banks and country clubs than in courtrooms. That the decision makers in government, in this latter, realistic sense, are on the side of civil rights is by no means clear in this "land of the free and home of the brave." It can therefore be argued that even in this nation we need to state our problem as that of continuing to live under hostile and unjust authorities, and fixing our strategy accordingly, rather than accepting the current democratic mythology and then feeling we have simply to mop up a few pockets of remaining discrimination.

As a matter of fact, democracy itself, not only when abused but actually when doing its best, continues to be an unjust social order.[20] It is a source of uneasiness to note to what extent certain civil rights workers seem to feel that if they get the vote they will solve their problems and African Americans will be given an equal chance. We sometimes even have painted for us the picture of a causal chain of unavoidable sequences beginning with the troops necessary to guarantee the franchise, assuming that when African Americans can vote the governments coming into power will be capable of dealing with all social evils in a rapid and effective way and thereby creating a just and equitable society. There is nothing in human nature or in the social history of democratic government to justify this kind of hope.

All of this is not to say that the Christian church ceases to be concerned for the *relative* improvement of the society under which it lives, improvements which certainly must go in the direction of a broader franchise, the elimination of discriminatory legislation, and everything else that causes men to suffer. Yet these efforts must not be carried on with a rationale which gives people the hope that somehow just around the very next corner "Freedom Land" will come into view.

It is in accordance with the proper place of the church in society that the real revolutions which change the nature of an entire civilization are those which take place in secret. They are those shifts in moral assumptions and in the availability of quality people which can take place only patiently and without notice. Those interpreters of the civil rights movement who speak of moving beyond the vote to jobs and beyond equal employment to the kind of society in which there would be no unemployment are certainly right if by drawing this kind of distinction they mean to point to the depths of society's sickness. Their analysis is however questionable if from it they draw a prognosis of violent revolution determined to smash even where they have no materials to rebuild. When the weapons of the strike and the nonviolent demonstration are contemplated as being capable of bringing the entire process of (segregationist) government to a standstill, this must be conceived of as a violent revolution, even if no demonstrator ever lifts

20. Numerous great minds, including Winston Churchill and Reinhold Niebuhr, are given credit for the dictum "Democracy is the worst form of government, except for all the others."

his hand to slap a neighbor. And such violence always does more harm than good, by destroying the fabric of society without being able immediately to restore it.

It is thus a mistake to concentrate on the absence of physical violence if one's actual intention is the total disruption of the present society's capacity to manage itself. The real revolution in race relations and the recognition of the dignity of the black people of North America has taken place in the last two generations not because of but in spite of the theoretical commitment of our government to democratic ideals. It has taken place by training strong personalities whose demeanor and whose gifts are even in silence a condemnation of those social structures which deny them their place. The current civil rights movement is simply the visible part of the iceberg. Although much remains to be "mopped up," and the process of carrying the revolution through to its necessary conclusion may still be long and will certainly be painful, there is no halting its movement. If therefore Christians are concerned that the continuation of this revolutionary movement be Christian, nonviolent, redemptive, their concern will be to continue to concentrate upon the identification and removal of one abuse at a time, rather than on theoretical sketches of the new order toward which we must move and whose attainment is thought to be the only justification for removing one abuse at a time.

The Church Should Be Not a Chaplain but a Conscience to Society

The function of the chaplain in any institution is to presuppose the adequacy and legitimacy of the structures of that institution, whether it be a hospital, an army unit, or a factory, and to deal with the "religious" needs of his parish within that framework. His attitude by definition must therefore be "positive" toward the rulers of the particular unit of society which he serves, toward its aims and toward its preservation. That the opposing army also has its chaplains makes evident the limits of the moral independence of both. Should he take a critical stance at all, this must be filtered through his fundamental acceptance of the system as it is.

Now the message of the Christian gospel is a promise of salvation.

It is in the deepest sense a "positive" message. Yet this message of promise comes by way of a condemnation of our self-centeredness, our self-satisfaction, and our self-confidence. To this the conscience testifies; its first incidence is critical. It is theoretically possible for one's conscience to approve one; but usually this is not what happens first and it can never be taken for granted. The clarity and the objectivity of the standards by which it measures are reflected in this readiness to judge man's motives and achievements, as is the need of one beyond oneself to forgive and to restore. So conscience, by definition, must be able to criticize.

Most of the discussion of the place of the churches in the face of the racial revolution seems actually to be balancing against one another two different conceptions of the "chaplaincy" role. On the one hand we see most of the churches, fearful and conservative, as chaplains of the segregated order — accepting it, accepting the authority patterns which prevail within it, and making the situation palatable. It has seemed to many that the only alternative is for the church to be in the same sense the chaplain to the revolution — accepting it wholeheartedly, agreeing with its new authority patterns, and receiving its support.

My suggestion is that our traditional assumptions have prevented the breakthrough of a new and more creative alternative; namely, that instead of blessing this cause or that in a blanket way, the churches might be the conscience of a movement whose dynamism (including its egoism) the church neither completely supplies nor expects completely to control. This vision of the stance of the church would seem to be a more discerning goal (and likewise descriptive of what has thus far actually happened) than to feel that the churches should, in a modern edition of the Social Gospel, proclaim that the liberation men need will be obtained through the abolition of certain of the most evident structural injustices.

Jesus Christ Is the Hope of the World[21]

The major loyalties of those who act in contemporary society are to objects of hope which can only be spoken of as "myths." We have been

21. Cf. my chapter by this title, pp. 192-218 in *The Royal Priesthood*.

educated, whether our ancestry is African or Caucasian, whether we go to church or not, according to the democratic mythology which holds that government is "of the people, by the people, and for the people" and that this form of government is intrinsically so effective and so reliable that it is the only ultimate possibility for all society. Our counterparts on the other side of the globe have been educated with an equal degree of self-confidence in the Marxist hope, according to which the economic mechanism of society drives inexorably toward the creation of a classless society. It is as such a myth that we must understand the concept of "freedom" as a hope for men.

Every secular hope is true and necessary as a criticism of ingrown and complacent "religion." The message of Old Testament and New is that God is intervening among men to change the structures of human relationship and that this is the ultimate hope of all men. Whenever men gather about a hope other than this, they thereby demonstrate that they have not truly heard what it really means, that in Jesus Christ the kingdom is near at hand. In this sense the critique even of "unbelief" can have a corrective function within the community of Christian concern.

Even beyond this, secular hopes are necessary because secular language is the only language there is. If we do not say "Jesus Christ is Lord" in language that men can understand, then we are not saying it at all. We should be worse than uneasy when we find the self-confident ease with which the word "freedom" replaces the name "Jesus" in the hymnology of an oppressed race; yet what is questionable about this should not be that a "translation" has taken place, stating the Christian claim in terms that men can understand. Our question should rather be whether the word "freedom," with all the freight of meaning which it has come to have in the contemporary movement, is big enough and true enough to say everything that the name of Jesus must mean.

As necessary as these "secular hopes" are, as ways of paraphrasing the gospel, they are not adequate and especially are not true predictions of what will actually happen even if things turn out according to the hopes and the plans of men with vision. The American Revolution began with the claim that "taxation without representation is tyranny"; yet before the young government even really existed new and higher taxes were unavoidable. The same has been true of the Marxist promise that once the proletariat controls society through the Communist Party, the apparatus of the state can rapidly wither away. In our age we are witnessing the bitter disappointment of the leaders of newly formed nations who discover that, even though the French, British, or Belgian colonizers were exploiting them, the expulsion of those imperialists does not necessarily provide an African or Asian people with either more political freedom or a better economic status. The same must be said of the promise of "freedom" held out before millions today by the civil rights movement. The legal possession of the franchise has never meant for the Caucasian majority in American society any solid guarantee of real moral or political freedom, and once every citizen has access to the polls it will become clear that injustice, economic disorder, and social division remain. What we are saying here is no "pessimistic" argument against doing anything, but rather a plea for reasonable realism in recognizing the limits of those goals which we nevertheless must continue with all our might to seek to reach.

The inadequacy of any translation of the Christian hope into contemporary options by no means should lead us to conclude that the transcendent goal of the kingdom of God is irrelevant; but we should be freed from the assumption that the relevance of a moral goal is primarily that it commands and enables us to sit down and calculate the safe and sure tactics which will enable us to reach it. Far more often, the relevance of one's hope is more profound *and more effective* when it bypasses this process of pragmatic calculation in favor of other modes of relevance.

a. There is the relevance of what its critics call the "absolute." There are times when the refusal to accept substitutes, the refusal to compromise, the refusal to be satisfied with any of the apparently available alternatives, is the most true and faithful and ultimately effective thing the Christian can do. This is not because he has any naive confidence in either himself and his righteousness or his "principles" and their clarity, but because this commitment to one thing most surely believed incarnates the only true liberation from the absolutism of our day-to-day routine slaveries and from the pride of the Constantinian assumption that it is our business to make history come out right.

b. The relevance of the Christian hope is sometimes that of *signs*. There are actions — and some of the most significant events in the civil rights movement would fall within this category — whose meaning is not "instrumental" but "significant." What matters about such a deed is not the changes it immediately brings about in the social order, nor the people who it pushed into a different position than they wanted to hold, but what it *signifies*. Since we are not the Lord of history, there will be times when the only thing to say is a word to which no one seems ready to listen and which will coerce no one; yet it needs to be said nonetheless, in the confidence that it is our Lord and his Holy Spirit and not we and our eloquence who will make of our sign a message. This is the hope which our efforts seek to proclaim. Perhaps Christians would be well advised to ask that the "demonstrations" of social protest remain more purely just that; namely, that they "demonstrate" something rather than being used as tools of social coercion and as pressures to force men against their will to bargain.

c. The relevance of a transcendent hope is sometimes that of the *wonder*.[22] Every account of the meaning of "the movement" gives some attention, and perhaps a discerningly Christian account would give more, to the dimension of the unexpected — another age would have called it the providential — at crucial turning points in the last decade. How often have not the great things, the brilliant solutions, the courageous resistances, the reconciling solutions been given to us at points where the outcome of the struggle was not the one predicted by the most careful planners but was a surprise, a revelation, "a wonder in our eyes," as things happened which would not have happened if the planners had had their way. And so it always is with the lordship of the crucified one. His power is not the divine rubber stamp with which he is obliged to seal our best efforts but rather a treasure in earthen vessels, a strength that is made perfect in weakness.

The last and deepest reason for considering Jesus Christ, and not democracy or justice or equality or "freedom," to be the hope of the world is not ultimately that the hopes are incomplete or disappointing nor even that they lead their devotees to pride and brutality. Their ultimate inadequacy is that in their search to be strong, in their urge to provide "justice" with "peace," they are not truly strong. They locate our worst need in the wrong place, namely, outside ourselves. "The weapons of our warfare *not fleshly, but mighty*." Those for whom Jesus Christ is the hope of the world will not measure their contemporary

22. The metaphors of "sign" and "wonder" to characterize the way Christian witness "works" are again used in my *The Original Revolution*, pp. 155ff.

social involvement by its promise of effectiveness tomorrow, not by whether it will succeed in providing jobs and freedom, but only by the identity of the Lord in whom they have placed their hope, and *this* is why they are sure to succeed.

CHAPTER 6

The Power Equation, the Place of Jesus, and the Politics of King

It was just days after the assassination of Martin Luther King Jr. that Herbert W. Richardson wrote in *Commonweal* that King had been

> the most important theologian of our time, . . . because of his creative proposals for dealing with a structure of evil generated by modern relativism.[1]

I do not propose now to follow Richardson in further describing the thought of King himself, by means of further analysis of his speeches and writings, as many have done and properly continue to do. Nor shall I dwell on Richardson's identification of "relativism" or "ideological conflict" as the essence of the modern challenge. I do however support Richardson in the claim that there is profound learning yet to be gained by the Christians of North America in the unfinished appropriation of the meaning of the black struggle and of its unfinished state.

We all shared, and we still all share in some way, in what King

---

1. Herbert Warren Richardson, "Martin Luther King — Unsung Theologian," *Commonweal*, 3 March 1968; reprinted in *New Theology No. 6*, ed. Martin Marty and Dean Peerman (New York: Macmillan, 1969), pp. 178ff.

sometimes called "the American dream." There was in that vision a deep optimism about the course of history, but also (more precisely) about the adequacy of the American social system and its ideals to become an effective vehicle of that historical process. Within biblical studies, and in social analysis, that kind of confidence has begun to be set aside, since the days when King studied at Boston, by various sorts of less confident prognosis: by learnings from Niebuhrian realism, from utopianism, from apocalypticism, from existentialism, or from the different shadings of Marxism. Some of these competing visions despair of history, and some of them retain the optimism but give it a new vehicle.

Many other topics within this story would also reward close-grained attention, but I propose to begin with this coarse statement of our present theme: how are we to respond to the waning of the simplicity of our hope for freedom?[2]

The American dream could be subdivided more narrowly into several strands. There would be philosophical evolutionism of the style of Hegel or Spencer, biological evolutionism derived from Darwin, can-do pragmatism derived from the American frontier experience, peda-gogical humanism stated by Dewey, and the growing confidence that this was a new world where we could escape the mistakes of the old one, confidence ratified year after year by the floods of new immigrants. The older Christian hopes, as they coincided more or less with the American dream, also had several strands. Some were more theocratic and "postmillennial," some more apocalyptic. In this temporary con-fluence of optimisms, Christian hope served not as an opiate but as a stimulant.

On the longer range, not all of the promises of this multifibered optimism turned out to be true. For generations, nonetheless, there was enough congruence between hope and achievement that at least the

2. This material was initially presented 6 October 1981 as an invited lecture to a "faculty enrichment series" sponsored by the Atlanta Theological Association, con-vened by Gammon Theological Seminary, at the invitation of President Major T. Jones. The assignment given me had been "to probe some unresolved issues within liberation theology." I could have done that around the growing Latin American liberation litera-ture, or around my own *The Politics of Jesus*, but it seemed far more pertinent to grasp the same issues in the form they were taking at the heart of America's own rights movement.

direction in which the achievement pointed seemed to confirm the hopes. We didn't seem to need to reckon deeply with failure. The impossible would only take a little longer.

The problem of suffering could be dealt with (it seemed) by instrumentalizing it. Unearned suffering can be redemptive, we were told.[3] This is a Hindu truth, revived by the mystical experience and spiritual discipline of Gandhi. It is also a Christian truth, although not all of the meaning of the cross in the Christian message is rendered adequately by stating it in terms that sound like those of Gandhi.[4] It may likewise be true as a form of psychological judo, using the adversary's strength against him, touching the conscience of the oppressor by obliging him to see the harm he is doing. Acceptance of innocent suffering is a demonstration of good faith on the part of the nonviolent lawbreaker. Facing the prospect of suffering is a kind of moral discipline which confirms the internal strength of people committed to the movement.[5] In all of those ways, the failure to find "Freedom Land" just around the corner could be kept from demoralizing us, and the promise that we shall overcome some day could still be sung as a promise and not a postponement.

In terms of ethics and pastoral theology, this congruence between our hopes and our successes laid the social analyst, the preacher, and the ethicist open to several levels of questioning. Is right action right because after all it "works," at least in the long run? Is it right only when we can see that it will "work" soon? How do we answer the

3. The phrase is routine in King's writings: cf. James M. Washington, ed., *A Testament of Hope: The Essential Writings of Martin Luther King* (New York: Harper and Row, 1986), pp. 18, 41, 47. Likewise in Gandhi, *NonViolent Resistance* (New York: Schocken, 1961), pp. 17, 63, 66, 72-77, 112-15.

4. It frequently needs to be pointed out, as, e.g., in my *The Politics of Jesus*, 2d ed. (Grand Rapids: Eerdmans, 1994), pp. 129ff., that the notion of "cross" is often appealed to wrongly. In the epilogue to this essay I shall comment on the inadequacy of one prominent journalist's sincere effort to interpret "the cross" in King's thought.

5. Nowhere in the thought of King does one encounter a methodologically sophisticated concern to choose among the several possible disciplinary settings (the psychology of the oppressed, the psychology of the actor, the sociology of public opinion) to explain further just why or how suffering works. There is more of that in Gandhi, or in Gandhi's Western interpreters from Shridharani to Sharp. Cf. my paper "The 'Power' of 'Non-Violence,'" Joan B. Kroc Institute for International Peace Studies working paper 6:WP:2.

younger, less patient leaders of the Student Nonviolent Coordinating Committee and Congress of Racial Equality, who already in 1965 were getting ready to say that the way of nonviolence should be abandoned because it was "no longer" "working"? Does this confidence in the congruence of hope and effectiveness boil down after all to a philosophical utilitarianism? In personal tactics? Does it permit or even foster a manipulativeness which trusts too much in the rightness of one's own perspective?

I began by noting that one of the points at which the waves of prominent historical change moved in such a way as to spare us some difficult adjustments was the passing, although more than ephemeral, coincidence between the Christian hope and the American dream. I say "more than ephemeral" because there are deep connections between the two. There are both analogies of structure and causal links. The power of the American dream would not be understandable, nor would it have arisen, without its cognation with the Christian hope. The subject of the American dream would not be thinkable if it had not been for the impact of the gospel upon the Western world through Renaissance, Reformation, and Enlightenment.

Yet there continue to be elements of abiding difference. The form in which twentieth-century schoolboys appropriated the American dream has been transmuted by at least two elements of learning, particular to Americans and to modernity, which substantially cheapened its promises. One of those borrowings was the global impact of the idea of progress, coming into the modern mind from many sources. It came from German idealism as a philosophical movement, from Darwinian biology as a model assumed to throw light on society as well, and also from other transmutations and reformulations of hopefulness, which seem similar to the Christian hope for history yet are founded on other kinds of warrants.

The second, specifically American, component was the success of the continental takeover by the Western European immigrants, the first and most successful specimen of the worldwide colonial expansion of European travel and technology. "Progress" had actually happened. The availability of apparently unlimited resources (without considering it as a moral problem that they were taken away by force from their previous occupants) and the aptness of the immigrant European culture to seize and to tap them all, and to build a civilization in what Europeans took for a wilderness (since the previous inhabitants did not count), reinforced still further the ethnocentric self-confidence which European culture had enough of to begin with and gave to the notion of a religiously founded civilizing mission the powerful amplification of several generations of impressive success.

Thus the American dream represents the twining together of at least three independently derived but very compatible strands: the aggressive hope for history of Puritan Protestantism, the philosophical credibility of progress as a cosmic drive, and the experience of white America's successful seizure of the continent.

There were always a few people at the time who, not always with the most convincing language, raised doubt about the rational or moral adequacy of that positive vision. But the times were against them. It cannot be our concern here to itemize the valid reservations, whose appropriateness we can perhaps perceive more easily today than during the first flush of liberal optimism. For our purposes it is useful, however, to name the points at which Christian hope for history tends to differ from one or the other of the strands of that rope.

Whereas the philosophical hope for history makes progress a cosmic necessity, sure to come with a certainty we can confess even when we do not see it, the Christian hope, which is also held to against the evidence, refuses to project by what dates or by what mechanisms God's victory will come, and does not expect to see it quite yet. In the vision of John,[6] the saints are under the altar, asking, "Lord, how long?" Their trust in God's ultimate victory has not been abandoned, but from the very earliest days their faith is strained by the fact that it takes longer to come than it should.

As over against the triumphant theocracy of a Cromwell or a Cotton Mather, there is in the biblical hope no correlation between the ultimate victory of God and the immediate prosperity or power of the saints. In fact, in the most important cases, the correlation is negative: It is the Lamb who was slain who is worthy to receive power. It is the victim who will see the victory. This negative correlation applies also, expressly, to the ethnic and cultural identity of the people of God. The coming of the Messiah means the coming of *all the nations* to the knowledge of Torah, not a privilege for the people who have been

6. Revelation 6:10.

sharing the witness of hope ever since Moses.[7] The biggest difference at this point between Jesus of Nazareth and his namesake of Jericho and Gilgal is his different attitude to the Gentiles. The prosperity of a distinctive people subjugating to themselves not only a territory but also the other peoples already living there would not count in the light of the Christian dream, as it did both for the ancient Hebrews and in the American experience, as ratifying the vision.

It then becomes clear at what point the American dream and the Christian hope for history will come unraveled. It will be at the point of short- and medium-range failure. Not always does this crisis need to be faced. The Montgomery bus boycott was "saved by the bell" of a federal Supreme Court decision that came just before the last minute. As the readiness of civil rights activists to break the law in the interest of a higher moral law escalated, so did their access to friends in Washington. It thus never really had to be decided, in the "progress" of the civil rights movement of the 1960s, whether the "higher law" which became effective was the moral law of God and nature, over against the laws of men, or whether it was federal law and the Constitution and Supreme Court as over against the laws of states and counties.

There have been those for whom the observation I have just made would count as an expression of disbelief or negative bias. That is not what it means here. It is rather the effort simply to label, in terms drawn from our common experience, the point of difference between the two so very largely cognate models of human dignity and liberation between which most of us are most of the time straddling.

The drama of our needing to disentangle the two visions becomes acute when one of them has really failed. Both the practical verification of the hope through the claimed moral success of white colonialism and the cultural convictions of evolutionary philosophy are falsifiable. There are certain grounds on which it becomes natural in some settings to believe them, and other grounds in other situations where they are no longer credible. Especially as the vision of the age of Martin Luther King Jr. intended to apply the American vision no longer merely to letting a few blacks in on the success of the whites but rather to the entry of all

7. Cf. my description of the prophetic vision of the "Hilltop City" in *He Came Preaching Peace* (Scottdale, Pa.: Herald, 1985), pp. 96-107.

American citizens into the fulfillment of those promises, it was possible for that vision to be proven to be *only* a dream. In a deeper way, the credibility of the vision has come to be seen as self-refuting, even for the heirs of the privilege. Now that those elements which were credible, because it seemed that they were being verified in history, have been undermined by the same judgment once held to support them, what now will come of their analogue, the Christian hope? Will it be possible to keep hoping as Christians when the other strands of the rope have frayed and broken?

Suffering once had seemed to some to be an instrument of social change, and thereby not profoundly or ultimately tragic. Suffering, when accepted, when innocent, made sense as part of a larger utility transaction. Whether the thought was that the acceptance of suffering generates spiritual power, or that the awareness that he is making you suffer touches the heart of the oppressor, or that the cultural perspective of the victim is a stance from which to see truth more clearly; . . . whatever be the detailed articulation of the relationship, the pain made sense as part of the promise of progress. But if the progress is slow, or if the promise of pie is reserved for the sky after all, how now can the pain be justified?

One answer is very simple. There were already some people trying it on for size during the last years of King's leadership. They said it in terms that sounded like an argument only about timing, opportunity, and the quantitative evaluation of how much good can be done by how much evil and how long we can wait. They said nonviolence had already begun to fail to produce the results we have a right to insist on, and that in a classical situation of last resort violence would now be both effective and (therefore) justified. My concern is not now how one could have evaluated that claim then, when Stokely Carmichael, H. Rap Brown, and Malcolm X were beginning to make it,[8] or how one would today evaluate the claim that black violence in America was or would be effective. Other segments of the necessary arguments would be

---

8. Since my assignment at the Gammon Seminary event (cf. n. 2 above) was to analyze the problematic of "liberation theology" as a whole, it should be pointed out that there was nothing about this pragmatic case for "whatever means necessary," as including violence, that was peculiar to the black struggle. That violence in the cause of freedom is morally in a different category from violence for other causes is an ancient notion, usually (in our history) correlated with white triumphalism.

equally difficult to parse.[9] I am concerned here only to account for the way in which that argument arose after 1965 as an early emergence of the difference between the American dream and Christian hope.[10]

This challenge was not only not surprising and not only inevitable; it was also fundamentally wholesome that after the successes there should have been the questionings, and that we should be driven to return to look at greater depth at the issues of the persistent power of evil and the temptations of triumphalism.

What is the validity of our cause when we are not winning? Does it change the affirmation of the human dignity of the adversary when (in the foreseeable future) the adversary will not be won over by our suffering love but keeps on unrepentantly oppressing? Does it reverse the pragmatic ethical commitment of the activist to truth telling, to breaking the law only in very exceptional circumstances, and to rigorous nonviolence, when those tactics achieve less? Should it increase our readiness to settle for half a loaf, for tokens of progress or bartered co-option? Does it open us after all to irrational destructive anger or to despair? Does the abiding power of evil downgrade for us that creative epoch and those leaders to the status of flukes, exceptions that prove the rule that God is not on the throne after all?

The text which Martin Luther King Jr. drew most frequently from his treasury of classical and popular poetry and hymnody was the verse of Lowell:

9. It was Malcolm X who most strongly argued the case for legitimate violence, *as an argument in principle* fitting the classical "just war" tradition. Yet Malcolm never in fact claimed that the time had come in the United States for the violence whose licitness he theorized about. Tactically, Malcolm's thought in his last weeks was moving rather toward King. Cf. James H. Cone, *Martin and Malcolm and America* (Maryknoll, N.Y.: Orbis, 1991), pp. 192ff.

10. During his last years and months King's thought was growing and changing in numerous ways. His focus moved from voting rights to jobs, he took on the Vietnam agenda, he granted the validity of "black power" rhetoric. . . . Yet this led to no shift at all in his basic affirmation about the moral imperative of nonviolence or "the power of suffering." He did not become any more tolerant of violence. If anything he became more overt about his nonviolent commitment. In any case this is not a study in the development of King's thought. Our concern is a theme in the common "canonical" witness of Gandhi and King.

Will the cause of evil prosper?
Yet 'tis truth alone is strong.
Though her portion be the scaffold,
    And upon the throne be wrong,
Yet that scaffold sways the future;
    And behind the dim unknown
Standeth God within the shadow,
    Keeping watch above his own.[11]

In what sense is this promise true? Is it a refusal of historical reality? Is it the kind of illusion Reinhold Niebuhr said people have to believe if they are going to make any difference, even though it is not true?[12] Or is it in some sense a real description of an undercover reality, some kind of subterranean causation or some invisible divine strategy according to which things do actually move forward by falling back? How can we affirm the sovereignty of God if we are still losing, and it seems that we stand to lose still more? The answer to this question, I submit, is a christological claim, although King in his public discourse did not formulate it that way.

Only when we are chastened by putting our problem this way are we fully ready to see it as part of the good news of the gospel that the New Testament affirmations claimed no instrumental linkage between their trust in God's future victory and their own present progress. The early Christians had no American dream to reinforce or to be reinforced by their messianic hope. Yet they said of their crucified Master that he

11. James Russell Lowell (1819-91) wrote the hymn "Once to Every Man and Nation." In addition to contributing to the American canon of popular poetry, Lowell served the United States as ambassador to Spain and England. King used this quotation six times in the talks collected by Washington. The same collection also carries six quotations of the parallel metaphor "truth crushed to earth will rise again" from William Cullen Bryant.

12. "There are no limits to be set in history for the achievement of a more universal brotherhood. . . . All the characteristic hopes and aspirations of the Renaissance and Enlightenment . . . are right at least in this, that they understand the *agape* of the kingdom of God as a resource for infinite developments toward a more perfect brotherhood in history" (*Nature and Destiny of Man* [1943], 2:194). "The truest visions of religion are illusions, which may be partly realized by being resolutely believed. For what religion believes to be true is not wholly true but ought to be true; and may become true if its truth is not doubted" (*Moral Man and Immoral Society* [1932], p. 81).

would come from heaven to judge: that he would bring down from heaven a new Jerusalem.

In our time both biblical scholarship and social analysis have acquired new respect for what they call "apocalyptic" patterns of reasoning. In scholarship there is increasing recognition that almost none of the New Testament writers can be understood without their sense of an imminent divine irruption in history. In social philosophy, capitalism and socialism, both major Western forms of social optimism, make promises they can't keep. Neo-Marxists talk of utopia in a positive sense.

The World to Come Is the Real World

To speak of "apocalypse" or "utopia" is no longer easily mocked as being otherworldly or spiritualistic. It is a way of talking critically about *this* world; yet it recognizes that one cannot be clear about how we shall get from here to there.[13] That uncertainty means that we have no simple basis for assigning ourselves the authority to manipulate history, no justification for lesser-evil calculations of consequential choice with the promise of "less evil" results. We need not assassinate Pharaoh or Nebuchadnezzar or Stalin or Hitler for it to be confirmed that the proud will be destroyed. We need not make ourselves the avengers to prove that God is not mocked. The point of this Semitic "apocalyptic" vision is not that we should not think or plan or analyze or intervene. It is not agnosticism or unconcern about social process, yet it does undercut the pragmatic case for casuistic compromise.[14]

The response of both King and Gandhi at this point was deeper than a mere debate about more or less effective means. They both

13. Cf. the closing chapter of my *The Politics of Jesus* and my essay "Ethics and Eschatology," *Ex auditu* 6 (1990): 119-28.

14. The word "compromise" serves us poorly. It gathers together a number of quite different phenomena. What it means in the pejorative sense just used above is the intentional decision to do *less than the best one can*, on the grounds that that will afford some kind of control over the system, to the end that one's goals will be achieved although through unworthy means. The word "compromise" can however also designate other, more worthy decisions to accept less than the ideal, without bearing that connotation of intentional evil and manipulative calculus. Such a "compromise" may be *the best one can do*.

affirmed the unity of means and ends as a philosophical, yea theological conviction.[15] Each rooted the unity of ends and means not *primarily* in a social-science analysis but in a fundamentally religious cosmology. This was natural for Gandhi within a Hindu worldview of reincarnation and renunciation.[16] It was reasonable for the Black Baptist King from within the experience of communities surviving under Jim Crow. It may have been made easier for King than for some other liberation thinkers, in view of his adversaries' Anglo-Saxon traditions of fair play and limited authority.[17] Nonetheless it is true as well in the perspective of the Christian faith in the resurrection and ascension of the crucified Jesus. If the Lamb that was slain was worthy to receive power, then no calculation of other non-lamblike roads to power can be ultimately authentic.

King's own restatement of his cosmic confidence did not regularly claim an explicit christological basis:

There is something in the universe that unfolds for justice and so in Montgomery we felt somehow that as we struggled we had cosmic companionship.[18]

15. The "ends/means" language recurs constantly. In Gandhi's *NonViolent Resistance* (cf. n. 3 above), cf. pp. 9-15, 42, 155, 183-88, 203, 213, 236, 252; cf. p. 199 in Louis Fischer, ed., *The Essential Gandhi* (New York: Vintage, 1962). Sometimes a causal connection between faithfulness (means) and victory (ends) is suggested; sometimes not. In King, see Washington, pp. 45, 102, 109, 214, 154f., 331, 482-85.

16. "The modern or Western insatiableness arises really from want of a living faith in a future state, and therefore also in Divinity. The restraint of ancient or Eastern civilization arises from a belief, often in spite of our selves, in a future state and the existence of a Divine Power. . . ." Gandhi in *Young India*, 2 June 1927; quoted in Fischer, pp. 289-90.

17. The standard putdown argues: "Gandhi's appeal to the British conscience would not have worked against a Japanese occupation. King's appeal to the Bill of Rights would not have worked against Hitler." This is partly true, though banal, as a way to avoid forgetting the problems of suffering and failure. It is however not pertinent as moral argument. It overestimates massively the generosity of British colonial administrators and of American police and politicians in the Jim Crow South. More important, if it is meant as an ethical argument, it fails. There are no success stories either of violent insurrection against Axis or Stalinist imperialism or tyranny.

18. Berkeley, 4 June 1957, in Washington, pp. 13f. King played with numerous other wordings equivalent to "something in the universe." Sometimes the phrasing is "the moral arc of the universe is long but it tends . . ." Sometimes there would seem to be an allusion to "the arm of the Lord" in Hebrew prophecy.

How long? Not long, because no lie can live forever.
How long? Not long, because you still reap what you sow.
How long? Not long, because the arm of the moral universe is
long but it bends toward justice.[19]

He could also restate it as a general truth of political science,
although even here the wording is confessional:

I believe that unarmed truth and unconditional love will have the
final word in reality. That is why right temporarily defeated is stronger
than evil triumphant.[20]

If the Lamb is worthy to receive power, then the only rational
worldview, in a cosmos where we have no control, will be apocalyptic.
This is the view of the Brazilian Ruben Alves and Uruguayan Miguel
Brun, some of the most perceptive among the Latin American liberation
theologians, who have long since added the image of exile to that of
exodus in order to understand more adequately the message of liberation.[21] It is true for the Soviet Baptists and for Solzhenitsyn.[22] So the
Apocalypse prolongs the message of Jeremiah: "seek the peace of that
city where the Lord has placed you as strangers." This is not an ir-
responsible dualism, writing off the agenda of the real world (although
the same language can be taken that way). It is not sectarian withdrawal
cutting off community with other believers, nor Tolstoyan purism (although, once again, some can take it that way). It is rather a prime
example of correlating the liberation promise with "the real experience
of the oppressed."

An oppressed community is sustained by a hope which is not
verified first of all by experience, and therefore cannot be falsified by
apparent defeat. The community which sustained the hope was first of
all authorized to hope not by its experience of effective militancy but

19. Montgomery, 25 March 1965, in Washington, p. 230.
20. Nobel Peace Prize acceptance, Oslo, 10 December 1964, in Washington,
p. 224.
21. My first statement of this point was "Exodus and Exile: Two Faces of
Liberation," *Crosscurrents* (fall 1973): 297-309.
22. This was of course written long before the collapse of Stalinist regimes in the
late 1980s.

by singing and preaching and mothering and eating together in the light of the good news. There is a pointer to this same insight in the way James Cone ended his concluding chapter in the book *Black Theology: A Documentary History* with attention to the problem of suffering.[23] The "problem of suffering" is more than an intellectual challenge to "theodicy," driven by an apologetic concern for having the God language of the community be credible. It is driven by more than an ethical concern, needing to behave in the right way. It is a concern for soteriology and eschatology. What is at stake is the authenticity of our proclaiming the hope which only God ratifies.[24]

The language of the Bible, we saw, is, "He will come to judge." That divine intervention is sure. It is this-worldly. It is not set apart from this world by an antipolitical or apolitical dualism or "division of planes." It vindicates our faithfulness, but without mandating us to be manipulative or coercive. It condemns the oppressor, yet without vengefully doing to him what he had done. The Lord's coming "to judge," i.e., to set things right, will be soon, but not right now. It does not bypass our ongoing struggle; yet the criterion guiding us in the struggle is not whether we win, not whether we can implement lesser-evil calculations to get there, but whether we keep the faith.

But the New Testament does not leave its hope dangling there. It teaches a coherent (though strange) cosmological vision whereby this world of faithful suffering can be understood. The apostles applied the words of Psalm 110: "The Lord said to my lord, sit at my hand until I make your enemies your footstool,"[25] to the ascension of Jesus Christ and his interim rule over the principalities and powers. That means that there are other patterns of power for change than the victory of the good guys. That the Crucified One is now "seated at the right hand of the Father" means that "he has the *whole* world in his hands," without its being in *our* hands. Thereby the apostles testified to their awareness of the patterned quality

23. James H. Cone, "Epilogue," in *Black Theology: A Documentary History*, ed. Gayraud S. Wilmore and James H. Cone, 2d ed., vol. 1 (Maryknoll, N.Y.: Orbis, 1979), pp. 436ff.

24. This might be related to what Richardson (n. 1 above) meant by "the structure of evil generated by relativism." King's cosmic appeal certainly reinforces a nonrelativistic reason for overcoming evil with good.

25. Strangely to us, this is the one text of the Hebrew Scriptures most often cited in the New Testament.

of the world, which is not a chaos but (even in its fallen state) a cosmos: created although fallen, yet not fallen out of God's hand, and brought under his control precisely by means of the cross.

This vision of the lordship of Christ over the powers made it possible for the first Christians to see even tragic events as having positive potential, like the cross itself. One could see the destructiveness of Assyria in Isaiah 10, or that of Rome in Romans 13, or one could see since then the menace of Islam facing medieval Europe or of communism today as paradoxically usable by God for good. Likewise the secularized values of post-Christian culture will be of use. Yet in seeing that tragedy has positive values we do not fuse those causes or agencies or strategies into Christian ethics or baptize their bearers, or substitute their role for our ministry of reconciliation.

This is then the immediate political pertinence, in a situation of frustration, of confessing with the Creed that it is Jesus who for us and who for our liberation was made human. This is the New Testament refutation of the definition of Jesus as apolitical. Gustavo Gutíerrez says this by denouncing the "distinction of planes." I said it simply by calling Jesus "political."[26] Any description of the human predicament in such terms that the answer Jesus gives is not an answer to our question must be a wrong question.

The full humanity of Jesus means that whatever else might be the grounds we might adduce for not following his ethical guidance, his not being fully human, or his being human but apolitical, is one which will not wash. This becomes year by year more the case, as scholars add increasing clarity to our knowledge of the real social setting in which Jesus and his followers led people by a concrete social strategy.[27]

---

26. J. Yoder, *The Politics of Jesus,* 2d ed. (Grand Rapids: Eerdmans, 1994). The use of the adjective did not mean a reduction; it rather sought to safeguard the wholeness of the classical Christology; cf. especially pp. 52f., 93-109, 226.

27. Cf. early witnesses to the rising seriousness with which the social shape of early Christianity is being taken: John G. Gager, *Kingdom and Community* (Englewood Cliffs, N.J.: Prentice-Hall, 1975); Gerhard Lohfink, *Jesus and Community* (Philadelphia: Fortress, 1985); Wayne A. Meeks, *The First Urban Christians* (New Haven: Yale University Press, 1983); Jonathan Z. Smith, "The Social Description of Early Christianity," *Religious Studies Review* 1, no. 1 (September 1975): 19ff.; Gerd Theissen, *The Social Setting of Pauline Christianity* (Philadelphia: Fortress, 1982). Since the mid-1980s the pace of publishing in this genre has been increasing; cf. works by Richard Horsley, John Elliott, Ched Myers, etc.

It may seem that in citing here the creedal phrase "he became human for our liberation" I avoid a needed logical demonstration by an appeal to dogma. True enough: to unfold the full meaning of the concept of incarnation for ethics would call for fuller argument. Yet those who define the human predicament in such terms that Jesus — either the Jesus of history or the one in the creeds — cannot by definition be its answer are appealing no less to traditional dogmatic categories.[28]

Hope When We Did Not (Yet) Overcome

One theme to which (it would seem to many) the New Testament cannot speak must be that of the ongoing quality of history after the end which after all did not come. If the hope of the apostles called for the world to end soon, are we not left to our own devices when we learn that the world is going on? Was not the apocalyptic vision refuted long ago? There are new issues which result in our being obligated, it would seem to some, to leave the New Testament behind. That forward movement is self-generating and self-governing. It leads organically to Constantine, to Christendom, to the Crusades, and to empire. It creates a vision of the unified and saved world; a vision which however is seriously qualified by the provincially divided and oppressive reality.

If you grant that God works in history, it would seem at first that that development, namely, the transition to Christendom, which actually happened, is the way God in fact did choose to work. Or if on the other hand you want to be more critical, then it would seem to some that the way to do that would be to deny history. If we wish somehow to stand in judgment upon what came of Christendom, some would say that we are driven to choose, with Tolstoy, "none of the above," in the name of a bloodless, gentle Galilean, not a liberator. It would seem that the New Testament offers too thin a slice of history, too fragile a fulcrum to bring to bear any creative and critical judgment upon what has come of God's world. Then we would be left, whether with a good or a bad conscience, to seek some other recourse: common sense or nature,

28. Standard, very traditional themes like the two natures of Christ, the distinctions between nature and supernature, the ordering of law and gospel, or the doctrine of the Trinity have all been appealed to toward this end.

reason or relativism, late Hegelian dialectic or modern social analysis, for a guide through a "real world" in which Jesus Christ is not Lord after all.

There would however have been another way to read the story: another vision of history implied in the notion of incarnation, distinct from the way that notion has been used in favor of patterns of religious establishment. It might be claimed that the meaning of Jesus is sufficiently clear and so normative that it can stand in judgment upon later departures from it.

Then instead of later developments being self-validating, they would be accountable to it as to a charter. It would then be possible for further development to be faithful; we would call that progress. It would also be possible for later changes to be unfaithful; we would call that betrayal or apostasy. It would not mean the end of history but would trigger a summons to repentance. Then history would be read not as unilinear but as a blend of faithfulness, apostasy, and renewal, each able to be and each needing to be identified in concrete cases. To construe faithfulness as a simple disjunctive choice between withdrawing from history and claiming responsibility to take it over would then be deceptive.

Christianity down through history is not the religion of the New Testament, and we could not ask that it be that. It has to be an array of alternative but not all equally appropriate ways of moving on from there. The New Testament, being the charter for that story, must be its critique. That is what the Protestant Reformation intended, although its vision soon became sidetracked through the premature creation of new political establishments and the development of a new doctrinaire scholasticism. New challenges pull out of the old story resources previously untapped. The continuing critical radicalization from which in the nineteenth century came the Disciples' patterns of "restoration," although naive, was still methodologically correct.[29] This stream of new biblicisms and "restorations" has contributed strongly to the black church experience and been led by it.

---

29. Cf. my interpretation of this more dialectical, more critical vision of historical betrayal and renewal in *The Priestly Kingdom* (Notre Dame, Ind.: Notre Dame University Press, 1984), pp. 63ff. and 123ff. Renewed recourse to the New Testament does not seek to take history "back to Go" but rather enables authentic progress.

It would follow that there is no point at which a renewed recourse to the apostolic writings and their pointing to Jesus cannot renew us. In every age it is possible that there may be a new and true witness. In every age there lurks the temptation to sell out to conformity to the spirit of that time. In every age there may be renewal through recourse to the irreducible "thereness" of the Jesus narrative.

Not only is this the pattern Christians confess themselves called to, when we read our history since Jesus as a mix of faithfulness to celebrate and apostasy to condemn. This is also what Jesus himself did as in his day he read his people's history. Jesus made no beginning from scratch. He claimed only to renew and fulfill, in the light of the original creation, of Moses and the prophets, what had already been commanded and promised, already betrayed.

Likewise the prophets to whom Jesus appealed had been doing in their time nothing brand-new; already then they were rereading their history in the light of the Hebrew story since the exodus, and especially (as far as our current agenda is concerned) they (followed by Jesus) were rereading in its light the long, failed history of kingship and statehood into which Israel had made such a tragic detour from Saul to Zedekiah.

That rootage of Jesus in Hebrew history gives to his ministry a depth in dialogue with community experience which was missing in the Jesus of Tolstoy and of Rauschenbusch, who became by a simple reversal of signs also the Jesus of Reinhold Niebuhr. That depth of social substance is missing as well in the Jesus of American fundamentalism.

When we see Jesus in the perspective of the Hebrew heritage, his themes of judgment and fulfillment take on far more substance. They are illuminated by the failure of the models of David and Solomon to give to God's people a king like the kings of the other nations. We are instructed by the collapse of the model of Ezra and Nehemiah, thinking through ritual purity to renew a nation without political sovereignty but with the coercion of a centralized cult backed by the authorization of the Persian empire. We are instructed by the failure of the Maccabean vision of holy liberation.

What Jesus brings is not a slightly more demanding ethic, escalating beyond the pharisaic ethic which was already demanding enough, so that Jesus can be dealt with by isolating the question, "What can a perfectionistic ethic be good for?" Jesus represents rather a paradigm of renewal taking up into itself all of the concreteness of the deuteronomic vision of faithful community under God. Jesus "renews" by judging in the light of the Hebrew hope. He "fulfills" by bringing the nations into that heritage, moving beyond Jewish ethnicity yet doing so in a forward direction, with and not against its earlier momentum.

The problem stated at the beginning of this review was generated by the deceptive and partial coincidence between the gospel's hope and the optimism of the West. I have been arguing that the gospel's hope need not be set aside in favor of consequentialist prudence on grounds either of Jesus' irrelevance, of the kingdom's not having come.

Now we may be able to ask again how to view the collapse of the confident cosmology of the West, in which all of us, even the dissenters and the underdogs among us, have been trained. This confident Western cosmology not only saw our kind of people as better than the other kinds of people and as favored by the gods. It also saw us all together as so centrally located in the universe that we can if we choose decide how things shall go. The structures of things are transparent. We know how it works and can manipulate it. Every decade we know more, and can manipulate better. Therefore morality does easily seem to boil down to the discussion of how we shall use the power we have, in order to direct the structures of society toward what we consider the proper purposes.

Yet somehow, as we know more, we find that we are not after all in better control. The machines we create, like the sorcerer's apprentice's servants, take on a character of their own and produce results other than those we had asked for. The more people are educated, the more people there are whose efforts to cheat the system will sabotage it. Thus instead of reducing the universe to orderly reasonableness and manageable docility, we face escalating complexity of powers beyond our control. Our ability to name them, to construct some of their mechanisms and trigger some of their reactions, aggravates rather than easing our sense of being their slaves more than their masters.[30]

It is increasingly appropriate to ask whether we have access to a cosmology for situations of weakness. Whereas the age of trust in progress counted on the gradual culmination of the promise of orderly world dominion and thought of magic, apocalypse, and poetry as vestigial

---

30. A deeper analysis of how progress in creativity increases our jeopardy is offered in the works of Jacques Ellul, most notably in his *Technological Society*.

marks of the areas where culture had not yet finished mopping up on primeval ignorance, now we must at the very least ask whether mopping up will take longer than originally expected. If so, it might be a help to have some magic or some poetry we could trust, a cosmos beyond our managing. Gandhi and King had that.

Epilogue: Failing to Understand "the Cross"

Although he chose the title *Bearing the Cross* for his encyclopedic biography of Martin Luther King and featured three quotations on the subject on his frontispiece, author David Garrow[31] is in fact very thin in what he has to say about the meaning for King of that classical Christian symbol. There are in Garrow's massive tapestry frequent references to three interlocking weaknesses which marked the work of King: namely, his feeling that his social prominence was unearned, his sexual diversions, and his recurrent depression. These themes too are described matter-of-factly by Garrow, without psychological or ethical analysis, but his documentation on them is full,[32] whereas when it comes to the cross, except in the title and frontispiece, it is not. Perhaps partly this is the case because Garrow attends little to the content of King's books and sermons,[33] although he does frequently report King's allusions to his ministerial calling. This thinness may thus be understandable. As a political scientist Garrow has the right to share his discipline's mode of reducing the language of piety into its institutional payoff before taking it seriously,[34] but that does constitute a significant reduction.

31. David Garrow, *Bearing the Cross: Martin Luther King, Jr., and the Southern Christian Leadership Conference* (New York: Morrow, 1986).

32. The historian who might wish, as I do not at this point, to check out some of the contestable details is not well served by Garrow's mode of clumping sources in his footnotes.

33. Much of the material in King's speeches and books was drafted by others. Yet they were persons who knew well the man and his voice. Numerous of the King quotations which Garrow provides are oral rather than written memories. That does not give us grounds to doubt their substantial accuracy, but it does limit our interest in seeking to exegete them carefully.

34. Garrow's tone deafness is well illustrated by his not recognizing as such King's quoting of refrains from gospel songs (p. 576) or the allusion to Moses in the last

It therefore must fall to others, and to us here, to interpret more carefully the place of cross language in the Christian movement, on whose resources King drew, as one of the common references bridging the distances between the mainstream white communities of his academic and institutional connections and the suffering of the black communities to and for which he spoke. This would have filled out Garrow's account very usefully.

The cross language which Garrow does cite, not often but prominently, does not belong primarily in the context of either King's conjugal inadequacies or his guilt and depression, where Garrow wants to locate it.[35]

a. The first citation on the frontispiece is from King's letter to Coretta on the occasion of his first incarceration: "This is the cross that we must bear for the freedom of our people."[36]

b. The second citation is from an address to a National Conference on Religion and Race in Chicago:[37]

> The cross we bear precedes the crown we wear. To be a Christian one must take up his cross, with all of its difficulties and agonizing and tension-packed content and carry it until that very cross leaves its marks upon us and redeems us to that more excellent way which comes only through suffering.

Memphis rally speech (p. 621), as by his not analyzing the weight of the James Russell Lowell hymn King so often quoted (cf. above, p. 133). There are six quotations of Lowell referenced in the index to Washington. Likewise for the biblical metaphor "the arm of the Lord is long . . ." (sometimes also "the arc of the moral universe"), already noted above, note 18.

35. I make this observation not only in terms of the logic of piety or that of moral thought, but also historically and literarily. The places where King uses the cross metaphor are in the frame of reference of innocent suffering as a strategic choice, and as a form of power. Looking carefully at the major quotes makes this clear.

36. Garrow, *Bearing the Cross*, p. 148.

37. 17 January 1963. Oddly, Garrow does not otherwise report the event where this was said. James Cone in *Martin and Malcolm and America*, p. 139, describes best the importance of that large ecumenical event. It apparently did not meet the criteria for inclusion in the Washington anthology. Practically the same words are reported as well from an Ebenezer Church sermon in September 1966 (Garrow, *Bearing the Cross*, p. 532) and in July 1965 (Garrow, *Bearing the Cross*, p. 707 n. 7).

The setting of this statement was the increasingly somber awareness, arising within the Southern Christian Leadership Conference (SCLC) staff, that the coming conflict in Birmingham could be very costly. In a planning session King just had said: "I have to tell you that in my judgment, some of the people sitting here today will not come back alive from this campaign."[38] In the same setting Andrew Young said of King: ". . . every time he made a commitment to something like this he was committing his life. . . . He thought in everything he did it meant his death."[39]

c. The third quotation is cited from another SCLC staff discussion, this one concerning the public relations cost to the SCLC of King's having taken on fully the second front of very publicly criticizing the Vietnam War. Criticism of the war had been building in his mind and in the movement for months, but only in the course of the spring of 1967 did he overrule those of his good friends who were warning him against that danger.[40] He spoke out publicly in Los Angeles 25 February and then most visibly in New York's Riverside Church 4 April. This was the end of his access to Lyndon Johnson: "When I took up the cross, I recognized its meaning. . . . The cross may mean the death of your popularity. It may mean the death of a foundation grant. It may cut down your budget a little, but take up your cross, and just bear it. And that's the way I have decided to go."[41]

Two of these three brief statements were unpremeditated. They are not in speeches written for King by others. None of them is about any of the three psychic or moral weaknesses identified above to which Garrow gives so much attention. All have to do with the suffering which results from a conscious choice to confront vulnerably the powers of injustice. All correlate with needing to decide, again and again amidst the tangles of tactics, to renounce the attraction of coercive means,

38. Garrow, *Bearing the Cross*, p. 229.

39. In view of the way Garrow clumps his quotes topically, it is not sure that this was said at the same time.

40. What finally made up his mind was seeing some battlefield pictures in a magazine he had picked up in an airport on the way to a vacation. In this May 1967 statement (Garrow, *Bearing the Cross*, frontispiece and p. 564) he said he had been lacking courage on the subject since 1965.

41. This was also the setting in which James Lawson spoke of the cross (Garrow, *Bearing the Cross*, p. 555).

whether those be the push of the angry rhetoric of justified insur-
rectional violence[42] or the pull of co-option by the government's
demand for a premature peace.

There are a few other uses of the term "cross" elsewhere in Garrow's account, and they differ in how the figure works. King's younger
colleague Bernard Lee used the phrase "the Cross that you must bear"
to designate King's financial sacrifices in contrast to his staff's need for
better salary.[43] Staffer James Bevel, projecting the kind of aggressive
campaign needed to change Chicago, said that "a crucifixion is necessary first."[44] Each of these echoes shows that the cross language was
familiar in the SCLC milieu, but each nuance is different; Bevel made
the cross a tactic and Lee made it an ascetic style commitment.

In addition to the book I have been discussing, David J. Garrow has
edited a valuable three-volume collection of essays about King's
thought.[45] In it he reproduces an essay of his own entitled "The Cross of
Leadership," giving the term yet another twist.[46] There it means King's
self-doubt, especially before the Nobel Prize, as to whether he was up to
the job. Garrow's observations are insightful and well documented, but
the term "cross" does not occur and the challenge is different.

For centuries the metaphor of bearing a cross had had multiple
meanings for Christians, many of them distracting from the center of
what it meant for Jesus.[47] While aware of some of these, and without

42. Garrow is good about King's very delicately balanced response to the blunt
rhetoric of "black power." Cone in *Martin and Malcomb and America*, pp. 124ff., is clear
about both the meaning of "cross" and its centrality for King.

43. Garrow, *Bearing the Cross*, p. 447. Another young staffer, Charles Jones, used
the imagery of "cross over career" rather lightly to urge King to go more readily to jail.
Taylor Branch, *Parting the Waters* (New York: Simon & Schuster, 1988), p. 615. It
became a code term in debates about tactical choices about when to go to jail: "I should
choose the time and place of my Golgatha" (Branch, p. 467).

44. Garrow, *Bearing the Cross*, p. 448.

45. David J. Garrow, ed., *Martin Luther King, Jr.: Civil Rights Leader, Theologian,
Orator* (New York: Carlson, 1989). Oddly it does not include the Richardson text with
which this essay began.

46. Garrow, *Martin Luther King, Jr.*, pp. 453-54.

47. I offer a brief summary of Protestant redefinitions of the cross in my *The
Politics of Jesus*, 2d ed. (Grand Rapids: Eerdmans, 1994), p. 129; there would be additional variations worthy of note were we to pursue the theme down through the history
of Christian spiritualities.

abstract ethical analysis or critical Scripture studies, King had got it right. Somehow the combination of straightforward Black Baptist preaching, Boston University personalism, and catching up with the legacy of Gandhi fell together in a fruitful and powerful synthesis, which Garrow, despite his use of the word in his title, missed.

Significantly, the cross analogy was not articulated in King's account of his midnight experience, alone in his kitchen in January 1956 after his first jail experience.[48] It would thus seem to be a mistake to juxtapose it to any kind of psychic or moral weakness, even though King had those weaknesses. Bearing the cross was for King, as it seems to have been mostly for the Gospel writers, an ethical and a strategic category. It signals the conscious choice of a path of vulnerable faithfulness, despite the knowledge that it will be costly. That makes it a piece of the cosmology already reviewed in other words above, according to which the shape of the universe is such that to return good for evil is functional.

48. Recounted in *Stride to Freedom: The Montgomery Story* (New York: Harper, 1958), pp. 134f.; Garrow, *Bearing the Cross*, p. 83; Garrow recounts, p. 89 and occasionally again later, how foundational this experience remained in King's memory.

CHAPTER 7

The Believers Church
and the Arms Race[1]

My assignment calls me to focus on three perspectives.

The code label "believers church" means first of all that *believing* is an alternative *stance* in the social order. It secondly means that to be a believing community represents an alternative *leverage* on the social order. Thirdly, the narrower, technical meaning of "believers church" serves as the mark of a distinctive denominational understanding. That may be the point our conference planners had in mind,[2] but that is not the place to begin.

1. Transcribed and edited from an address delivered at Goshen College, Goshen, Indiana, 15 March 1978, as part of "No More War Week" activities. Reprinted for discussion at the Mid-America Region of the New Call to Peacemaking for its gathering, 8 March 1980, at Wichita, on "The Abolition of the War System." The New Call to Peacemaking was a grassroots educational effort of Brethren, Friends, and Mennonites, concerned to hold together piety and politics, evangelism and Bible study. The slogans in the titles, whether "Arms Race" or "No More War," should be understood as calling for clarification not of a macro political utopia but of the believing community's understanding of its role. This chapter is thus not narrowly about the arms issue, any more than the two previous ones were specifically about race. It is about the church in the world. The peacemaking mission of the church is not a theme for its own sake but an especially evident specimen of the larger question of mission in the world.

2. The label "believers church," derived from the German sociologist/historian Max Weber and given currency in the United States by Donald Durnbaugh (*The Believers' Church* [New York: Macmillan, 1968; Scottdale, Pa.: Herald]), was a favored

148

I. What Does It Mean to Be "Believing"?

There is an obvious response in the Jewish story where we all begin, a text that is often (usually, in fact) interpreted in a way different from the way I think it ought to be taken. When interpreted in its total context, in the thrust of the total passage, this passage says something that we properly should begin with: "Faith is the assurance of things hoped for, the conviction of things not seen" (Heb. 11:1, RSV).

These words have been taken traditionally to mean that faith means affirming something for which there is no solid reason to say it is true, except that you swallow real hard. It is taken to be a virtuous exercise to be able to swallow harder than other people. To believe is to trust the undemonstrated.

If, however, we read the rest of the passage — namely, the whole of chapter 11 and the beginning of chapter 12 of the letter to *the Hebrews* — it's quite clear that something more precise and more substantial is being said. Faith is what it takes to obey. We have first the model of Abraham, then a series of other models from Abel down through the immediate predecessors of the confessing community, winding up with Jesus. For these people, to be *believing* meant acting in obedience despite the lack of evidence that obedience would "work."

So as the primary model, to be believing is a posture in the midst of the poverty of history. To be believing means that caring is useful, and that the usefulness of caring or of obeying is not dependent on whether our optimism can be documented. To believe, demonstrated by all these people in the story, most prototypically by Abraham, means to obey when you are not sure it is going to pay. That's what it meant to be a believer. That's what Abraham did; he obeyed when he wasn't clear how it was going to work out. That's what Jesus did, "for the joy was set before him" at the end of the passage.

What does that tell us about our kind of subject? What does this have to do with the arms race? Since faith is not a human possibility, it isn't something we can do simply by ourselves, then neither are the products we hope to achieve, neither are the goals we set for ourselves. It's not really possible, humanly, to do what we set out to do in faith.

---

way for historic peace church thinkers to locate their identity in the wider ecumenical world together with Baptists and Disciples.

Thus the believer will be fundamentally pessimistic about the good the powers of this world can do, or about what we can do among the powers of this world in their own wisdom. So the believer agrees, along with the people we typically call "radical," that we can't use the present system for much good.

But the believer also agrees with the people we call "Niebuhrians," that the hopes of both conservatives and radicals (who *both* say we can do *something*) will deceive us. And that applies to the hopes of doing something significant in a manageable range with SALT, or to stopping the B-1 or using a UN disarmament conference to get somewhere. There isn't much ground for hope.

But not only is faith something we can't do. It is something God does. Then the potentialities of faith are not bound by the limits of the system. And therefore the believer is fundamentally optimistic. The believer agrees (despite the evidence) with the liberal that persistent pressure on the system is important. The believer agrees with the utopian that the fact that there is no clear line from here to where we have to get to is no reason to be quiet. This stance, which the Bible calls faith, believingness, faithfulness, frees us from the bondage of an engineering model of the social order. It frees us from thinking that all we can do is what we can see ourselves doing through our wisdom about the system, and by virtue of our strength in using the handles on the system which we can get our hands on. It frees us to make a new impact from within our own identity, rather than trying to reason back from how the world's system likely will respond to our input. To believe in this sense is to hope, to love, on grounds that the world can't take away.

But when I say we are free from the engineering model of the social process, that does not mean we stand its analysis on its head and say we don't care about planning, thinking, analyzing. To challenge the model of manipulation and management is not to replace it with another bondage, with anarchy or the refusal to analyze, with the flippant claim that we don't know *anything* about how the system works, or that it doesn't matter to try to watch how our contribution to the system changes it.

No! We do need to think about mechanisms, causality, probabilities. Yet the effect of the management model on our thought on this issue, so far beyond our reach, has been not that it fosters concern but that it pushes us to despair. So we may keep the pragmatic analysis as one servant. Many manifestations of hope are at the same time realistic. Many hopeful things are also possible things to do. Thus when I say we are freed from the pessimism of system-immanent analysis, that does not mean that we don't care about mechanisms and social analysis, political analysis, and calculation of results. It means that that caring is held within a wider trust.

You will have noticed how I have been referring to the word "system" as if it has a certain simplicity, so that you could fight "the system," join "the system," critique "the system" as if there was something rather clear about that term. That's true in a New Testament worldview. "This present evil age" in the language of Paul, the "cosmos" (world) in the language of John, is pretty clearly being thought of as a coherent unity, polarized over against the new world of the gospel, the message of the new age. But there are times and places where that simplicity doesn't fit and we can't reason that clearly. There are times and places where or when the presence and ministry of the people of God, or the workings of Providence, have interpenetrated with the rest of the process in such a way that it's much more complex.

It is not an available possibility simply to apply or naively to update the New Testament polarity. We can't simply say "yes" or "no," the world is out there and we are over here. There are good reasons for that. Complexity is not all the work of the devil. Partly it is the progress of the gospel. H. Berkhof, in his interpretation of what the apostle Paul thinks about the "principalities and powers," speaks of progress in "domesticating the powers."[3] Those forces in and behind the cosmic order, which are intrinsically good for us because they are part of creation but have become bad for us because of the fall, can (Berkhof suggests) again be sobered, limited, and made useful, thanks to the presence of the believing people proclaiming Christ in their midst. They can be divested of their autonomy and destructiveness and used for some good. (If the language of "principalities and powers" from the apostle Paul is new to you, it would take us too long to fill that in, but the Berkhof book is available as a source of introduction to one of the ways that the New Testament thought about these matters.)

If then it is the case that the powers can sometimes be "sobered";

3. Hendrikus Berkhof, *Christ and the Powers*, 2d ed. (Scottdale, PA: Herald Press, 1977).

or if it is the case (in contemporary language) that social pluralism and limited government can open some spaces for creativity and freedom; and if it is the case that churches over the years have actually done something, have ministered, have established ways of meeting certain needs; *then* it is no longer the case, in many elements of our present society, that the world with its rebellious destructiveness is over there, the evil system, and we over here. Thus, if our theme were "Christian higher education" or "the church and the arts" or "democracy," we would have a different set of questions before us than we have tonight.

But with the arms race, the New Testament's polar image seems pretty largely to pertain. It would be hard to argue that preparations for reciprocal mass destruction have been in any way "tamed" or "Christianized."[4] The arms race, whether it be the race of the superpowers themselves or the competitive huckstering to the small nations of more conventional arms, is one of the simplest analogies to the monster language of the Apocalypse: technology gone idolatrous; nationality, rationality, technique, science gone crazy. What is the difference between a 700 percent and an 800 percent overkill? It does not make any difference to the ability of the balance of terror to keep the peace, if that is what it is supposed to do. The combination of SALT negotiation on the surface and the introduction of other destabilizing weapons at the same time cannot be called rational. International politicians who justify the tactics of totalitarianism used by our CIA and other agencies, on the grounds that they claim to save the very freedoms that they are subverting, cannot be called rational. Or what about covering corruption and profiteering on the grounds of security, the multinational distortion of the market that is being argued for on the grounds of free economy?

In this realm, which is more than the arms race — the multi-national, international competitive economy seeing the arms race as the tip of the iceberg — the Berrigans and Stringfellow are right. The language of the Apocalypse is the right language to describe what's going on. You can't get to peace from here! This is not a matter which can be dealt with commensurately to the reality by sober planning, careful working within the system, detailed think-tanking. That "business as usual" mood does not begin to fit the size of the problem. The problem is still one that fits the apocalyptic language of dragons and angels and

---

4. Unless it be in the worse way; cf. Harold Brown.

the sky falling down. That is a better description of what we are up against than the more sober formulae to which the liberals are trying to reduce it. So the imagery of the hope that makes no sense but keeps us obeying even when we don't see the victory behind it is still, for this theme, the clearest way to live in a biblical cosmology.

II. What Does It Mean to Be a Believing Community?

What I'll be saying here may seem to be the least original for me and you.[5] It needs to be said, but it isn't new. What difference does it make, as we witness against the monstrosities, that we are a community and not just individuals or angry people? A community, to use the newer fad language of the sociology of knowledge, is *an alternative construction of the world.* To live in a community, to celebrate and share and talk the same language as one's fellows, cultivates and celebrates a consciousness. It teaches us another way to respond to reality than the way that other world teaches us to perceive reality. It aids our perception; because we are in this alternative community we see things other people don't see, we notice things they don't notice, we make connections they haven't seen. But it does more than that. It enables perseverance, it motivates, it protects us from the erratic and the impulsive, because the stance we take is a shared and a celebrated stance. We live with one another the maintenance of the language that gives meaning to our countercultural identity.

That is the case on the level of values and perception. Second, to be a believing community has some practical values. In the believing community we receive *training in styles of conflict resolution.* We encourage ourselves to believe that you can solve problems together. The community provides moral and material support for risk taking. This has been said about the Hutterian communities in the sixteenth century, which regularly sent off people two by two to go out for several months on missionary circuits, very often with the awareness that they might

---

5. The New Call to Peacemaking, in whose name the meeting was convened, was sponsored by Brethren, Friends, and Mennonites, groups very conscious of their status as unpopular voluntary minorities. I invite the reader to observe the dimension of denominational self-consciousness in this text not as a folkloric peculiarity but as an instance of the integrity problem which every communion faces.

not come back. It has been said about the early Quaker missionaries in seventeenth-century England that the reason they were free to go was that they knew their family would be taken care of if they didn't come back. Their model of meaningful risk-taking was supported by the fact that the community that sent them shared their responsibilities. The *holding power* of people in such a social movement was rooted in a commonality of style. The movement enables the division *of labor*, whereby we all don't work at the same thing, yet because we are together we are all working at what all of us are working at. This is a possibility only in structured sharing. The capacity to be *effective* in obstruction, in lobbying, in continuity is dependent on having a community in the stance of opposition.

Now this possibility, the advantage of community as over against the freelancing prophet, applies more directly on localized issues than on global issues like the world arms race. It can apply locally to the slavery issue, because every slave and every slave owner is local. It can apply locally to a civil rights struggle, because an instance of racism is in a particular town and a particular place. It can apply locally to criminal justice and offender issues, because there the offender, the victim, and the penal institutions are local. But we can't in the same sense immediately get a hand on the institutions of the arms race. So some of these values of the countercultural community are not as visible, not as directly and pragmatically pertinent as in some other cases.

Still it is worth reminding ourselves that the value of the believers church approach to problems is partly that it offers, practically, better ways to do things. I just said it is not as easy to apply it to global issues. Yet it is not quite fair to say that you can't, because we haven't really tried it. We have seldom thought to give priority concern to solidarity over against the system at this point. Mennonites have sought solidarity when their conflict with the system led them to migration. Then we had a strong worldwide network of economic solidarity, created to help people move from Russia to the North American plains, or later from Germany to Paraguay. For that kind of response to the system there was solidarity. For individual conscientious objection to military service, there has been in North American Mennonite experience considerable solidarity. There has been less organized solidarity for the maintenance of the Pietist and conservative social style (on alcohol, tobacco, abortion) as themes around which to gather concerted resistance. Once the civil rights movement was underway, there was even a degree of support from Mennonites for that kind of nonviolent movement for social change.

But regarding the global arms race, or with regard to the armament establishment, we haven't really tried solidarity. We don't really know it wouldn't work. We have no grounds to say it would have no impact. It's rather like the standard dictum "It isn't true that Christianity has been tried and found wanting; it has been found hard and not tried." This is the case with regard to a North American church impact on the armament system, by means (for instance) of tax objection or other forms of civil disobedience, if conceived of as supported by a sizable community. Although our theology says our stance over against the destructive powers of the world is a stance we take together, with regard to this issue we have always let a few people go ahead on their own if they want to make some visible extreme protest, while the rest of us wonder if their lonely step was wise.

But when I spoke of "the believing community," illustrated just now by reference to North American Mennonite experience, that let a certain confusion into the picture. It is not sure that North American Mennonites are a believing community on this matter. It might be that this definition might apply more closely to other groups, to certain humanists, certain kinds of human socialists, or perhaps to certain groups of Jews, than to the positions held by the denominational organizations called Mennonite, Brethren, Friends.

III. The Believers Church as Type Identity

This phrase appeared on our conference program because it is as a self-image some of us try to live up to, as a label for the way to try to be different from other Christians. There is establishment Christianity, mainstream Christianity, and then there is this alternative.

If you think you are in the mainstream, then you attempt to take responsibility for managing the culture. That gives you one set of assumptions. If you are in the believers church, you know you can't be in charge of managing the culture. I suspect this meaning to be in the minds of the people who chose my topic for this evening. We must come to this use of such a phrase with some hesitancy. That way of identifying a position, by describing or locating it as over against something else, may give to some, even to some of us, the impression that this position is a derivative position. It negates what most normal people affirm. It corrects, or compensates for, or objects to the normal stream of things, and therefore can only be seen in its negation.

There are points in Western history where that derivative, reactionary quality cannot be denied. But we don't have to theologize from there. Faith, after all, the faith of a minority group, if it is faith in the God of history, is not a quirk or a sectarian hobby. It's not something worse than, or weaker than, some natural baseline where ordinary people make sense. Belief is not making less sense.

Thus it causes confusion if we ask, "What can we do that would be *specifically* Christian?" as if we always had to be different. It is intelligent, it is normal, it is humane, or democratic or scientific to object to the arms race. It might be that what is different about being Christian in some cases is not what we do or whether we do it, but only why we do it, how hard we try, or how long we stick with it without success. Or the distinctiveness may lie in the explanations we would teach our children, to show why we keep on doing it when it doesn't seem to be working. It might be that what makes a believers church different from decent, human objections to evil in the wider culture isn't an ethical difference at all, but only a matter of the meaning framework in which we put the fact that, like anybody else who is intelligent, we're against it, for pretty much the same reasons and more.

So the believers church position should be expected to be a rational, factual realism about the arms race. It's the other positions that are irrational, unbalanced, and compulsive! Nationalism is nonrational. The arms race is compulsive. Crusading is fanatical. A really religious crusade is blasphemous. Thinking that the way the CIA and the FBI work is a good way to manage a society is not simply somewhat unbalanced, but structurally crazy.

So we shouldn't be trying to "back into" a consistently "sectarian" position in our social critique. Once in a while we do find ourselves in a situation where faithfulness to rationality or to the Bible makes us a minority. Then we'll have to be willing to be that. But as a minority we shall not concede that rationality or objectivity or respect for scientific data lies on the other side of the debate. So I suggest that our understanding of what we mean by the label "believers church," when we apply it to ourselves as a distinguishing characteristic, has to be defined a little more deeply than we usually do. It needs to be taken out from the shadow of an inferiority complex where it often puts us.

There have been in the history of reformation many models of reform. Especially we need to discern two that look alike but are deeply different. One projects a fixed pattern. You have a reformation and then the reformed position has become fixed and it doesn't need to be reformed anymore. You just keep it solid. Reformation is to restore a fixed proper pattern, and then to keep it. The other vision of reformation is that it must be an ongoing process, never finished, because one never gets a grasp of all the errors and all truth at once. And even if at one particular point all the right moves were made, in the next generation or the next century more right moves will have to be made. So reformation is an ongoing process, never finished.

Those are two different visions of what it means to reform Christianity and two different visions of the believers church. My understanding, from what I have been assigned to interpret in the story of Anabaptism, Quakerism, and Radical Reformation through the centuries, is that it is definitely the latter pattern that obtains. It's not the creation, over against the world, of a "church" that just sits there at odds with the world, but rather an ongoing critical process. And that means an ongoing critique relative to our own identity. This must apply to our present problem, namely, how we respond to rampant superpower nationalism in the present world? Especially when we live within the superpower.

One part of our own identity, which we need to be critical of, is the impact upon our social and moral stance of the fact that so many of our fathers migrated selectively. There is no more politically important gesture of loyalty than to migrate selectively into a place where you have it better. Our grandfathers told themselves that they were not being political, but they did so by going to the places where they were better off. If we watch Mennonite migration patterns across the centuries, across the globe, not only in the North American experience, we discover that Mennonites generally went to places where the authority patterns of the host government were hierarchical and authoritarian. The reason is because they could trust the prince to keep the promises of privilege he made to them. Whether it was southern Russia, western Canada, eastern France, or the mountains of Switzerland, it happened over and over again that we found ourselves in positions of privilege over against the natives who had been there before us. We came in under the protection of an authoritarian government which would rather have us, which favored us over its own people.

What has that to do with the arms race? It has something to do with whether we are able to talk back to the authorities, whether we have the psychic wherewithall to see our world the way the New Testament saw its world. It has to do with whether the gratitude we feel because we have been taken in by authorities who are good to us because we're good to them — we pay our rent, we don't revolt — whether that gratitude has destroyed our capacity to see the monstrosity of rampant nationalism for what it is. It has to do with the ease with which we have fallen into a simplification of the problem in the past, assuming that the relation of church to world is a stable polarity. The world's out there, we are over here, we are polarized, but we are also settled into that differentness, so that we have to let the world go its way while we go our way.

The connections between the two historical streams, "church" and "world," are numerous. We want them to give us religious liberty. We want to be able to evangelize individuals out of that stream into this stream, but we expect that "worldly" stream to go on in its own violent, selfish, nationalistic identity, just as we hope it will let us do our thing.

But simple, stable duality is not really true in logic. The definition according to which the duality is stable is itself a biased definition. It assumes that first there is normalcy, reasonableness, order, nature, and that that faith is something peculiar pulled out from that, stuck onto it, in a relation of tension with it, rather than perceiving that that way of putting the question together is itself predisposed by wanting that answer. That is, predisposed by wanting to affirm the autonomy of the secular order in its fallenness.

Such a stable duality is not biblical. The language of the Bible, in all the major strands of New Testament thought, does not say to the world that it's all right for the world to be world in the fallen sense. It doesn't say that you do your thing and we do our thing. The language of the Apocalypse, proclaiming that the Lamb is at war in the world and is vanquishing the world, is not used to accept that kind of simple complementarity between the minority church and the violent world.

Nor is it true historically that we ever have that kind of stable social divide. The living church has always made more of an impact on the world, and the world has always been more destructive, more selfish, more idolatrous than that stable vision. We must not accept the slogan conclusion, "you can't impose Christian ethics on non-Christians." Of course you can't. It's true on one level. Ethics can't be imposed, because Christians can't impose anything, can't coerce. If they did they wouldn't be behaving as Christians. But that's not the whole truth. It's not true that, because we can't impose Christian standards on other people, therefore we should affirm that it is OK for them to live according to other standards. As one Mennonite minister said at a meeting at the time of the Cuban missile crisis fifteen years ago, "War is wrong for us and right for them."

But that would be to make a balanced, even comfortable complementarity out of what should remain an apocalyptic tension. We can't grant that to the wider world, even for an inconclusive and not very true bomb-rattling bluff, as might have been the case of Cuba. We can't confirm that other standards are "all right." We can't leave the world in peace with its commitment to other standards. So we can't get ourselves off the hook of needing to have something to say, by saying ahead of time that the world can't or shouldn't listen. The fact that we are a minority, the fact that we are what the church historians label as the type of group that is not in touch with the world, does not discharge us. Being "sectarian" may free us from despair at our failure to get things done fast, but it won't free us from responsibility.

These comments are only orientation. As I said at the outset, I can't really offer more than orientation; i.e., getting ready for the kind of social study that a group like this needs to go on with. I intentionally haven't started with specific witness or action tactics, though it is obvious that what we have talked about raises certain questions about tactics. Just this week there came to my desk two documents proposing very specific things to do about the arms race. One of them comes from Sojourners and the Church of the Savior, two Christian congregations, friends of ours in Washington, D.C. This strategy is to make a statement — five pages saying why it is so important just not to wind down the arms race; they want to aim this statement at the coming International Disarmament Conference. They hope it will get several hundred formal sponsors and then tens of thousands of signatures, so that this can get into the channels of the process of diplomatic policy making at just the right time, so that when the American delegation goes to the UN conference, they'll go with some openness.

The other letter came from some other friends on the other side of town, Jonah House, inviting a handful of people not to sign a statement but to come and get in the way, to interfere with patriotic preaching services, to get in the way of traffic at the Pentagon, and in legal and not always legal ways to make it visible that they are on the other side. Not to make statements, and not to talk to diplomats, not really to propose any alternative, but simply to make it dramatic that the whole system is insanely wrong.

Now which of these is the right thing to do? Both? Neither? The one thing that we can't get away with is *not* dealing with them — unless we come up with something else.

Of course it is also possible to deny that this issue is an issue in its own right. After all, others would say the arms race is just the normal outworking of a capitalist system, of nationalism and its military system, so that what we have to attack is the fact that our government uses our money for all kinds of war preparations, not simply nuclear items. It's the whole military economy we have to get in the way of, so we shouldn't pay our taxes. That too again is being done in different ways. Some of us say we ought to do our tax refusal carefully, by working for a law that would permit us to be legal conscientious objectors with our tax dollars, by way of the World Peace Tax Fund. Others say, no, we will refuse to pay under the present system, because that's the way we are supporting the war now.

If we take a critical position with regard to all kinds of war, we are obviously clear as to the arms race itself. But does that dispense us from denouncing Trident and Cruise and Rocky Flats in particular? This is only one more sample with which to work, in the light of the hope that it means to be believing, the solidarity that it means to be a community. To hope and solidarity let us add the accountability that means that we won't go off alone. We must do these things together, with responsibility for one another.

I could try to be abstract about more guidelines with which to do this. I could go into logical questions like whether the logical polarity between "effectiveness" and "faithfulness" that we so often try to get some light from is any help. But I really meant it when I said I can't bring answers. What I can bring is a description from history and from logic of one approach, one self-aware orientation, and I'll leave the rest up to you. If I thought I knew where to go from here, I wouldn't have the right to come and say it, because that wouldn't have been believers church process. If I had been sure that you don't know anything either, it wouldn't have been worth coming. Part of what it means to be the believers church is to believe that there are answers that we don't have yet. And that we get them, not by inviting someone from twelve miles down the road to talk from a distant history, but by working together at specimens, symbols, celebration, studies that say what we can say, even though we know that we don't yet know it. That stated hope is all I intend to offer. The rest is for you.

PART 3

Basics

CHAPTER 8

The Original Revolution[1]

1. The Old Words and the New Agenda

So wonderfully has he dealt with me,
   the Lord, the Mighty One.
   His name is Holy;
his mercy sure from generation to generation
   toward those who fear him;
the deeds his own right arm has done
   disclose his might:
the arrogant of heart and mind he has put to rout,
he has torn imperial powers from their thrones,
   but the humble have been lifted high.
The hungry he has satisfied with good things,
   the rich sent empty away. (Luke 1:49-53, NEB)

In the whole body of Jewish and Christian liturgy, only a very few texts might be more widely known — and more vainly repeated — than the two songs from the beginning of Luke's Gospel. One of these songs is found on the lips of the maiden Mary. Catholic tradition knows it by its opening

---

1. A sermon preached first in Central Methodist Church, Buenos Aires, in 1966 and last in Eisenhower Chapel, Penn State University, in November 1968. Previously printed in *The Original Revolution* (Scottdale, Pa.: Herald, 1972). Reprinted by permission of Herald Press.

word, *Magnificat*, "My soul doth magnify the Lord." But what it says is the language, not of sweet maidens, but of Maccabees. It sings of dethroning the mighty and exalting the lowly, of filling the hungry and sending the rich away empty. Mary's praise to God is a revolutionary battle cry.

That simple observation should suffice to locate our topic. The fad word in the last few years of both Protestant and Catholic social thought is "revolution." From the black ghettos of the United States to the 1968 World Council of Churches Assembly in Uppsala, from the archbishop's residence in Recife to the Ivy League seminaries of the American Protestant establishment offices in upper Manhattan, from Peking to the Sorbonne, the slogans are the same. The system is rotten. Those whom it oppresses should submit to its tyranny no longer. It deserves nothing other than to collapse in upon itself, a collapse we will engineer.

It would be worthwhile sometime to dwell at more length on the way in which the term "revolution" confirms the intellectual relevance of Gresham's law, according to which the coinage with the least substance, value, and character will get the most circulation. The word "revolution" has passed through so many hands, over so many tongues and pens, that most of its meaning has worn off. Shaving cream is revolutionary if they put lime perfume in the can with the soap. The compulsory village relocation program in the Mekong Delta was rebaptized "Revolutionary Development" after the 1966 Honolulu conference where the United States sought to dress up the Vietnam War as an alliance for freedom. But the fact that a word can be prostituted or violated does not take its proper meaning off our serious agenda.

The old word, the technical term, for the change Mary was rejoicing in is "gospel"; but "gospel" has become a tired old word. For some it means the invitation to an individual to accept the forgiveness of sins, so that to preach the gospel, to "evangelize," is to spread the message of this invitation. For others it means correct teaching about the work of Christ, so that "evangelicals" are those who hold to traditional doctrines. Elsewhere "evangelical" simply is the current word for "Protestant." For still others "gospel" represents a particular kind of country music.

If we are ever to rescue God's good news from all the justifiable but secondary meanings it has taken on, perhaps the best way to do it is to say that the root meaning of the term *euangelion* would today best be translated "revolution." Originally it is not a religious or a personal term at all, but a secular one: "good news." But *euangelion* is not just any welcome piece of information, it is news which impinges upon the fate of the community. "Good news" is the report brought by a runner to a Greek city that a distant battle has been won, preserving their freedom; or that a son has been born to the king, assuring a generation of political stability. "Gospel" is good news having seriously to do with the people's welfare. Today we might speak of the end of the Vietnam War in this sense; not merely an event that makes some of us happy, but one which shapes our common lives for the better.

This is not only true of the meaning of the word we translate "gospel" in its ordinary, secular usage outside the New Testament; it is true as well of the story the New Testament calls by this name. Mary's outburst of social enthusiasm in the Magnificat is only one sample; but the response of her kinsman Zechariah to the birth of his son is to sing of the fulfillment of God's promise:

> Age after age he proclaimed
>> by the lips of his holy prophets,
> that he would deliver us from our enemies,
>> out of the hands of all who hate us. (Luke 1:70-71, NEB)

When this son John began his own preaching, Luke describes as "evangelizing the people" his predictions: "Already the axe is laid to the roots of the trees; and every tree that fails to produce good fruit is cut down and thrown on the fire." To those who asked him, "What shall we do?" he answered: "The man with two shirts must share with him who has none, and anyone who has food must do the same." Once again, whatever it is that God is about to do, it will be good news for the poor, bad news for the proud and the rich; and it will be *change,* including changed economic and social relations.

This was the expectation that Jesus himself picked up when in terms almost identical to John's he announced that the "kingdom of heaven is near," and then more precisely:

> The spirit of the Lord is upon me because he has anointed me;
> He has sent me to announce good news to the poor,
> To proclaim release for prisoners and recovery of sight for the blind;
> To let the broken victims go free,
> To proclaim the year of the Lord's favour. (Luke 4:18-19, NEB)

The "year of the Lord's favour" or his "acceptable year" is the Jubilee, the periodic economic leveling-off provided for every half-century by the Mosaic law.[2] Such a change is what Jesus says is now coming into view in his beginning ministry. It will involve attitudes, so it can be called "repentance," *metanoia*, "turning-the-mind-around." But it also involves social practices, "fruits worthy of repentance," new ways of using possessions and power. The promised coming change involves social and personal dimensions *inseparably*, with none of our modern speculative tendency to dodge the direct claim on us by debating whether the chicken or the egg comes first.

This was John's agenda, and Jesus'; but it is also ours. Between their time and ours, there have been other ages when men were more concerned with other questions, other priority agendas. There were centuries when men were especially aware of the fragility of life and its brevity; they wanted a word from God that would speak to their fear of death and the hereafter. Man's basic need was seen as his mortality. In this context it is no surprise that Christian preaching and poetry dealt with mortality and that the good news man needed was spoken in terms of eternal life.

In other societies, other cultures, peoples are plagued by anxiety, guilt, fear of judgment. In this context the good news is stated in terms of forgiveness, acceptance by God, and acceptance by other people. Today some rephrase it as self-acceptance. In still other ages, other cultures, need is primarily thought of as help for getting a job or in facing sickness or poverty. To this as well the Christian message can speak. People are still asking these questions, and Christian preachers are still proclaiming good news in all these ways; why should they not?

But for Jesus in his time, and for increasing numbers of us in our time, the basic human problem is seen in less individualistic terms. The priority agenda for Jesus, and for many of us, is not mortality or anxiety but unrighteousness, injustice. The need is not for consolation or acceptance but for a new order in which men may live together in love. In his time, therefore, as in ours, the question of revolution, *the judgment of God upon the present order and the imminent promise of another one,* is the language in which the gospel must speak. What most men *mean* by

2. Cf. a review of its meanings, and its significance as backdrop to Jesus' ministry, in my *The Politics of Jesus*, 2d ed. (Grand Rapids: Eerdmans, 1994), pp. 60-75.

"revolution," the *answer* they want, is not the gospel; but the gospel if it be authentic must so speak as to answer the *question* of revolution. This Jesus did. He accepted the phrasings John had made current; he proclaimed the coming kingdom and let himself be called (though reticently, and subject to misunderstandings and redefinitions) the Anointed One *(Messiah)*, or the Awaited One.

2. The Four Ways

Time has not changed as much as some think. In any situation of social conflict and oppression there are a limited number of possible strategies. Born a displaced person in a country under foreign occupation and puppet governments, Jesus faced the same logical options faced in 1778 by a Pennsylvanian, or in 1958 by an Algerian, or today by a Vietnamese or a Guatemalan. As he set about being the expected Messiah and representing in the world the cause which he called a kingdom, the situation surrounding him, the men whose expectations he spoke to, and the tempter who accompanied him through his career all joined to ask of him a particular kind of behavior to reach his goals. He had four choices.

One way to begin, which was open to Jesus as it is today, was that of realism: to begin by accepting the situation as it really was. The Romans were in control of Palestine (much more solidly than the French in Algeria in 1958 or the Americans in Santo Domingo in 1968); any hope for change must begin with that reality. A brand-new start is not an available option; we must save what we can by aiming at what is possible. This was in Jesus' age the strategy of the Herodians and the Sadducees. These were not, as a superficial reading of the Gospel narrative might make one think, nasty and scheming people; they were intelligent leaders following a responsible strategy. Their concern was to do the best one could in the situation. Their rationale was simple and honest: one could not change the fact of Roman rule whether one desired to do so or not. "Let us then save what we can by aiming at what is possible." These were the people who were able to keep the temple worship going, to maintain the public recognition and teaching of the Jewish law. They preserved a breathing space for the Jewish people and culture — a unique, legally guaranteed status for the practice of a non-Roman, monotheist religion. It will not do to condemn them all unheard, any more than it is honest today to condemn some people unheard as "establishment." They were working for justice and for change, and not at all without effect. Their work included some very costly — and effective — nonviolent direct action against the desecration of their temple by the Roman armies. But of course, in order to change it they accepted and directly sanctioned the social system of Roman occupation under which they lived, and from which they profited. Yet this was in the interest of doing the best one could with the options available, only biding the time till more sweeping change could be engineered.

This stance is still very much alive today. For some it is taken in an uncritical, proestablishment way. Despite the theoretical separation of church and state, our society is never without a chaplain in the army, in the Congress, and in the Memorial Day parade. It is the service of the chaplain to sanctify the existing order with the hope of being able progressively to improve it. A powerful publicity organization bears the name Religion in American Life. These are the people who advertise that by the use of religion "you can lift your life." What the religion is does not matter too much. It is assumed that it can be Protestant, Catholic, or Jewish; and if it were Buddhist or Muslim that would not change the point very much. This is likewise the concept which is at work when the interpreters of politics tell us, quite independently of any particular moral choices he might make, that President Eisenhower or Kennedy or Johnson or Nixon can be called "a very religious person."

But a similar stance is taken as well by many who are more critical. Much of the noisy social criticism of our day comes from "established" agencies: from the staff of councils of churches or of mainstream denominations. Criticism of American military policy in Vietnam, or of investment policy in South America or South Africa, has in the late 1960s often come from the tenured faculty of the endowed Ivy League universities and seminaries, trying to turn America's "good guy" self-image in upon itself as a judgment instead of a justification.

But for Jesus, the strategy of "infiltrating the establishment" was not a temptation at all. Of the four available options, it was the only one which never could have come to his mind. This party was against him from the beginning; in fact, from the time of his birth. It was their head, Caiaphas, who stated that it was expedient that one life should be sacrificed — whether justly or unjustly mattered little — for the sake of the community.

For it does come to this: if religion is to sanction the order that exists, it must defend that order even against criticism by the prophetic word, even at the cost of the life or the liberty of a prophet. The critic-from-within-the-establishment, the house prophet, will, if he stays inside when the crunch comes, be with Herod after all. This has not changed in our day.

The starkest alternative to the establishment path was that of righteous revolutionary violence. It was presented in Jesus' time by the underground political and military group called the Zealots, men in the heritage of Joshua and the Maccabees, for whom the "zeal of the Lord" was to express itself in holy warfare against the infidel Romans. The Romans understood no other language than that of force; no other means can be effective than a response to them in their own kind. Zealot revolutions rocked Palestine about once a generation in the decades before and after Jesus.

Today as well the Zealot temptation is beckoning. In Christian student organizations, both Catholic and Protestant, and in the 1966 conference on Christian Responsibility in Modern Society in Geneva, voices are loud which proclaim that the only option for the Christian church is to "take sides" with those forces which demand immediate social remodeling, even at the cost if necessary of much bloodshed. Such an attitude fits the mentality of youth in many civilizations. Anything would be better than what we now have; what we need is a whole new start.

This Zealot option represented a real possibility, in fact, a real temptation for Jesus. It was this possibility to which he was particularly drawn in his debate with the tempter in the desert at his baptism, and again at his last trial in Gethsemane. More of his disciples came from the Zealot group than from any other part of Palestinian society, and their expectations were clearly along this line. Recent scholarship has clarified the extent to which Jesus' ministry must be understood as representing a constant struggle with the social option of revolutionary violence. This possibility was close enough to Jesus to constitute a genuine temptation. Jesus was perceived by some of his followers, and by the Herodians and Sadducees, as the nearest thing to a Zealot, and was executed by the Romans on the grounds that he was one. He used their language, took sides with the poor as they did, condemned the same evils they did, created a disciplined community of committed followers as they did, prepared as they did to die for the divine cause.

Yet Jesus did not take the path of the Zealots. When the end finally came it was in fact one of the former Zealots on his team, Judas, who turned him over to the authorities. He rejected this path not, as some of us might, because, being secure, he would stand to lose in a revolution, or being squeamish, he wanted to avoid social conflict. At those points he was with the Zealots. His rejection of their righteous violence had another kind of reason. He did not agree that to use superior force or cunning to change society from the top down by changing its rulers was the real need. What is wrong with the violent revolution according to Jesus is not that it changes too much but that it changes too little; the Zealot is the reflection of the tyrant whom he replaces by means of the tools of the tyrant. The Zealot resembles the tyrant whom he attacks in the moral claims he makes for himself and his cause: "In the world, kings lord it over their subjects; and those in authority are called their country's 'Benefactors'" (Luke 22:25, NEB). One of the clear differences between Jesus and the Zealots was his readiness to associate with the impure, the sinner, the publican, the Roman. What is ultimately wrong, for Jesus, in the righteous arrogance of the revolutionary is not the fact (which is historically demonstrable) that insurrectionary movements most often fail and thereby actually make worse the situation of the oppressed. Nor is the decisive failure the fact (also historically demonstrable and psychologically normal) that successful insurrectionary movements most often are corrupted by the temptations of the very appeal to righteousness in the use of power which brought them to victory. It is not even that most often (though perhaps less uniformly than for the other arguments) the revolutionary is immature, incapable of self-criticism, with little sense of history or of social determinants. If these were the only arguments against the Zealot model, they would convince an ethicist but they might not have convinced Jesus; they all leave the door open a crack for an exceptional case which might succeed after all.

What is wrong with the Zealot path for Jesus is not that it produces its new order by use of illegitimate instruments, but that the order it produces cannot be new. An order created by the *sword* is at the heart still not the new peoplehood Jesus announces. It still, by its subordination of persons (who may be killed if they are on the wrong side) to causes (which must triumph because they are right), preserves unbroken the self-righteousness of the mighty and denies the servanthood which God has chosen as his tool to remake the world.

But we are ahead of ourselves. Jesus had some other, less extreme choices. He could have rejected the Roman rule and the compromises of the Herodians without necessarily joining the Zealots.

A third logical possibility available to Jesus was the desert. He could withdraw from the tension and conflicts of the urban center where government and commerce constantly polluted even the most well-intentioned son of the law, seeking to find a place where he could be pure and perfectly faithful. In the last decades we have come to know much more about the "monasteries" around the Dead Sea. These sizable colonies of people were doing just this: maintaining faithful copies of the text of the Old Testament Scriptures, living a life unspotted by the outside world and in literal conformity to the rabbinic rules.

There are some who have thought that this is the path of Christian faithfulness. The Amish, migrating every other generation, or the hippies in California canyons are only the extreme forms of such withdrawal. The rural community has often been praised as the place where it is easier to be Christian, because life is more simple and one has to deal with fewer people; the village has a minimum of government and all economic organizations are man-size.

The days of real rural withdrawal are fast passing, but the synthetic countryside we call the suburb, with its artificial old swimming holes, artificial expanses of meadow, and artificial campfire sites, set up to maintain an artificial distance from the city's problems, still represents some people's vision of what to live for. This is supplemented by the still more complete withdrawal of the weekend lakeside and the camping trailer. But Jesus, although his home was a village, found no hearing there, and left village life behind him. He forsook his own handicraft and called his disciples away from their nets and their plows. He set out quite openly and consciously for the city and the conflict which was sure to encounter him there.

There is yet a fourth possibility which, like the first, lay close on the path of Jesus. This was the option of "proper religion," represented in his society by the Pharisees. The Pharisees lived in the middle of urban society, yet they sought, like the desert sects, to keep themselves pure and separate. The root of the word "Pharisee" means "separate." These people kept themselves pure in the midst of the city by keeping rules of segregation. Certain areas of life were to be avoided; certain elements of culture are not for the Pharisee. Certain coins, certain crops, certain persons, certain occupations, certain days were taboo. So it is in our day; there are many who feel that it is both possible and desirable to distinguish by a clear line the "spiritual" or the "moral" issues, to which religion properly speaks, from "social" and "political" issues, which are not the business of religion. The theme of "revolution" in our society is the prime example of what is not the Christian's concern.

But their separation is really not that clean. To avoid revolution means to take the side of the establishment. To say that the church should not meddle with the problem of open housing is to conclude that the house owner and the real estate agent, even if members of the churches, receive no concrete moral guidance from beyond themselves. To say that it is not the business of the church to second-guess the experts on details of political or military strategy, to have judgments on the moral legitimacy of particular laws, is to give one's blessing to whatever goes on. Those who object to the church's having something to say about economies, especially if that be critical of the existing capitalistic order, have no qualms about seeing the church on the other side of the economic question, or about economies having a say in the life of the churches.

So it comes as no surprise to be reminded that in the case of Jesus, the Pharisees as well, although deep moral and theological differences separated them from the Herodians and the Sadducees, finally did make common cause with them in the crucifixion because Jesus threatened their position of noninvolvement.

3. Light to the Nations

But what then is Jesus to do, if he rejects at the same time the established order of the Herodians and the holy, violent revolution with which the Zealots sought to change that order: both the outward emigration of the Essenes and the inward emigration of the Pharisees? We need not meditate long to see that this question is our own.

To answer our question as it has been sharpened by a survey of available social strategies in Jesus' time and in ours, we must look back to what God had been doing or trying to do for a long, long time. The Bible story really begins with Abraham, the father of those who believe. Abraham was called to get up and leave Chaldea, the cultural and religious capital of the known world in his age, to go he knew not where, to find he knew not what. He could not know when or whether or how he could again have a home, a land of his own. And yet as he rose to follow this inscrutable promise he was told that it was through him that the nations of the world would be blessed. In response Abraham promised his God that he would lead a different kind of life: a life different from the cultured and the religious peoples, whether urban or nomadic, among whom he was to make his pilgrim way.

> From the rocky heights I see them,
> I watch them from the rounded hills.
> I see a people that dwells alone,
> that has not made itself one with the nations. (Num. 23:9, NEB)

Yet in that apartness how present! This is the original revolution; the creation of a distinct community with its own deviant set of values and its coherent way of incarnating them. Today it might be called an underground movement, a political party, an infiltration team, or a cell movement. The sociologists would call it an intentional community. Then they were called "Hebrews," a title which probably originally meant "the people who crossed over."

Abraham's children did not always keep God's promises, but God remained steadfast in his loyalty to them. His promises of righteousness to be brought to the nations through his servant Israel were from year to year reiterated, reinforced, clarified, even though the likelihood that the Israelites would become the instrument of their fulfillment seemed less and less evident. These were the promises, Christians believe, which Jesus came to keep.

Jesus did again what God had done in calling Abraham or Moses or Gideon or Samuel: He gathered his people around his word and his will. Jesus created around himself a society like no other society mankind had ever seen:

a. This was a voluntary society: you could not be born into it. You could come into it only by repenting and freely pledging allegiance to its king. It was a society with no second-generation members.

b. It was a society which, counter to all precedent, was mixed in its composition. It was mixed racially, with both Jews and Gentiles; mixed religiously, with fanatical keepers of the law and advocates of liberty from all forms, with both radical monotheists and others just in the process of disentangling their minds from idolatry; mixed economically, with members both rich and poor.

c. When he called his society together Jesus gave its members a new way of life to live. He gave them a new way to deal with offenders — by forgiving them. He gave them a new way to deal with violence — by suffering. He gave them a new way to deal with money — by sharing it. He gave them a new way to deal with problems of leadership — by drawing upon the gift of every member, even the most humble. He gave them a new way to deal with a corrupt society — by building a new order, not smashing the old. He gave them a new pattern of relationships between man and woman, between parent and child, between master and slave, in which was made concrete a radical new vision of what it means to be a human person. He gave them a new attitude toward the state and toward the "enemy nation."

At the heart of all this novelty, as we said already in explaining Jesus' response to the Zealot option, is what Jesus did about the fundamental human temptation: power. This was part of the promise:

> Here is my servant, whom I uphold,
> my chosen one in whom I delight,
> I have bestowed my spirit upon him,
> and he will make justice shine on the nations.
> He will not call out or lift his voice high,
> or make himself heard in the open street.
> He will not break a bruised reed,
> or snuff out a smouldering wick;
> he will make justice shine on every race,
> never faltering, never breaking down,
> he will plant justice on earth,
> while coasts and islands wait for his teaching. (Isa. 42:1-4, NEB)

Jesus not only thought of himself as doing somehow the work of this chosen "Servant"; he also saw this as his disciples' way.

You know that in the world, rulers lord it over their subjects . . . but it shall not be so with you. Among you, whoever wants to be great must be your servant . . . like the Son of Man; he did not come to be served, but to serve, and to surrender his life as a ransom for many. (Matt. 20:25ff., NEB)

All of this new peoplehood, the being-together with one another and the being different in style of life, his disciples freely promised to do, as he renewed the promise that through them the world should be blessed and turned right side up. Now the usual name for this new society which Jesus created is "church." But when we use the word "church" in our day we mean by it a gathering for worship, or the group of persons who gather for worship, or who might so gather, and who otherwise have little to do with each other. Sometimes it even means the building they meet in, the organization which provides that there will be an officiant at the meeting, or even the national agency which manages the pension fund for the officiants' widows. But the word Jesus used in the Aramaic language, like the equivalent word the New Testament writers used in the Greek language, does not mean a gathering for worship nor an administration; it means a public gathering to deal with community business. Our modern terms *assembly, parliament, town meeting* are the best equivalents. The church is not just a certain number of persons nor a specific gathering of persons assembled for a particular religious rite. The church is God's people gathered as a unit, as a people, gathered to do business in his name, to find what it means here and now to put into practice this different quality of life which is God's promise to them and to the world and their promise to God and service to the world.

Jesus did not bring to faithful Israel any corrected ritual or any new theories about the being of God. He brought them a new peoplehood and a new way of living together. The very existence of such a group is itself a deep social change. Its very presence was such a threat that he had to be crucified. But such a group is not only by its existence a novelty on the social scene; if it lives faithfully, it is also the most powerful tool of social change.

4. And Now?

> The kingdom of God is at hand:
> repent and believe the good news!

To repent is not to feel bad but to think differently and therefore to act differently. Protestantism, and perhaps especially evangelical Protestantism, in its concern for helping every individual to make his own authentic choice in full awareness and sincerity, is in constant danger of confusing the kingdom itself with the benefits of the kingdom. If anyone repents, if anyone turns around to follow Jesus in his new way of life, this will do something for the aimlessness of his life. It will do something for his loneliness by giving him fellowship. It will do something for his anxiety and guilt by giving him a good conscience. So the Bultmanns and the Grahams whose "evangelism" is to proclaim the offer of restored selfhood, liberation from anxiety and guilt, are not wrong. If anyone repents, it will do something for his intellectual confusion by giving him doctrinal meat to digest, a heritage to appreciate, and a conscience about telling it all as it is. So "evangelicalism" with its concern for hallowed truth and reasoned communication is not wrong; it is right. If a man repents it will do something for his moral weakness by giving him the focus for wholesome self-discipline, it will keep him from immorality and get him to work on time. So the Peales and the Robertses who promise that God cares about helping me squeeze through the tight spots of life are not wrong; they have their place. *But all of this is not the gospel.* This is just the bonus, the wrapping paper thrown in when you buy the meat, the "everything" which will be added, without our taking thought for it, if we seek first the kingdom of God and his righteousness.

The good news of God's original revolution is not, as the Zealots of right or left would say, that violence is only wrong when the bad guys use it or that enmity is only wrong when it is violent. It does not say, with the emigrant to the desert, that you can cop out and do your own thing unmolested. It is not concerned with the inner-worldly emigration of the Pharisees, to refuse cooperation only at the point of personal complicity. It does not promise, with the Herodians and Sadducees, that if enough morally concerned people sign up to work for Dow, Du Pont, and General Motors, we can beat the communists yet at feeding the world. All four of these classical strategies have in common that they dodge the duty of beginning now, first, with the creation of a new, voluntary, covenanting community in which the rejection of the Old is accredited by the reality of the New which has already begun.

The question for our time, in the world which awaits and aspires to revolution, is not whether the kingdom is coming but what we will do about it. It continues to be possible, and in fact likely, that we may choose the strategies which Jesus rejected. We could find most respectable company in any of these four camps, as did our fathers. Or we could, if we chose, accept in all its novelty and discover in all our creativity the kind of life together as fully human men among men which he came to live and to give, including the kind of death he came to die. We could accept, if we would repent, that novelty in our ways of dealing with one another, with ethnic differences, with social hierarchy, with money, with offenses, with leadership, and with power, for which "revolutionary" is the only adequate word.

The kingdom of God is within your grasp:
repent and believe the good news!

CHAPTER 9

The Biblical Mandate for Evangelical Social Action[1]

There are two reasons not to make things easy for ourselves today by simply restating the common convictions which have brought us to this working consultation.

First: it is one of the peculiarities of contemporary evangelicalism that the average congregation or the average Christian is trusted to read the Bible for herself or himself. This expectation of immediacy, sometimes spelled out more fully in a doctrine of perspicuity, has its good, strong, historically attested gospel reasons. However, when standing alone, it also has some limitations. One is that a person's confidence in the accessibility and the authority of the meaning of Scripture can very soon slip over and take the form of confidence in the adequacy of her or his own interpretation. How often in recent years we have read articles or have heard sermons on such themes as "the biblical view of . . ." or "the biblical mandate for. . . ." Yet what followed was not an inductive biblical study, was not derived from carefully reading a par-

---

1. Address assigned for the constitutive meeting of Evangelicals for Social Action, Chicago, November 1973, reproduced by permission from Ronald J. Sider, ed., *The Chicago Declaration* (Carol Stream, Ill.: Creation House, 1974), pp. 88-116. After that initial event, Evangelicals for Social Action became a panevangelical agency for education on matters of social concern. I commented on the event and its importance in the article "Evangelicals at Chicago," *Christianity and Crisis* 34 (18 February 1974): 23-25.

ticular text, was not the fruit of a new testing of the witness of Scripture, but rather took for granted the general evangelical stance which the communicator already held and knew that her or his listeners or readers also held, and then related the known values and familiar phrases of that stance to the new question.

The corrective for this overconfidence in one's own grasp of the message of the text is not to deny to the laity the use of the Bible. It is rather to take serious responsibility for the theologian's task of making visible the structure of interpretation. This is the point of the science of hermeneutics. What is the process which authorizes me to say I am interpreting the biblical view of something or other? Can I go at that task in such a way as to merit the claim that my Christian brother or sister should read it the same way?

The second reason for care as we enter our subject matter is that once we have identified the problem of hermeneutics in its historical and linguistic dimensions, we are forced to recognize as well the historic fruits of that problem in the variety of positions held by various Christian traditions, all of which today would be classified as "evangelical." Evangelical Anglicans, evangelical Calvinists, evangelical Lutherans, Methodists, Baptists, Mennonites, and Pentecostals each have a different thought structure. Some of those differences will matter for the way we approach the mandate for social concern. It may help us if we face quite openly the fact that there are diverse strategies, and that these strategies operate differently for different purposes with regard to what we ought to do about the varieties of "evangelicalisms."

For some purposes, the differences are downplayed and the parallel focus is accentuated. The common purpose behind such a reduction may be common tasks of service, publication, evangelism, or the battle against modernism. Often this tendency prevails when a transdenominational meeting of evangelicals, like this one, is brought together: commonalities tend to be emphasized and the challenges of diversity played down.

This is fine for program projection and for doing battle against unbelief, but it is of questionable adequacy when what is needed is, as in this setting, to find a way to meet a *new* challenge, concerning which our several traditions have inherited approaches which genuinely differ from one another.

The obvious alternative is to take the distinctiveness of structure very seriously and to limit cooperation to that which does not in any way jeopardize distinctiveness. This has happened in past debates, when our several movements found their origins. It is a position usually taken again in times of economic or structural retrenchment, and often in that kind of psychological retrenchment which is sometimes provoked by the encounter with a new set of challenges for which we do not have answers easily accessible in the tradition.

There might be a third possibility, which would be the outworking of one definition of evangelicalism, although different from other traditional definitions. This would be to say that while placing only limited confidence in past answers, either in their commonality or their differences, we trust that in a *renewed* approach to Scripture, in full awareness of the diversity of our approaches, we might find some new light. We might find a *new* way to submit to the bar of Scripture those places where we have traditionally differed, trusting that more careful hermeneutical perspectives drawn from history and language, renewed concern for the shape of the questions the world puts to us, and renewed openness to one another and the Spirit could move us toward a commonality of stance which would not be merely the negotiated common denominator of strategy of parallel focus nor static pluralism. It is with a view to laying the groundwork for such a hope that my response to my assignment today shall be focused not so much on a mere recital and synthesis of biblical affirmations and commandments as upon dealing with the existent variety of hermeneutical orientations.

The purpose of this typological background review is not to renew the arguments of history or even to claim to be fully fair to the reality of past argumentation, but rather to refocus the question which we seek to take back to Scripture for new light.

A multiple mandate. We would not be gathered here if we did not believe that the love of a sovereign God drives us into concern for the social order. We would not be gathered here if we were not convinced that the shape of that concern is at least partly a critical one. God does not simply tell *us* to accept the existing order; he tells us also that it must change. We probably all agree as well that the bindingness and the vitality of our concern for the shape of society will be derived from more than one stream within the salvation story:

To affirm God as a loving Creator, the earth as our home to be stewarded, and the life of our neighbor as entrusted to our care, is one way to say it. . . .

To affirm the covenant with Noah, with its divine protection of life, with its promise of the seasons as the structure of cultural life and divine protection of blood as the presence of personal life, is another. . . .

To affirm the covenant with Abraham, with its call to faith and its promise of a blessing for all the nations, is still another. . . .

To affirm the Mosaic covenant, whose Torah is an abiding testimony to the wholeness of God's concern for the shape of the life of his subjects, is another. . . .

To recount the Hebrew history, with its repeated rhythms of obedience and disobedience, temptation and renewal, is yet another. . . .

To proclaim reconciliation through the blood of the cross is another. . . .

To respond in faith to the kingdom proclamation of Jesus as an authoritative reordering of the relationships of those who hear and follow him, and potentially of others as well, is still another. . . .

To recount in faith the story of the apostolic missionary community as it spread a new lifestyle across the Mediterranean world is another. . . .

To proclaim the hope of a new city whose Builder and Maker is God, where a tree grows whose leaves are for the healing of the nations, is yet another.

All of these drive us into active social concern. Few of us would declare there must be but one way of stating the mandate for Christian social concern, in only one verbal form, or only one scriptural image.

But that still leaves us with our present agenda. There would not be the need we now acknowledge for a process of common search and formulation, which has not yet been completed, if "Bible-believing Christians" had not somehow in the past seriously failed to put their thoughts together on this subject, in a way which would responsibly illuminate their obedience and protect them against the temptation of Constantinian conformity to which we have been especially subject in recent generations.

So the biblical mandate we are to be looking for must be more than the imperative to love the neighbor socially. It must contain a corrective for the tendency to define the neighbor too locally and individualistically. It must not only explain that it is our duty to respect the powers that be, but also provide leverage for formulating the limits of that respect, and for articulating our resistance when those limits are overrun. It must not simply affirm the obligations of community and of righteousness. It must also equip us to respond when the very structures of community and righteousness become destructive.

All of the themes noted above in passing will be of substantial usefulness in this task. I hope we all affirm them all, even if in different sequences and proportions. My search is for those which can be the most formally constitutive of that understanding of the social task which can provide the instruments of its own self-discipline.

The paradigm of peoplehood. Evangelical preaching and practice in certain classical forms has trusted the will of the regenerate *individual* to be the bridge between grace and structure. The individual in a position of authority, whose heart has been changed by the gospel, will, it is claimed, use his power more unselfishly, more creatively, more industriously for good. This is not false, but it is far too small an answer, and one which is more modern than biblical. Among its limitations are the following:

a. It provides no substantial information about what are the particularly more righteous ways in which power should be used. It must assume either that they are self-evident to the whole society or that they are known somehow intuitively by the converted statesmen. Neither of these assumptions can be supported either by experience or by theology.

b. It ascribes little significance to the ethical insights, concerns, rights, and decisions of people who are not in power.

c. It fosters the already too great evaluation of coercive power and prestige in society. It makes it still harder than before to put the question whether certain particular powerful positions should exist at all. Certainly, as Frank Buchman, founder of Moral Rearmament, once argued, if Mussolini had been converted he would have had great power, which he could have used for good. But if you place your hopes for the welfare of Italy and the glory of God in Italy on the conversion of Mussolini, you are no longer genuinely free to ask whether Fascism is wrong.

d. It dodges the fact, which a truly honest individual in a high position is very clear about, that many evils are matters of structure and not of inner disposition, so that the most unselfish heart in the world cannot necessarily "use for good" or "clean up" a fundamentally vicious structure.

This approach when taken straight fosters an unevangelical understanding of the *station* or *office*, i.e., the person's place in the social order, as a relatively autonomous vehicle of moral insight. That the liberty of the Christian consists of his/her being released from inauthentic constraints and irrelevant laws, in order to do what belongs to her/his station, was in the sixteenth century an understandable corrective against the overvaluing of monasticism, against clericalism, and a potentially useful fulcrum to criticize the crusading glorification of the state as an instrument of divine righteousness. But when taken alone, it is not true. The insight or the role definition of the banker, the businessman, the legislator, the educator, the soldier is not sufficiently sanctified that he or she can read off the surface of the social order a definition of the duties of the child of God in that slot, as the frequent celebration of the effectiveness of the sanctified important individual would lead us to try to do.

Now I have suggested that the Christian church as a social reality is the needed corrective. The alternative to the focus on the redeemed individual is not to pay attention only to structures or to massive movements of the mob and the media, but rather to recognize that there is a particular point where the redeemed individual and social structure are both present, namely, in the Christian community as a visible body within history. Workshop coordinator Sider, in his instructions, quoted back to me, in his invitation, my statement, "The primary social structure through which the gospel works to change other structures is that of the Christian community."[2] How can it be claimed that the choice of God to work with persons in community rather than alone provides correctives for the shortcomings indicated above?

Sometimes the experience of the Christian community is a *paradigm* in the simple sense. The Christian community does things which the world may imitate. The Christian community feeds the hungry and cares for the sick in a way which may become a model for the wider society. The Christian community makes decisions through group process in which more than one participates, and moves toward decision by consensus rather than by virtue of office and authority. Historians of democracy have seriously suggested that the basis for the concept of the Anglo-Saxon town meeting was the experience of disputation and decision making in the independent Puritan congregation. Today, even

2. *The Politics of Jesus*, 2d ed. (Grand Rapids: Eerdmans, 1994), p. 153.

secular business management circles are adopting the concept of decision making through conversation which stems from the Radical Reformation.

The Christian who does have a position of relative power in the wider society, far from claiming autonomy in that station by virtue of God's having made it an authority unto itself, can be trusted relatively in his role only if he will listen to the admonition of his sisters and brethren regarding the way he discharges it. Thus the Christian community is not only a model as community; it is a pastoral and prophetic resource to the person with the responsibilities of office, precisely in order to keep the office from becoming autonomous as a source of moral guidance. Sometimes the function of the community will be simply to encourage him to have the nerve to do what he already believes is right. At other times, other church members, thanks to their participation in other parts of society, will bring to his attention insights he would have missed; sometimes the community's proclamation of the revealed will of God may provide for him leverage to criticize the present structures.

Serious sociological and psychological analysis should have made it clear to us that there is no such thing as an individual functioning all by himself out of the definition of who his "self" is, standing alone.[3] The person is aware of his being himself and being alone precisely because he is the member of more than one group, and because at some points the claims of several groups upon him conflict. The service of the Christian community to the businessman, the politician, the communicator, the worker, or any other molder of the shape of culture is not to promise and to glorify heroic individual integrity, but rather to provide a reference group which is both accepting and demanding, more reliable and more critical than the other groups and structures in which the socially responsible person is otherwise bound.

The peoplehood which the apostles after Pentecost led in self-understanding called itself the *ekklesia*. That did not mean what *church* means in modern usage: it meant parliament or town meeting, a gathering in which serious business can be done in the name of the kingdom.

---

3. It might be more correct in contemporary style to continue here to write "her/his" or "s/he"; yet in the history of European ethical thought, here being reviewed, this notion of the *station* or the *office* as defining what a person ought to do has usually been patriarchal, so that a superficial style correction would be anachronistic.

In other words the Christian community is a decision-making body, a place where prophetic discernment is tested and confirmed, the organ for updating and applying the understanding of the revealed law of God, the context for the promised further guidance of the Spirit.

Evangelical thought in recent decades has often been hampered by too naive an understanding of how the Bible can function authoritatively in social ethics. On the one hand there has been naive trust in the insight of the regenerate man of God; just as naive on the other side has been the trust that a few phrases from the Bible could be translated directly into social policy without any discipline of translation across cultures. The alternatives to these oversimplifications are not relativism or selling out to some contemporary social-science insight, but rather the functioning of the congregation under the guidance of the Spirit. The New Testament does not claim that Scripture contains all the answers. It rather promises us (John 14:25ff.; 16:12ff., as samples only) that there will be adequate and binding further guidance given to the church as it goes along, and that this further guidance will be subject to the judgment of the community, oriented by the fixed points of the apostolic witness in the canon.

The peoplehood called *ekklesia* is different from other peoples in its composition. It includes Jew and Gentile (not simply two ethnic groups but two cultural types). It includes both masters and slaves and makes them brothers "both in the flesh and in the Lord" (Philem. 16, RSV). It includes men and women, replacing their hierarchical relationship in pagan society with mutual subordination (Eph. 5:21). It shares money and bread and the gifts of the Spirit in a way that is a radical alternative to the authority structures of Gentile society. In all of these respects and more, the Christian community provides both a place to stand from which to say to the world something critically new and a place to keep testing and exercising the understanding of that critical message.

The Christian community is also a *means of influencing* other groups. The simple fact that the church is intractably present on the social scene as a body with its own authority, economic structure, leadership, international relations, openness to new members, conscientious involvement in society at some points, and conscientious resistance at others means that the social process cannot go on without taking account of her presence and particular commitments.

Permit me to recount a personal experience of a decade ago. In an ecumenical conversation circle in Evanston, we were discussing what might be the Christian responsibility for the racially segregated housing picture in that town. The self-evident need, from the point of view of some of the participants in the conversation, mainstream Protestants, was for the ministers of the community to ask the mayor and city council for municipal administrative measures in favor of open-housing practices. This would be the church operating, in the person of the ministers, to discharge her social responsibility. The conversation was brought into some disarray when one of us asked whether the real-estate dealers and the sellers of houses were not mostly members of the Protestant churches in Evanston. The answer was that they probably were, but that the preacher was powerless to get his own members to take Christian ethics seriously on the grounds of their faith, without appealing to the coercion of government to get "the church" *as membership* involved in lay professions to be less unchristian.

This anecdote is a specimen of the recurrent temptation to expect other forces in society to be more morally effective, or other authorities to be more morally insightful, than the body of believers in their structured life together. As Franklin H. Littell analyzed the failure of Prohibition,

> Politicians in the churches attempted to secure by public legislation what they were unable to persuade many of their own members was either wise or desirable. . . . Lacking the authenticity of a genuinely disciplined witness, the Protestant reversion to political action was ultimately discredited, and the churches have not to this day recovered their authority in public life.[4]

The lesson drawn from the defeat of Prohibition is sometimes thought to be that political action against social evils is self-defeating. That is to misread the point. The lesson might be that drinking alcohol is the wrong sin to prohibit. That too would misread the point. The point is rather that legislative implementation is only meaningful when it extrapolates or extends a commitment on the part of the Christian community which has already demonstrated the fruitfulness of that commitment.

4. *From State Church to Pluralism* (New York: Doubleday, Anchor Books, 1962), p. 20.

I could go on with the list. The church as a network of complementary charismata is a *laboratory* of social pluralism. The church as educational community is a nurturing ground for countercultural values. The church as community of forgiveness is a live alternative to a society structured around retributive sanctions.

So the foremost political action of God is the calling and creation of his covenant people, anointed to share with him as priests, prophets, and in the servanthood which he revealed to be the human shape of his kingship. The church is both the paradigm and the instrument of the political presence of the gospel.

But around that center we should fill out the picture. In seeking to organize what more there is to say, I have followed two formal concepts. One, already stated, is the awareness of past unfaithfulness and failure. This is not an area where we can start simply from the beginning, unfolding either fight ideas or fight strategies straight out of the Scriptures as if their guidance had always been clearly seen.

Parenthetically, it may clarify the picture if I pause to recognize a tension widely present in evangelicalism between formation and reformation as ways to see oneself. Often the claim is made to be unfolding the truth straight from the center, timeless and unconditional. Yet in actual historic experience, the need has more often been to critique and restore: to admit unfaithfulness and seek renewal. It is this latter view of our task that I assume. I am not asking why Christians should care about the political realm, but why they so often have been involved wrongly. That is why I propose to develop my further outline by itemizing some of the challenges, beginning with the questions, not the answers.

Secondly, I have for this introduction chosen to accentuate multiplicity, not simplicity. Both preacher and theologian tend to look for one key thought to bring all the rest into line. It could be done. Everything could be seen in the light of creation, or covenant, justification by faith, conversion, love, or hope — or the church. For two reasons I here avoid the path of simplification:

1. It tends to invite fruitless denominational debates about whether one center is better than another.
2. It might leave unchallenged the trend in our midst toward intellectual compartmentalizing, which would see social responsibility

as one ministry beside many others, or one good deed beside others, or one chapter of ethics beside others.

I thus willingly pay the price of a certain scattering of my remarks in testimony to the roundedness of what we are trying to describe.

Power is the name of the game. The political realm is the realm of power. Power is the ability to make things happen. The political process channels and distributes this ability. If bad guys have power, bad things will happen. So we good guys must get power to make good things happen. But unfortunately, to get the power for good uses, even the good guys must do some less good things. This way to open the problem leads to some unhelpful blind alleys:

a. It may lead to arbitrariness in judging how much evil is necessary to attain how much good, in which the privilege of person or party rate higher than the competing values.

b. Moral leadership may be replaced by finesse in drawing lines between shades of gray, as estimates of "how much" and "how far" replace "who" and "whether."

c. To say no to the process of seeking power may seem — to those who say no as well as those who go along — like just another reading on the "how far" kind of question, and as having chosen the purity of noninvolvement as the better part.

I must already object to this analysis as naive political theory. The person who in a given situation "withdraws" as a result of careful moral choice, or is defeated end excluded from power, is not necessarily any less responsible, active, involved than the one who makes it to the top.

But a deeper cost of the call for the good guys to get power is the quantifying of what they may sacrifice to get it. The just-war theory quantifies the lives you may take for the sake of some other political good. "National security" justifies the crimes you commit to weaken your critics. The "safety of our troops" justifies unconstitutionally expanding a war. That peace must be "with honor" justifies prolonging a war.

But the focus on the good guys getting control does not first become wrong when they lie or bribe or cheat or kill to win. It becomes wrong before that, when control itself is seen as the goal and when power is seen as a neutral quantity easily usable for good. Seen politically, power tends to corrupt: you need no theology to be more realistic than the American mood has been about "government by the people" through their elected representatives.

But you do need the New Testament to see Jesus' alternative: "The kings of the Gentiles lord it over them; and those who have authority over them are called 'Benefactors.' But not so with you" (Luke 22:25-26, NASB).

Jesus recognizes — as Luke reports it — that "doing good" is a claim the powerful make for themselves. He does not say outright that the claim is false. Nor does he affirm it. He simply sets the issue aside in favor of servanthood as his way to be the expected King, and therefore his disciples' way as well.

But servanthood is not a position of nonpower or weakness. It is an alternative mode of power. It is also a way to make things happen, also a way to be present. When we turn from coercion to persuasion, from self-righteousness to service, this is not a retreat but an end run. It brings to bear powers which, on balance, are stronger than the sword alone:

- the power of the truth rediscovered when obscured,
- the power of the dissenter willing to suffer,
- the power of the people to withhold confidence,
- the attraction of an alternative vision,
- the integrity that accepts sacrifice rather than conformity to evil.

We can be protected from absolutizing power for its own sake and from the betrayals of good causes which such thinking has justified

- by a vision of Christ's servanthood as a live alternative to lordship;
- by awareness of the many other kinds of power on the side of truth and humanness; and
- by realism about the precariousness, the real weakness and the temptations, of the top of the heap.

There's no place like home. Another besetting sin of the political realm is provincialism: the limitation of one's love to one's own kind of people. One of the main reasons Reinhold Niebuhr could rightly say that groups tend to be more selfish than individuals is that a leader's bid for recognition most easily appeals to group interest *against* those of some other class, race, nation, etc.

Narrowness of world awareness may be the fruit of misinformation, of traumatic experiences of migration, or of oppression. A wider than provincial vision may be fostered by education, by travel, and by good experiences with people of other cultures. But the alternative vision which it is our business to proclaim is more than cross-cultural education; it is a spiritual mandate. "If anyone is in Christ — there is a whole new world!"

The New English Bible rightly translates 2 Corinthians 5:17 not "he is a new creature" in the individualistic sense but "there is a new creation." Paul says that about Jews and Greeks. He says it as well by extension about the divisions between classes and between the sexes. It is just as true by implication of the divisions of tribes and tongues, peoples and nations, which Revelation 5 tells us are overcome by the power of the Lamb that was slain.[5]

We already know, from the development of secular culture, that wider unities are economically and culturally imperative. We have learned to see the region as a wider unity than the village, the nation than the state. But unless the wider vision be spiritually rooted, it will not hold in the crunch against the instincts of group enmity. It is not enough when a few groups join — as in the American melting pot — against a more distant common enemy. Cosmopolitan vision is not enough. Unless the *positive love of the enemy* stands behind the affirmation of the dignity of other groups, unless divisions are transcended by a dynamic rooted in the divine nature (Luke 6:36) and in the reconciling work of Christ (2 Cor. 5:16ff.), it cannot tame our demonic native ethnocentrism.

Refusal to hate or to sacrifice the "enemy" is one safeguard against provincialism, and since our world is already organized in the shape of military nationalisms, our defense must begin there. Yet the Christian

---

5. Cf. my attention to this witness in: "The Social Shape of the Gospel," in *Exploring Church Growth*, ed. Wilbert R. Shenk (Grand Rapids: Eerdmans, 1983), pp. 277-84, as well as previously: "Church Growth Issues in Theological Perspective," in *The Challenge of Church Growth*, ed. Wilbert R. Shenk (Elkhart, Ind.: Institute of Mennonite Studies, 1973), pp. 25-47. Behind these dialogical texts is the exegetical argument in "The Apostle's Apology Revisited," in *The New Way of Jesus*, ed. William Klassen (Newton, Kans.: Faith and Life Press, 1980), pp. 115-34.

offensive focuses at another point, namely, at one more dimension of the peoplehood we call the mission of the church. The people of God are by nature a supra- and transnational reality. Ever since Constantine, Western Christians have been unclear on how and whether Christian brotherhood relativizes national loyalties and identities. Even our overseas missionary efforts have not always been untainted by linkage with the cultural and economic interests of the homeland. The structural looseness of evangelicalism has made it still easier not to hear the voices of our brothers and sisters overseas when they critique the narrowness of our "Christian Americanism."[6] My point is not that we do not care about the rest of the world. The investment by evangelicals in missionary activity shows this clearly enough. But how do we care? Is it to share with them our superior way of life and save them from socialism? Or is it to take counsel with them about what it would mean for us, in the world's most powerful nation, to be accountable beyond our borders?

This may be a good place to stop for a question that goes beyond the Bible itself. Jew and Gentile are reconciled in Christ; but can that "whole new world" be implemented in the political realm? Jesus' disciple will love her or his enemies; but can that love be imposed on the world? Of course it cannot be imposed; nothing of the meaning of the Christian faith can be imposed upon the unbeliever. But that is not the question. The question is whether, when the Christian acts according to his faith in this way, relativizing provincial selfishness and defending the rights of other parties, he is thereby being apolitical or irrelevant. The answer would seem to be clear: How you see the adversary and the wider human community is the very substance of politics. Love of the enemy and respect for the out-group is not politically *popular*, but it is politically relevant and politically right.

Means and ends: principles or providence. When I speak of what is "right," I have identified another abiding issue. What is the place of pragmatic compromise? Are "right" and "wrong" timeless and clear? Or situational and calculating? The justification for specific political activi-

6. At the time of the November 1973 meeting I did not sign the programmatic statement which had been drafted in the course of the meeting; not because of anything it said, but because of what it failed to say against ethnocentrism and nationalism, proceeding as if concerns of Christian identity and social action could legitimately be focused only on America.

ties which are not evidently expressive of the love of God and immediately productive for the welfare of the neighbor is usually given in terms of calculation of the projected effects of a given action or of the evil events which would take place if such questionable actions were not taken.

To use a traditional label, contemporary political ethical thinking is practically without exception "utilitarian." The structure of a utilitarian calculation may be complex or simple, long or short range. One may speak immediately of some particular threat to be warded off, or one may use long-range "prudential" considerations like "Honesty is the best policy" or "I do not want to be responsible for eroding the constitutional prerogatives of my office."

Utilitarianism as a style in ethics is so prevalent in our culture as to be hardly challengeable. It would take too long to argue carefully here the philosophical inadequacy of simple utilitarianism as an ethical system.[7]

7. Among the logical shortcomings of utilitarianism as a full ethical system are the following:

- Effectiveness in reaching a goal can be measured only if the goal itself has been justified by some other criterion than utility, and if the price that must be paid for reaching the goal can also be quantified in terms that reach beyond the situation, in order to permit weighing the price and the goal against each other.
- There is a hidden nonutilitarian assumption when I say, "I *should* make the course of events come out right."
- Dealing with the *effects* of a decision in terms of causal process presupposes a closed causal system enabling me to evaluate my action in terms of its predictable results; yet the fact that I am making a decision whose effects have not been calculated assumes in my own person an openness within the system. If I am to take seriously that the system is open where I make *my* decision (even if it be on the basis of my calculation of utility), I can hardly justify assuming that all the other agents within the system are completely docile to mechanistic causation, having no mind of their own.
- He who phrases an issue in terms of the tension between "impersonal principles" and "effectiveness toward good goals in the situation" thereby obfuscates another basic ethical dimension: that of the agent of decision. The language of "principle" — whatever its limits — at least safeguards the concept of accountability beyond oneself. The justification in terms of projected results on the other hand tends to assign to the agent himself both projection and evaluation. What the Watergate burglars and the White House plumbers said was, "Legality is less important than national security" — a formally perfect example of pragmatic reasoning. But what they said in fact was, "We are accountable to no one."

Right now, as this nation rehearses daily the destructive effects upon our community of the liberties taken by those who felt that whatever they needed to do for the sake of a very good cause was justified, we have again begun to see the human side of the argument for a morality of principle. But now our question is the narrower one. Is there anything particular about the biblical message or about evangelical Protestantism which could speak with a fitness of its own to this question? Does biblical theology push us toward a particular mood or structure in ethics, as well as setting basic ethical norms?

I suggest that it does, and that one element of the correction for a self-justifying and self-accrediting pragmatism is a mood of *doxology* or trust, in which believing behavior is seen as an effect and not only a cause. Right action is a reflection of a victory already won as much as it is a contribution to a future achievement. It is more an act of praise rather than an act of simple servile obedience. We do not enter responsibly into the structures of social concern because we are sure of what we can get done there, but because we are proclaiming the lordship of Christ and predicting the day when every knee will bow before him.[8] Thus our conviction and our commitment are not dependent on our predictable effectiveness, nor on our confidence in our analysis of the mechanisms which we are attempting to manipulate. I do not mean to suggest any lack of concern for the study of the structures and the mechanisms of social change; but we do not canonize our interpretation of those structures in such a way that it could at certain times tell us to do the wrong thing for a good cause. If we saw our obedience more as praising God and less as running his world for him, we would be less prey to both despair and disobedience.

Another side of the corrective for self-serving pragmatism is the ancient Hebrew *denunciation of idolatry.* Idolatry means the willingness to honor, and to sacrifice for, other values, other loyalties than God himself. Radical monotheism exorcises the spirit of compromise by challenging the merit of the causes which are absolutized when truth or life or health is sacrificed to them. But idolatry means more than that. The difference between the true God and an idol is not only that one is

8. I have written more fully about the doxological base of ethics in "To Serve God and Rule the World," in my *The Royal Priesthood: Essays Ecclesiological and Ecumenical*, ed. Michael G. Cartwright (Grand Rapids: Eerdmans, 1994), pp. 128-40.

worthy of honor and the other is not. The idolater uses his prayer and offerings to manipulate the powers of fertility and strength. The Canaanite did not sacrifice to Baal because Baal was holy, worthy, or righteous. His cult was for the sake of his culture. Ancient Near Eastern idolatry, in other words, was the pragmatism of that age. The gods were used for human purposes, whereas Yahweh was to be honored for his own sake.

None of these considerations sets aside the need to think practically, to weigh the likely effects and the relative costs of available strategies. But they may help diminish the arbitrariness, the self-confidence, and the shortsightedness with which deeper values tend to be given up for apparent immediate effect.

Reverence for language. When the Decalogue forbids the false oath, and when Jesus "fulfills" the law by forbidding all oaths, this is by no means a ritualistic taboo or inexplicable prescription which only the finicky and legalistic will respect and the more enlightened may properly authorize themselves to pass over. We must rather learn to see here a double truth:

- the fragility of all human relations, depending as they do on words which may be distorted, colored, and on commitments which may be broken; and
- the self-giving divine presence to re-create and guarantee the reliability of language. In a kind of type of the incarnation to come, Yahweh comes among men, putting at our mercy the mystery of his name, subject to our misuse, inviting our respect. Jesus extends that same care over the rest of our language.

Open, true communication in place of the fabrication and management of information is a prerequisite of social health. Truth telling as moral ultimate is rooted in God's own nature; truth telling as social *sine qua non* has yet to be firmly anchored even in the most civilized democracies. When a press secretary can without apology declare his prior statements "inoperative," when an ethos of secrecy is so self-evident that "leaks" to the public are considered a worse offense than the misdeeds they betray, we see again the need for what Jesus meant when, sweeping away all asseverations as coming "from the evil one," he simplified and sanctified words: "Let yes be yes and no, no."

Postscript. This should be sufficient to exemplify — though not to exhaust — my claim that many strands of Christian faith point us into responsible, distinctive social presence, and that we may find our way farther and faster if we begin — rather than starting "from scratch" or "ideally" — with what has obviously gone wrong:

- individualism in faith and ethics,
- the search for power,
- pragmatism as a justification,
- provincialism,
- the abuse of communication.

I have left to one side — because it does not arise in the Bible itself — the issue which historical theology calls "spiritualism"; namely, the idea that religious reality is best identified — or safeguarded — by fencing it off from the real world, whether in the "heart," in mystical "insight," in "meditation," or in revealed mysteries. Then the transition from the spiritual realm to the social, or from "being" to "doing," is a new problem. The problem *is* real, for some of us. For more of our evangelical constituencies, it is the first question. But it is not a problem in the Bible. It is the product of our postbiblical experience, and therefore it belongs only at the edge of my assignment.[9] To deal with it we would have to move into historical and systematic theology. Creation, covenant, incarnation, reconciliation, kingdom, church — all the major biblical themes are rooted socially in common history.

I have dealt here with form more than content, with the why of social concern more than the what. I have not itemized liberation, violence, peace, economic justice, productivity, ecology, gender equality, generational justice as value definitions. This is not because the Bible would not speak as well, or because we should not, to the matters of content signaled by these slogans: it certainly does. But what has been holding us apart from one another and holding us away from the task has been the debates about the *whether* rather than unclarity about the *what*, and the *what* will vary according to context. The *why*

9. Cf. my "Experiential Etiology of Evangelical Dualism," *Missiology: An International Review* 11 (October 1983): 449-59.

is the same hope as of old; but a hope whose fulfillment we claim Jesus began:

> It shall come to pass in the latter days
>> that the mountain of the house of the LORD
> shall be established as the highest of the mountains,
>> and shall be raised up above the hills;
> and peoples shall flow to it,
>> and many nations shall come, and say:
> "Come, let us go up to the mountain of the LORD,
>> to the house of the God of Jacob;
> that he may teach us his ways
>> and we may walk in his paths."
> For out of Zion shall go forth the law,
>> and the word of the LORD from Jerusalem.
> He shall judge between many peoples,
>> and shall decide for strong nations afar off;
> and they shall beat their swords into plowshares,
>> and their spears into pruning hooks;
> nation shall not lift up sword against nation,
>> neither shall they learn war any more;
> but they shall sit every man under his vine and under his fig tree,
>> and none shall make them afraid;
>> for the mouth of the LORD of hosts has spoken. (Mic. 4:1-4, RSV)

CHAPTER 10

Are You the One
Who Is to Come?[1]

"Prophetism can be defined as that understanding of history that finds its meaning in the concern and purpose of God for that history, and in the participation of God in that history."[2] One might do well, in some context, to invest some time in unpacking the assumptions and implications of this compact and formal way of putting our question. What would be the alternative understandings? Would there be a God who would not care about history and not act in it? Or a God who would act within it without caring about it? Or who would care without acting? Does it make a difference which "history" one is talking about? Is there only one history, namely, something like "history as a whole" or "history as such"? Or is history necessarily particular, so that the God who called the Jews might not be identical with

---

1. Initially presented 22 March 1984 as one of six Parker Lectures in Theology and Ministry at the Institute of Religion, which is linked to the Texas Medical Center at Houston, Texas. The series title was "The Pastor as Prophet," which also became the title of the book based on the lecture series, which was published by Pilgrim Press in 1985 (editors Earl E. Shelp and Ronald H. Sunderland). Reprinted by permission of Pilgrim Press. The editors changed the title of the published version to: "The Prophetic Role of the Pastor: The Gospels." I here have returned to the original title, and have restored a few paragraphs which did not get into the book.

2. This phrase was part of the programmatic instructions sent to all the speakers by the series planners.

the God of whom the Bantus speak? Is the choice of histories itself a choice of Gods?

For present purposes, however, we need to lean in the other direction. I seek here simply to disengage from the Gospel narrative a description of the specific ways in which Jesus said his "Father" cared for and intervened in the life of people.

If we were conversing with Platonism or with Buddhism, it might be appropriate to discuss *whether* God is interested in history at all. From some religious and philosophical perspectives, the question may be whether God can care about history: whether it is compatible with the nature of Deity to be concerned about the realm of the finite and the particular. Is not Deity, by definition, infinite and incompatible with taking with ultimate seriousness any one time, any one place, any one practical goal, any one set of people?

That is not a question which can be meaningfully addressed to the Gospel accounts; they stand on the shoulders of centuries of Hebrew history, where that question had been resolved with such resounding certainty as not to be a possible question. The question that was evident from the perspective of Greek or Roman antiquity and that in the West became visible again in the age of Enlightenment — "how odd of God to choose the Jews" — did not strike the Gospel writers as odd at all. That YHWH of Hosts cares about a particular people is the specific definition, the identity of YHWH, as the one who chooses to be and to bring into being, more than it is a description of anything meritorious or lucky about the lineage of Abraham. Jesus presupposes and prolongs that understanding of the uniqueness of YHWH as the one who chooses.

The story about the Jew Jesus between the Zealots and the Romans, between the Essenes and the Sadducees, does not show him as being tested or tempted at all to conceive of God as not in history. The questions were in *which* history and in which *direction,* toward what end, that caring divine intervention was to be discerned and obeyed.

In this essay I have been asked to discuss the witness of the Gospel texts themselves: It cannot be my task to seek to reach past the specific texts into the critical reconstruction and deconstruction of the events or the redactional processes behind them. A gospel is, by nature, a witnessing document, and it is that dimension of witness that we want to hear. Rather than distill from the Gospel accounts a few timeless generalizations about a vision for history, I propose to review a series of the more dramatic vignettes within the narrative. Each implies and affirms certain deep certainties about God's intention for the human story.

The Promise Is Fulfilled

The private beginning of Jesus' ministry, according to three of the Gospel accounts, was a conversation with Satan in the desert, after Jesus had been baptized (like many other people) by John. What was being tested was his understanding of the way in which he was to proceed to be the liberator-designate. Will he do it as showman, as thaumaturgic welfare distributor, as multiplier of loaves and fishes? Will he do it by appearing suddenly in the temple to claim effective sovereignty, in the style of the Maccabees? Will he enter into a pact with the powers already ruling the globe?

None of these options would take Jesus or his people out of history. None would denature history as unimportant over against some other realm or kind of being. Jesus' answer is in the same world. It is a concrete alternative to those forms of the messianic temptation. His way will be an alternative to the way of the demagogue sweeping crowds along by his unique power, to that of the Zealot seizing the city by surprise violence, and to that of the collaborator scheming his way into the existing structures' domination.

The way of the demagogue, the Zealot, or the Herodian collaborator is not set aside because his goal of serving God's purposes is too concrete or too historical or too "political," but because it is historical differently. It is that differentness for which Jesus was first to live quietly half a lifetime in simple subordination to the Galilean family structure, from which he then emerged as a self-educated rabbi (something of a contradiction in terms) and peripatetic prophet, and finally, by living just as he did, gathering disciples just as he did, dying just as he did, and rising just as he did to plant in the midst of history a new kind of social phenomenon. He reformulated what it means to be the people of God in the world.

The Platform

According to Luke's Gospel, the first milestone of Jesus' public ministry was the time when, in his hometown synagogue, he was given the scroll of Isaiah to read. It was already open, or he turned it open, to chapter 61 (vv. 1-2), where Messiah is speaking:

> The Spirit of the Lord GOD is upon me,
>> because the LORD has anointed me
> to bring good tidings to the afflicted;
>> he has sent me to bind up the brokenhearted,
> to proclaim liberty to the captives,
>> and the opening of the prison to those who are bound;
> To proclaim the year of the LORD's favor. (RSV)

There is no way to take history in general or God in general more seriously than to say of a divine promise, as Jesus did in Nazareth: "Today this word is fulfilled among you."

History is a process in which specific events can be identified as links in the chain leading from God's past to our common future. What it was that was fulfilled, according to this prophetic text, was the promise of a transformed set of human relations involving the forgiveness of debts, the liberation of prisoners, and the renewal of the agrarian economy. What the Authorized Version translated impenetrably by "the acceptable year of the Lord" clearly meant in the Isaiah text the promulgation of the year of Jubilee, the arrangement under which, in the Mosaic order, every family would be reinstated every half-century in the possession of their ancestral land. If their fathers had lost it through bad luck, it would be restored to them; if they had come into wealth because of their fathers' astuteness, they would give it back as a celebration of the year of grace.

Such a vision is obviously not a literal model for other times and places. It presupposed the patterns of kingship and of landholding of ancient Israel, giving no guidance (if taken with picayune literalism) for urban economies or for the landless. Jesus' vision was not antiquarian. It would be equally inappropriate to read with picayune literalism the analogous vision of the book of Micah, according to which all people will be unafraid, owning their own vines and fig trees, and to complain that it would not be an interesting promise for the Wheat Belt. What counts is the simplicity with which both visions use the stuff of common economic reality to concretize the divine presence.

This direct description of liberation as the assignment of Messiah, and as the mark of this present instant, lays claim on the historical moment in a more radical way than do those eschatological visions that project unthinkable cosmic catastrophes in the distant or even the imminent future. Jesus is saying that a new quality of human life is beginning to be operative in his time and place: in Nazareth and, more broadly, in Galilee, and all the way to Jerusalem in those weeks and months when his presence will force decision on his listeners. The decision his presence imposes is for or against a new order that can be likened to the new beginning prescribed by the "year of the Lord's favor." That proclamation was unacceptable in Nazareth: it rejected the insider privilege of those who thought of themselves as especially God's people.

The Precursor's Doubts

The prefaces to all three of the Synoptic Gospels report Jesus' baptism at the hands of John as the beginning of his public ministry. Luke's Gospel reports a more formal crossing of the threshold from the age of John to that of Jesus, when emissaries from John visit Jesus while John is in prison to allay John's doubts about whether what Jesus was achieving was what John had been predicting.

Jesus had been one with John in the confidence that the impact of the promised kingdom was to be a profound reversal: the axe at the root of the tree, the unproductive branches thrown to the fire, the flail attacking the threshing floor, the chaff being blown off to burn. . . . That is what made of John's question a most fitting challenge: "Are you the one to come, or do we wait for another?" The question makes clear that the framework of historical meaning is a temporal expectation, which a given historical figure can either live up to or fail to live up to. The present moment either is or is not the time of fulfillment. John has earned the right to ask.

Jesus accepted the question but did not answer it with a sentence or a "yes." He answered by pointing to events in process, to miracles of healing. That kind of healing, it appears, should sustain the faith of those who were probably looking for a different kind of liberation.

Detailed biographical or historical reconstruction, to the extent to which scholars can risk it at all, points up differences between contrasting pictures of what various people thought John might have wanted and what Jesus wanted: Was John more like a Zealot or an Essene? Were the connections between the two movements or the two men as direct as Luke says? How do we interpret the difference between the Lucan account, with the appearance of a positive transition from John to Jesus, and the picture that John's Gospel gives of some competitiveness between the two movements, and some need for the disciples of Jesus to disavow John in order to affirm Jesus?

We need to name those questions, as part of the necessary seriousness of real history; yet for the purposes of this essay they do not matter. In any case, the Gospel account affirms a sequence of historic projects in which precursor and successor both understand God to be working in the real world to establish justice. Neither gives an independent value to contemplative or ritual religion, even though both spent long seasons in solitude and both laid claim to immediate understanding of the identity and purpose of God characterized by an immediacy quite different from the religions of tradition and authority. Their witness is not like what the Social Gospel vision of sixty years ago proposed by way of the reduction of religion to ethics. What they bring is not a reduction but a rise to a higher power. They offer not "ethics" in the sense of a set of behavioral imperatives for good people, but the proclamation of a new social possibility for the human story. Both of them affirmed the real alternatives of first-century Palestine as the place where, thanks to a renewed transcendent intervention, God's will is known and achieved.

Jesus both does and does not take over the mantle and the prophetic style of his cousin John. His answer to the emissaries from John who asked whether he is what John was looking for is affirmative; yet the evidence he tells John's disciples to convince their leader is his own ministry of healing, not his projected takeover of the palace. He does not even join John in scolding Herod for his blatant public and probably politically motivated immorality. He does not let his prophetic mission be downgraded into telling rulers what not to do. Yet he is with John in seeing what he is doing as an alternative to the way the elders proceed.

The King in the Desert

The hinge of the public ministry of Jesus, to the extent to which creative historical empathy can reconstitute anything of the way in which that ministry might have developed, is the feeding of the multitude. Until then, the crowds following Jesus were mixed in their composition and their expectations. His closest disciples are described as not yet understanding the core of what he was proclaiming. The miracle of the loaves and fishes had fulfilled in powerful public drama the prediction of the tempter: if Jesus would feed the people, if in the face of the privation and vulnerability that being in the desert has always meant for the human organism Jesus were to provide abundant sustenance for the body, he would be accredited as the coming king. John's Gospel, the most interpretative account, makes that most clear.

This event is the peak of the readiness of the crowds to acclaim Jesus as their anointed liberator. This had to mean (although our habits of interpretation have hitherto not taken it very seriously) that they would also be committed to supporting him in the military defense, against the Romans, of the kingdom they wanted him to set up. Now, for the first time, Jesus directly rejects that prospect. Now, for the first time, he tells his disciples of his coming suffering in ways that they are unable to understand and unwilling to accept. It is not that Jesus withdraws from having a messianic project for his people. It is that that project is defined with increasing clarity in ways that reject the temptations of holy violence. He joins the rabbis who had already decided that the Maccabean experiment had been a mistake. He prefigures a later rabbi like Johanan ben Zakkai, who was to disavow the Zealot rebellion of A.D. 66-70. That did not mean acquiescence in the Sadducean strategy of negotiation with the Romans within the framework of colonial status. It did not mean Essene quietism. For the present, Jesus does not say what alternative social project his message will mean. It has, in any case, meant a renewed claim to the mantle of Moses as the instrument of God's sustaining the people with bread in the desert, at the beginning of a new exodus.

The Disciple's Choice: *Caveat Emptor*

For Luke's account, the most dramatic statement of the alternative way toward which Jesus has been leading his disciples since the episode of the loaves in the desert is chapter 14. The sequence of account that describes Jesus' movement toward Jerusalem (chap. 9) had been marked along the way with reminders of his political vision. At the beginning of chapter 13 are two references to episodes of Zealot violence: the incident of the tower of Siloam and the massacre of some Galileans by Pilate. "Great multitudes" are still following Jesus (14:25); it is to them that he addresses his dramatic warning against a too-easy decision to join his movement.

Any normal notion of wise leadership would have one make the most of a moment of popularity, while it lasted, to enlist more people, to make it easy for them to extend and deepen their commitment to him, to move them from mere awareness to commitment. . . . We are accustomed to seeing it as the task of leaders, especially of the pastor, to make people's decisions easier. We believe we are serving people when we help them picture life in God's cause as the attainable goal of an easy transition. We assume that loyalty grows through involvement; they should not be frightened off at the outset.

Yet Jesus moves the other way. He warns his listeners against being too willing to follow him. Anyone who will follow him must be ready to jeopardize immediate nuclear family loyalties. The phrase he uses is "hate his own father and mother." Certainly this reference to division within the family does not mean preoccupation with psychic problems of internal family dynamics. It is, rather, that the unity of the family as the basic social cell is sacrificed to the values of the larger social cause to which a follower of Jesus becomes committed.

That cost is also described as the loss of one's own life. The way one might lose one's own life is described as one's "own cross." The "cross" in that connection can obviously not mean what it has come to mean in later Protestant pastoral care: neither the inward suffering of struggle with self nor the outward suffering of personal ill health or difficult social relations.[3] The "cross" could only mean (in the setting

---

3. Cf. "The Cross in Protestant Pastoral Care," in *The Politics of Jesus*, 2d ed. (Grand Rapids: Eerdmans, 1994), pp. 129ff.

that Luke's account means to narrate) what the Romans were wont to do with people threatening their political hegemony. Jesus warns the crowd that to follow him means exposing oneself to the reproach of causing political unrest.

He goes on to reinforce the warning against a too-easy adhesion to his cause by recounting two anecdotes concerning public figures who found, to their shame, that they could not complete an ambitious project they had undertaken: a building project and a war. King Herod had just done both these things. If he had been speaking in March 1984, Jesus might have referred to a former astronaut who thought he could get himself nominated to the presidency or to a president who thought he could pacify Beirut by sending the Marines. Better not to set out for battle if you are not ready to give your life for the cause. What more dramatic demonstration could there be of the irrevocably historical shape of Jesus' project?

What is the cost one should count? The family is the basic cell of society. Yet in a serious missionary situation, to decide in favor of Jesus may have to be done at the cost of other real values, especially one's commitments to family and ethnic group. Jesus uses the verb "to hate" with regard to the values of family loyalty and one's own life. "Hate" here does not mean a malevolent emotion or a desire to destroy someone; it must however mean a conscious decision to put those values in second place.

The other word for the cost of following is "the cross." By the time Luke wrote his Gospel, he and his readers of course knew about Jesus' own death; yet for the account of Jesus' speaking to the crowd, that meaning cannot be assumed. What the cross *then* had to mean was what the practice of crucifixion by the Roman army already meant in that setting, namely, as the specific punishment for insurrection. Followers of Jesus, he warns them, must be ready to be seen and to be treated as rebels, as was going to happen to him.

The Liberator's Choice

The most outright and overt explanatory statement of what he is doing that Jesus ever gives is probably his word to the disciples in "the upper room." Luke has placed here in the middle of the passion account a word that in Matthew and in Mark is found at other points in Jesus' ministry. It is framed between the breaking of bread, in which Judas's betrayal is foretold, and two other words about rejection: the prediction of Peter's denial and the word about the two swords. Certainly we are not pressing the text when we understand Luke to be illuminating all those conflict words with this one general teaching, and illuminating the teaching with the words of conflict. When Jesus says, "The kings of the Gentiles exercise lordship over them; and those in authority over them are called benefactors" (22:25, RSV), he is describing his own temptation. When he says, "But not so with you; rather let the greatest among you become as the youngest, and the leader as one who serves" (22:26, RSV), he is describing not only his own decision about his own path but also the prophetic perspective on the moral resolution of conflict. He is restating, in the form of a moral teaching, his own choice, which he had been making and renewing weekly since his baptism and day by day from the triumphal entry until that upper room conversation, and which he would be renewing again that night in the garden. It is the choice between violence claiming to be sanctified by the good it promises to do (those in authority calling themselves benefactors) and the authentic good done by one who serves.

Jesus thereby first of all makes clear that the most fundamental decision he had to make in this world was how to be that kind of benefactor. At the dramatic turning point of this passion Passover, he best describes his path by contrasting it — but that also means comparing it — with what the rulers of the peoples claim to do. He does not suggest that he has an alternative way to be a priest, although later Christians rounded out their picture of him by saying that too.[4] He does not claim to be a better prophet, although he acknowledges the line of prophets culminating in John as his precursors. Later Christians have properly also used the language of "prophet," as this book does, to describe his achievement. Yet the comparison and contrast with which he does define his mission are that of kingship. Lords in this world claim to be benefactors; he claims to be benefactor. They claim to be great; he provides an alternative vision of greatness. They dominate; he serves;

---

4. When apostolic writers called Jesus a priest, their accent fell on how he differed from ordinary priests; namely, by sacrificing himself. They were not interest in priesthood, or in the pastoral role, as a fixture in the life of religious institutions.

and there is no more profound description of what he asks of his disciples than that they be servants, with him and in his way.

That contrast is not meant as one moral hint among many, as Luke recounts it. It is not merely one scrap of political wisdom among others. It is a capsule statement of Jesus' own key self-definition, as he was torn between quietistic and Zealot models of the messianic role. The difference is not simply between ways to run a battle or ways to be socially responsible. It is between definitions of salvation.

What we learn from Jesus is not a suggestion about strategy or skill in the discharge of those particular leadership responsibilities ordinarily associated with the pastorate. What the gospel tells us is rather what kind of word we are called to minister in and toward. In a world of greed and self-aggrandizement, whose technology and dominant philosophy foster selfishness more than ever before, the people of God, as a whole, are called to be the firstfruits of an age of redistribution and shared sufficiency. In an age of rampant and in fact renascent nationalisms and of imperialisms whitewashed with the ideology of liberty, we are called to be heralds and instruments of the one word already created at the cross and at Pentecost, whose ultimate triumph we are to proclaim despite its evident present defeats.

Yet what is most striking about the way in which Jesus serves those goals is not the stated ends — which many another sage had dreamed about and many another activist promoted. What is original and redemptive is that he does it with his own blood. The community he creates is the product and not the enforcer of that new regime. His followers will live from, not toward, the victory of Christ. Our life is to proclaim, not to produce, the new world.

Our series of vignettes could be extended through the rest of the Gospel accounts and on through Acts; but for now, with this word from the upper room, we may leave the narrative and move to analysis.

Not Engineering, but Doxology

The standard account of the challenge of social concern would have us believe that the most difficult problem is to describe with some precision what kind of world we want: Do we want property to be owned socially or privately? Do we want prices to be set by the marketplace or in some other way? Do we want decisions to be made by an aristocracy or by a referendum? Do we want the races to mix or to live at peace apart? Once those broad goals have been set, the standard account of our social ethical agenda would have us believe that then the rest is only a matter of engineering, of bringing to bear toward that end whatever power we have available. Those who know which way the course of events should go can, with moral propriety, push them in that direction, and the clearer they are about that direction, the more authority they have to take control. The worse the situation is, the more violently they have the right to take over.

Jesus does not reshape the question by choosing a different social goal behind which to place his prophetic authority, and toward which to legitimate the application of power. His social goal is utterly traditional: It is that of the Mosaic corpus, with its bias toward the sojourner, the widow, and the orphan. It is that of Isaiah and Micah, the vision of a world taught the arts of peacemaking because they have come to Jerusalem to learn Torah and to hear the judicial oracles of YHWH. It is the ingathering of the nations in the age of the anointing. What differs about Jesus is not a different goal; it is that he sees, for both himself and his disciples, a different mode of implementation. They are not to be content with the existing order, as if it were close enough to what YHWH wants that one could get from where we are organically to where YHWH wants to take us. It is not the path of the quietists or the Essenes, who went to the desert to wait for God to act, or of the Pharisees, who kept themselves pure within society, disavowing the present world's structures but leaving it to a future divine intervention to set them straight. It is not the path of Zealot presumption, claiming to be the party of righteousness authorized by God to trigger the coming of the new age through a paroxysm of righteous insurrection.

Each of those standard type responses to "the mess the world is in" is a different answer to the question, "How do we get from here to there?" Jesus' alternative is not to answer that question in a new way but to renew, as the prophets had always been trying to do, the insistence that the question is how to get from there to here. How can the lordship of YHWH, affirmed in principle from all eternity, be worthily confessed as grace through faith? How can the present world be rendered transparent to the reality already there, that the sick are to be healed and the prisoners freed? We are not called to love our enemies in order to make them our friends. We are called to act out love for them because at the cross it has been effectively proclaimed that from all eternity they were our brothers and sisters. We are not called to make the bread of the world available to the hungry; we are called to restore the true awareness that it always was theirs. We are not called to topple the tyrants, so that it might become true that the proud fall and the haughty are destroyed. It already is true; we are called only to let that truth govern our own choice of whether to be, in our turn, tyrants claiming to be benefactors.

It is thus a profound misapprehension of the messianic moral choice to think that in his rejection of violence, Jesus was led by methodological purism in moral choice, choosing to be an absolutist about the sacredness of life. It would be an equally profound misapprehension to think that he was the world's first Gandhian, calculating the prospects for a social victory as being in his particular circumstances greater for nonviolent than for violent tactics. Both of those interpretations of what Jesus was doing as a social strategist follow the "standard account of social ethical discernment" that it is precisely the purpose of all the prophets to free us from. Jesus' acceptance of the cross, from which we throw light on his rejection of both pietism and Zealot compulsion, was not, in the first analysis, a moral decision, but an eschatological one. It was dictated by a different vision of where God is taking the world. Or, we may say it was an ontological decision, dictated by a truer picture of what the world *really is*.

As a final exercise in clarification, perhaps the originality of the prophetic vision of Jesus can be brought out by an effort to contrast it with the other models that have tended to dominate this discussion and to teach us how to think.

For four centuries now, it has been especially the Lutheran believers who have tirelessly reminded us that in soteriology we are not supposed to achieve, but to trust. Salvation is not a product, but a presupposition. We do not bring it about, but we accept it as a gift of grace mediated through faith. Jesus and the early disciples did not let that understanding dictate for them only what to do about "salvation," in the sense of the present integrity or the ultimate destiny of the soul. They applied it as well to shalom as the social historical purpose of YHWH. We do not achieve it so much as we accept it. It is not as basic to engineer it as to proclaim it.

For still longer than the Lutherans, Roman Catholics, or at least the Schoolmen among them, have been concerned to clarify that nature and grace stand not in opposition but are integrated in a complementary or organic way. The behavior God calls for is not alien to us; it expresses what we really are made to be. Yet, unfortunately, later Catholic strategy has foreshortened the critical potential of that vision by confusing the "nature of things" with the way things are now in the fallen world, especially in ethnic and national definitions of community and patriarchal definitions of order. When society has been defined as the nation and social order as patriarchy, then it is no longer true that grace completes nature; in the face of that definition of "nature," the word of YHWH has to be like a fire, like a hammer that breaks rocks into pieces.

Yet when the "nature of things" is properly defined, the organic relationship to grace is restored. The cross is not a scandal to those who know the world as God sees it, but only to the pagans, who look for what they call wisdom, or the Judaeans, who look for what they call power.[5] This is what I meant before, when I stated that the choice of Jesus was ontological: it risks an option in favor of the restored vision of how things really are. It has always been true that suffering creates shalom. Motherhood has always meant that. Servanthood has always meant that. Healing has always meant that. Tilling the soil has always meant that. Priesthood has always meant that. Prophecy has always meant that. What Jesus did — and we might say it with reminiscence of Scholastic christological categories — was that he renewed the definition of kingship to fit with the priesthood and prophecy. He saw that the suffering servant is king as much as he is priest and prophet. The cross is neither foolish nor weak, but natural.

A form of Catholic moral discernment older than the Scholastic vision is the culture of the early medieval period, between the old Caesars and the new Carolingians, an age during which civilization had to survive without the support of the preferred vehicle of righteous royalty. If you look at that epoch with the eyes of Justinian or of Charlemagne, it was the "dark ages." If, however, we ask of those ages what kind of light people had to live by, the answer is that it was the culture of the saints. Moral education was a matter of telling the stories

5. 1 Corinthians 1:17f.

of holy people. Holiness included patterns of renunciation and withdrawal, but it was also the age when a hermit would be called from his cave or an abbot from his monastery to be made a bishop. It was an age when the bishop, through his control of the sacrament of absolution, was the community's main moral teacher and, through his administration of the right of sanctuary, was its most solid civil peacekeeper.

It has been one major impoverishment of our Western moral universe that first the Schoolmen and then the Reformers, the former looking for something more intellectually generalizable and the latter denouncing abuses, have robbed us of the place of hagiography in morality. Not only did that mean a loss of the human concreteness of biography as a way to talk about being human. It also led to forgetting wholeness. It predisposed us to pulling love apart from justice, purity from practicality, and leadership from servanthood, dichotomies that have dominated moral analysis ever since. When God chose Jesus as the way to come into the world, when Jesus chose disciples as a way to make his message mobile, and when the disciples chose the "gospel" as preferred literary form of witness, each meant the choice of the story of the holy one as the dominant prototype not only of communicating, but of being good news. Jesus' parables, like his presenting himself as model, did not represent a mere pedagogical choice of "storytelling" as a more understandable way to communicate to illiterate crowds; the story is rather in the order of being and in the order of knowing the more fundamental mode of reality.

Yet older than our teachers from the "dark ages" is the Hebrew heritage which taught generations of Jews and Christians that law is a form of grace. Christians have been busy since the second century weakening that awareness. Hellenistic apologetes felt that the Jewishness of Torah would keep them from reaching nonbelievers. Reformers feared it would let religious performance stand in the way of saving grace. Both of these forms of anti-Judaism have profoundly impoverished us. It is only now, in the shadow — or should we say the light of — the Hitlerian Holocaust, that we are beginning to renew the recognition of all that was lost with the Jewishness of the original meaning of Jesus. Jesus' insistence, at the center of the Sermon on the Mount, which is itself the literary-catechetical center of the Gospel account as structured by Matthew, that the law is fulfilled and not forgotten is indispensable to understanding his claims in his time and even more for our time.

Thinking that we are freed from the law instead of *through and for* the grace of Torah is at the root of the anomie of our age, even though regrettably most of the preachers who proclaim that sorry truth seem to be interested in restoring a law that was not fulfilled in the Sermon on the Mount, one that would not relativize the family and favor the outsider.

The point of these side glances at the Lutheran, the Scholastic, the hagiographical, and the nomic visions has been not to reject them as wrong but to englobe and transcend them as true but inadequate. To make the claim with the simplicity of caricature: The prophetic vision does more wholly what each of those other modes seeks to do. Its vision of the priority of grace is more fundamental than that of the Lutheran mode, since it applies justification by grace through faith to morality as well as to "salvation" — or, as I hinted earlier, because its picture of the shalom that is given us by grace is both morality and what used to be called "salvation." It affirms "the nature of things" more profoundly than the Scholastic vision because it reads the substantial definition of nature from the incarnation and holy history, not from medieval culture *or* Greek philosophy. It affirms and transcends the culture of saintliness by planting in our midst the magnetic story of the model of all models, whom to follow is first of all a decision and a path before it becomes goals and principles. It fulfills the vision of the law of God by focusing the deep meaning of not swearing falsely, not committing adultery, loving the neighbor not as a mere holding pattern to save the civil order but as the design for restoring the cosmos.

To confess and to celebrate the healing of the world and to distinguish authentic healing from idolatrous and blasphemous counterfeits, the prophetic community is indispensable. The transformation of the world will proceed sometimes through the conscious exercise of discerning insight by believers, but also by others of good will, and even (despite themselves) by others of good will being providentially used, carrying out the imperatives and skills, of their vocations, i.e., those definable skills and goals of which the social organism is constituted. Yet to discern how those structures can be defined as servants of the "divine purpose" and be rescued from the idolatrous claims that their imperatives are univocal or their value autonomous, which led the apostles to describe them as rebellious principalities and powers, for the faith community is again instrumentally prerequisite. How do we know which vision of the vocation of motherhood is redemptive and which oppressive? How do we know which vision of national dignity or world liberation is true and which tyrannical? A doctrine of the vocation, or an affirmation of the orders of nature or creation, is powerless to answer if abstraction is made from the prophetic.

If then we confess the world as the ontological locus of God's sovereign intentions, and the believing community as its epistemological locus, the imperative is not first to stoke up our motivational devotedness, nor to develop more powerful sociological tools of persuasion or coercion, but to nurture the organic integrity of the community charged with the task of insight. The agents of coordination the apostles called "overseers and elders," the agents of community memory they called scribes, the agents of perception they called prophets, the agents of critical linguistic awareness they called teachers,[6] the agents of more-than-rational sensitivity they called discerners of spirits, the agents of doxology they called speakers in tongues, to say nothing of the healers, the administrators, and the bearers of other forms of charismatic empowerment which did not happen to occur in the apostolic lists but will be needed, and will be provided as need arises — must all be created anew and integrated repeatedly in the ongoing presence of God the Spirit in the body.

Cop-out or *Pars Pro Toto?*

If the gospel logic does not follow the standard account in centering the ends of Christian historical concern in the specific project to be achieved through the prophets' influencing the bearers of power, and if the model of the cross remains normative both in its particular historical orientation to the man Jesus and in its principled renunciation of coerciveness in implementation, is this not some kind of otherworldly quietism?

The possibility has always been open that it could be read that

6. This review of the variety of distinct roles within the community's process of discernment harks back to my listing in my *The Priestly Kingdom* (Notre Dame, Ind.: Notre Dame University Press, 1984), pp. 28ff. It is because of their diversity that the focus of the 1984 Houston conference on just the pastor was counterproductive.

way. It is intrinsically not that. They do not crucify quietists. A more adequate description would be to say that in its most formative stages this view is "apocalyptic"; but to sort out the multiple meanings that that term has in recent usage would be beyond our scope. What can be said most simply is that the future toward which the prophet knows God has already effectively begun to move the world is prefigured in the possibilities offered and to some modest extent fulfilled in the believing community. Sometimes it is the Holy Spirit, sometimes it is the church that the apostolic writings refer to as the *arrabon* (the pledge, or down payment) or as the "firstfruits" of God's impending victory. Here already the lame are healed, here the underdog is honored, here bread is shared and ethnicity is transcended.

The people of God are not a substitute or an escape from the whole world's being brought to the effective knowledge of divine righteousness; the believing community is the beginning, the pilot run, the bridgehead of the new world on the way. Its discourse may be called "apocalyptic" if by that — without disregard for other meanings the term may have — we designate a portrayal of the way the world is being efficaciously called to do that does not let present empirical readings of possibility have the last word.

I have used the phrases "believing community" and "people of God" instead of the other apostolic term *ekklesia*, because one learns from the literature concerned with this theme that reference to the community is often taken pejoratively; that is, the term "church" is often defined not by the apostolic and prophetic vision but by the abuses of sectarian, triumphalist, or ritualistic experience of the past.

None of those abuses is founded in what the prophets, Jesus, and the apostles were talking about. The believing community is the epistemological prerequisite of the prophetic confession. Whether it is God's intent to restore the world does not depend on faith, but faith is an instrumental precondition of knowing the shape of that restoration and defending it from our own foreshortened perspectives, whether foreshortened by selfishness or shame or by a too simple hope or a too weak one. As Yahweh could use famine and pestilence, Midianite merchants, and pagan emperors for his purposes in the Hebrew story, so tomorrow we may be confident that powers beyond the confines of faith can be instruments of judgment and of construction; yet to confess and celebrate that work, the prophetic function of the confessing community is indispensable.

By the nature of the case, the life of this kind of community cannot be cared for only by one specialized functionary named "the pastor"; that understanding of the pastoral task would be a contradiction in terms. How such a community would be appropriately structured, in the diversity of ministries or charismata distributed by the Holy Spirit, can, however, not be unfolded on the basis of the Gospel texts. For the Gospel texts, Jesus himself is the shepherd.

Nonetheless we do well to recognize that as the messianic community continues to minister to a still not-yet-messianic age, there will be need, in order to maintain and propagate the community and to illuminate its interfaces with "the world," for skills and perspectives that our parlance calls "pastoral," focusing on a style more than an office. The bearer of the prophetic task is the whole people of God. Specific ministerial gifts within that work are to be measured by their congruence with the whole community's calling to be the advance agents of the coming realm. Each of the partial perspectives we have recognized — vocation, nature, sanctification, law — will call for specific people to help articulate the shape of the prophecy needed. Scribes will need to be "pastoral" rather than legalistic. Elders will need to be "pastoral" rather than patriarchal. Prophets will need to be "pastoral" rather than neurotic. Teachers will need to be "pastoral" rather than abstruse. The one who consoles will need to be "pastoral" rather than manipulatively therapeutic. Those who plan and lead assemblies for worship and those who "preach" will need to point beyond themselves to the realm, and beyond the aesthetic to the prophetic. In our age's thought forms, the term most apt to preserve this accent will probably not be "pastor," with its overtones of professionalism and privilege; the place of the cross as a model for ministry will often better be rendered by the language of servanthood. Yet watching our language is not enough; "servicer" or "ministry" can also come to mean privilege.

The closest the Jesus of the Gospel accounts came to projecting the shape of the church was the description in Matthew (18:15-20) and in John (14–16; 20:19-23) of the coming guidance of the Paraclete to empower forgiveness and discernment. That is the warrant for continuing prophetic clarity. It is also the reason that the shape of the ministries contributing to that clarity must be renewed in every age. This is not a blank check for future impulsive, intuitionistic, or situationist "flexibility," for the Spirit's task is to remind the disciples of Jesus. The "more truth" that the Spirit interprets is coherent with its origin. Yet its coherence is not timeless rigidity; it is like that of a plant's organic growth, the implementation of a new regime. For this all the ministries in the body will be drawn on. Yet here I have let Jesus' pointers send us beyond the Gospels to the Epistles, beyond annunciation to unfolding.

The doctrine of the two natures of the divine Son, enshrined in the formulae of Chalcedon, has come to be a metaphysical puzzle. Yet what these notions originally meant, and should still mean, is that God takes history so seriously that there is no more adequate definition of God's eternal purposes than in the utterly human historicity of the Jew Jesus. That same prophetic condescension makes of the believing community — i.e., of the human historicity of those who confess Jesus' normativeness — God's beachhead in the world as it is, the down payment, the prototype, the herald, the midwife of the New World on the way. The ultimate test of whether we truly believe that God's purposes are for the whole world, that they are knowable, that they are surely about to be fulfilled is whether we can accept that in the present age it is the circle of his disciples who by grace are empowered to discern, more visibly and more validly than the Caesars and the Cromwells, what it means when at his command they pray,

Your kingdom come,
your will be done
on earth as in heaven.

PART 4

Ecumenical Testimonies

CHAPTER 11

The Spirit of God and the Politics of Men[1]

I. God and Politics

We do well to begin our treatment of this theme by protecting our title against some very easy misinterpretations of its meaning. It should not be taken to mean — as many like to think — that God and his Spirit are in one world and "men" and their politics in another. Some religious people believe that about God, and some politicians believe it about politics, but both are mistaken.

A. Where Does That Division Come From?

It would take a long historical study to uncover and disentangle what people mean when they understand such a division to be correct.

We could study the institutional history of the people of God in relation to pagan empires, from the Pharaohs to the Caesars, but we would not find "men" or politics on one side and religion on the other.

---

1. Lecture topic assigned for a sectional assembly of the South Africa Christian Leadership Assembly (SACLA), Pretoria, July 1979. Reproduced by permission from: *Journal of Theology for Southern Africa*, SACLA edition, no. 29 (December 1979): 62-71. Out of respect for the historical datedness of the text, the generic language of the assigned and published title has not been changed, but the term "men" is sometimes put in quotes to signal that I recognize that datedness.

We would rather find people on both sides, politics on both sides, and gods on both sides.

Or we could study the institutional history of Christendom for the past sixteen centuries, since civil rulers have been within the churches. Church and state are then seen as two different kinds of institutions, but there are Christian men and women in both of them, both claim to be under the Spirit of God, and both are political.

Or we could study intellectual history — the development of our concepts and our languages and our piety — to observe how the notion of "spirit" came, in some connections and for some purposes, to be thought of as opposed to or unrelated to matter, power, and the visible world. We cannot help using this warped language; but it cannot help us with our theme.

Our concern in speaking of "the politics of 'men' under the Spirit of God" is thus not to solve a linguistic puzzle, or a philosophical one, as to how two categorically unrelated realms can be connected, but rather to discern and be guided by the claims of God upon the one real world which he intends by the power of his Spirit to redeem.

The choice or the tension which the Bible is concerned with is not between politics and something else which is not politics, but between right politics and wrong politics. Not between "spirit" and something else which is not spiritual, but between true and false spirits. Not between God and something else unrelated to God, but between the true God and false gods. Not between the politics of "men" and something else that would not be "of men," but between men and women under God and men and women in rebellion against God's rule.

B. Is There Such a Thing as Being "Apolitical"?

A related misunderstanding is the notion that it might be possible for Christians to avoid or withdraw from the political realm simply and entirely. Some who believe this to be possible, and who ask it of others, mean that "the church" as organization, or pastors as its employees or its spokesmen, can avoid taking sides on some issues. That may be, but this does not keep the church as people from being involved. Others may truly believe that all Christians can be authentically "un-involved," and they may appeal to the example of the early Christians. Yet that notion can only be sustained by a very narrow idea of what "involvement" means, and only where Christians are very few. It may be possible in some situations (and it may be unavoidable in others) that Christians stand outside membership in political parties or can renounce candidacy for elective office, but this nonparticipation does not avoid being a positive political act. It is possible to avoid having a common witness or commitment on political issues by not speaking about them together, but then each Christian individually will have an implicit position and witness. It is possible to avoid having an outspoken political witness or to avoid criticizing existing structures, but then that silence is also a positive political action, accepting things as they are.

I suggest therefore that for our purposes we give up trying to define what is political and what is not, what is "involvement" and what might be abstention. Is military service political? is conscientious objection to military service? is paying taxes? not paying them? voting? not voting? having an opinion?

The root of the word "political" is the Greek word for "city," i.e., for organized living together of numbers of people. Anything is political which deals with how people live together in organized ways:

- how decisions are made and how they are implemented;
- how work is organized and its products shared;
- who controls space, land, freedom of movement;
- how people are ranked;
- how offenses are handled. . . .

Activity and passivity, speech and silence, are equally "political" when these are the matters dealt with.

II. The Spirit's Mandate of Old

Several songs in the book of Isaiah reveal to us a personage named "the Servant of the Lord" whose calling points us to an understanding of the political intentions of the Spirit of God.

> Behold my servant, whom I uphold,
>   my chosen, in whom my soul delights;

I have put my Spirit upon him,
he will bring forth justice to the nations. (Isa. 42:1, RSV)

Students of the Scriptures are not fully sure who this Servant was.
A prophet? a crown prince? the remainder of the Jewish nation? Christians (following Jesus himself in Luke 22) see in these texts a fore-
shadowing of Jesus' own work. Whoever he be, the intent of the Spirit
of God in calling and sending the Servant is that justice shall be brought
to the nations — a preeminently political purpose.

The Servant is identified with the Jewish people in their suffering
and captivity, but his mission is more than Judah's restoration. This
is stated in so many words in the next of the Servant Songs. Here
the Servant speaks, in the first person, of his being prepared for a
task:

The LORD called me from the womb. . . .
He made my mouth like a sharp sword,
in the shadow of his hand he hid me;
he made me a polished arrow,
in his quiver he hid me away.
And he said to me, "You are my servant,
Israel, in whom I will be glorified." (Isa. 49:1-3, RSV)

But then nothing happened. The mission never was undertaken. The
sword was not unsheathed, the polished arrow in the quiver never put
to the bow. The Servant admits his failure:

I have labored in vain,
I have spent my strength for nothing and vanity. (Isa. 49:4, RSV)

But God does not leave it at that. Nor does the Lord console the Servant
in his frustration as he wanted to be comforted. Instead there comes
another, still higher mission than the one still unaccomplished:

[The Lord] says:
"It is too light a thing that you should be my servant
to raise up the tribes of Jacob
and to restore the remnant of Israel;

> I will give you as a light to the nations,
> that my salvation may reach to the end of the earth."
>
> (Isa. 49:6, RSV)

The restoration of Israel, yet unachieved, is too little: the Servant will be used by God to save the world. For this reason the song had begun:

> Listen to me, O coastlands,
> and hearken, you peoples from afar. (Isa 49:1, RSV)

How does the Servant proceed to bring justice? Other texts will tell us more, but in these songs it is clear that what is to be tested is his gentleness, his patience, his persistence in defeat, his willingness to suffer.

> He will not cry or lift up his voice,
> or make it heard in the street;
> a bruised reed he will not break,
> and a dimly burning wick he will not quench;
> he will faithfully bring forth justice.
> He will not fail or be discouraged
> till he has established justice in the earth. (Isa. 42:2ff., RSV)

The drama of his suffering for others and his restoration to glory by the power of God is of course still clearer in the last of the songs, Isaiah 52:13–53:12. He is obedient, he must listen and learn:

> Morning by morning [the Lord] wakens,
> he wakens my ear
> to hear as those who are taught. (50:4b, RSV)

Being a disciple, he can sustain others:

> The Lord GOD has given me
> the tongue of those who are taught,
> that I may know how to sustain with a word
> him that is weary. (50:4a, RSV)

He trusts his Lord without seeing the path:

> [He] walks in darkness
>   and has no light,
> yet trusts in the name of the LORD
>   and relies upon his God. (50:10, RSV)

"Trust," "patience," "obedience" are qualities we are accustomed to honoring in an individual. We see them as personal virtues, but we assume they are unrelated to communities, to structures and to the world of power and injustice. Yet these texts are about a political mission. They describe the qualities of the Servant whom God can use to bring justice to the nations. Trust in the Spirit of the Lord is the alternative to trust in alliances, horses, and chariots, as Isaiah had said earlier (chaps. 30, 31).

The figure of the servant is but one specimen. It is clear from Moses to Malachi that the Lord God of the Bible demands political righteousness. In many parts of the Bible it would in fact seem that he cares more about such matters than about how many prayers and sacrifices are offered to him or whether he has a temple to dwell in. From that broad observation, we turn to the New Testament to see how that righteousness is to come and what is its shape. A few samples, to which we now turn, will need to suffice.

III. The Spirit's Mandate in the New Age

From Luke's first chapter, we hear the song of Mary:

> He who is mighty has done great things for me. . . .
> He has shown strength with his arm,
> he has scattered the proud in the imagination of their hearts,
> he has put down the mighty from their thrones,
>   and exalted those of low degree;
> he has filled the hungry with good things,
>   and the rich he has sent empty away. (vv. 49ff., RSV)

As Jesus said more than once elsewhere, the first shall be last and the last first. The coming of his rule is a great reversal, and the words chosen to describe it are economic and political: *thrones, riches, rank,* etc.

From Luke's second chapter, we hear the song of the angels:

Glory to God in the highest,
and on earth peace among men.

This is the echo to the announcement that in the city of David a liberator is born. Here we find the message of joy to balance the suffering of the Servant Songs. The hope the Spirit gives us is a call to praise God, not merely a task to which to put our shoulders or our minds. The context of the political obedience of Jesus as savior is the praise of God; our political mood must be doxological. We do not follow the Servant in his patient struggle to bring justice to the nations because an oppressive commandment obliges us to struggle on. We struggle on because thereby we proclaim glory to God in the highest. The shalom which God sends among the men to whom he is gracious is the foundation of our servanthood, not only its goal. It is the gift of his grace and the proof of his glory, before it is the product of our industry.

From Luke's third chapter, we hear the preaching of John: "Bear fruits that befit repentance. . . . He who has two coats, let him share with him who has none; and he who has food, let him do likewise" (vv. 8-11, RSV). The great reversal is not only the Lord's unseating the mighty and raising the humble; it is also our own repentance, and its most fitting examples are the change in our dealing with food, clothing, and (in the next verses) the power to tax and to coerce.

From Luke's fourth chapter, we hear Jesus' first reported extended discourse:

The Spirit of the Lord is upon me,
because he has anointed me to preach good news to the poor.
He has sent me to proclaim release to the captives
and recovering of sight to the blind,
to set at liberty those who are oppressed,
to proclaim the acceptable year of the Lord. . . .
Today this scripture has been fulfilled in your hearing.

(vv. 18-21, RSV)

What is all of this if not political — freeing the oppressed, establishing peace, upsetting the mighty, sharing bread with the hungry? All of this, Jesus and his disciples called "the kingdom," God's rule. This was his favored word to designate the shape of the working of the Spirit of God in the politics of men and women. We are called to live, and by the Spirit we are empowered to live, in the reality of that new order, and to trust and suffer and serve and wait as God brings that justice to the nations.

IV. The Kingdom and Our Kingdoms

Now it is clear how we need to redefine the alternatives in our title. The choice is not between God and politics, nor between the Spirit and "men," but between the politics of men (and women) in their (our) rebelliousness and the politics of men (and women) under the teaching and empowerment of God's Spirit. The difference is not one of realms but of paths; not of levels but of options.

My theme today is very near to that treated by David Bosch under the title "The Kingdom of God and the Kingdoms of This World."[2] All that he said could be repeated here. He reinforces, clarifies, explains the other option, which is neither sweeping withdrawal nor unquestioning involvement. What I seek to do here is to itemize a number of samples of how that new option looks, by lifting up for attention the most important contrasts. I shall treat only very briefly, because he said it so well, one major theme: the fact that the believing community *as a structured entity*, i.e., as *political*, is a foretaste, a testing ground, and a model of the Spirit's sociopolitical work.

In the politics of rebellious mankind, merit is to be rewarded and offenses are to be avenged. If I have power, I have earned it; if you wish to be respected, you must merit it. Justice means a precise fitting of rewards to performance.

The Spirit of God on the other hand enables a justice of grace. We pray to be forgiven as we forgive others. That one phrase of the

2. Dr. David Bosch, professor of missiology at the University of South Africa in Pretoria, was one of the coconvenors of the SACLA. This phrase was the title of his keynote address. It was printed on pp. 3-13 in the same issue of the *Journal of Theology for Southern Africa*.

Lord's Prayer, if prayed sincerely, would upset the entire correctional system of our societies. God's justice, as we are told in John's first epistle, is at work in his forgiving our sins. Since the cross, "punishing" sins is revealed to be not justice but vengeance.

In the politics of rebellious mankind, domination is the rule. Jesus said it bluntly: the kings of the nations lord it over them, and the rulers let themselves be called benefactors. In many cultures, only the style of the tyrant, the *caudillo*, the *Führer*, the *baas* is thought to be automatically worthy of respect. "Power" is understood as the capacity to destroy or to coerce by threatening to destroy or punish.

The Spirit of God on the other hand shows us the power of meekness, of patience, of service. Truth telling is powerful, as Gandhi showed us by entitling the story of his nonviolent struggle for justice "my experiments with truth." Creativity is power when beyond a desperate dilemma it sees new options. Love is power when it denies to the enemy, the oppressor, the last word in defining his relation to us. Community is power. The apostle Paul said once of his own combat that his weapons were "not carnal but mighty."

In the politics of rebellious mankind every concession is a defeat. A person in authority can never give in, for that would be to lose ground. One must not grant that the other party has even a part of the truth, for that would be the thin edge of a wedge. Error has no rights; truth can admit no compromise.

In the Spirit of God, on the other hand, truth is patient, as the righteous judge of the Old Testament vision is marked by his mercy, not his intransigence. Truth can accept risk or even defeat, for it knows it will rise again. Truth can afford to distinguish essentials from non-essentials and to accept delay or defeat for the latter. Truth can be pastorally patient with the weak brother, and ecumenically patient with the yet ill-informed brother. Creativity can find a new middle ground where both parties can meet without either having gone over halfway. But more than that: the Spirit of the crucified one can be redemptively patient with impatience and with enmity, can be nonresistantly patient with situations it does not control and cannot change, yet without mitigating at all the proclamation of God's demands or one's own obedience.

In the politics of rebellious mankind, information is a means of dominion. Secrecy, selective reporting, propagandistically biased language, and even falsehood become instruments of control. The media of communication serve not the readers and listeners but the owners, the rulers, or the advertisers.

The Spirit of God on the other hand demands and enables openness to all the truth, enables us to admit admission of various perspectives and contested evaluations, and trusts that truth will be served by the open encounter. Freedom of speech, assembly, and movement does not weaken a society but strengthens it. Proclamation, the specific biblical style of communication, differs from other styles (propaganda, indoctrination) in that:

- information is not controlled or sorted, but exposed;
- the hearer is not constrained but free in response;
- all hearers are on the same level.

In the politics of rebellious mankind, the world is a closed causal system, with no newness, no hope. How often is a destructive political decision justified by saying that there is no other choice, that all the other possibilities have been exhausted? Politics, they say, is "the art of the possible." Such a slogan serves easily to deny that anything less selfish, less defensive, less violent, more just, could have been tried.

The Spirit of God on the other hand gives hope: not groundless optimism but the promise of new possibilities in an open future, made real by creative imagination actually finding new paths, proving that there are other choices.

In the politics of rebellious mankind, the other side of the view of the world as a closed causal system is that my neighbor, and especially my adversary, is to be dealt with as a means to my ends, as an object upon which pressure is to be applied, a resistance to be pushed aside or destroyed. Resort to falsehood or to violence begins by denying the personhood of the other person.

The Spirit of God on the other hand restores for us the inviolable dignity of the other, the irreducible integrity of a fellow bearer of the divine image.

One aspect of this deterministic or fatalist view is what the people who analyze social process call the "zero-sum game pattern." It is assumed that if I win, you must lose. There is only so much value to go around: if you get more, I must get less. That is the logic. Yet in real life there are many other ways it may go. In some circumstances, such as war, both parties lose. In some creative social experiences — such as the division of labor, invention, education — all parties gain, each gaining more as the others gain as well.

In the politics of rebellious men all history is a zero-sum game. Pillage is as good as cooperation as long as you get what you need.

In the Spirit of God, on the other hand, we hope, we communicate, we invent. We are free to improve the rules of the game so that you can win without my losing. One very simple way to say what the South Africa Christian Leadership Assembly (SACLA) is about is: to proclaim Christ as Lord means that there are no dead ends. A climate of hope and inventiveness can make room for new patterns where fatalism knew very well that there were none.

Another specimen of this fatalism is unquestioning reverence for those patterns of behavior which are so widespread that we call them "laws." The "laws" of the marketplace, the "law" of profit. Does the Christian obey that law? Or should we bend it by providing more jobs or better jobs at the cost of lowered profits? The laws of the marketplace dictate for town development that upper-class housing and lower-class housing must be in different areas and must be served by different schools, so that the next generation will again grow up without an experience of cultural plurality. Must that law be obeyed?

In the politics of rebellious mankind, it is claimed that even the gods are in favor of a hierarchical world. Differences between classes and kinds of persons are immediately evaluated as differences in dignity. It is the business of politics to assign us our different ranks.

In the Spirit of God, on the other hand, while rejoicing in differences — Jew and Greek, male and female, old and young — we are liberated to proclaim the equal dignity of all, which means, as the apostle Paul says it, that we intentionally give more respect to the less honored members of the body.

In the politics of rebellious mankind, it is permissible, even proper, even desirable, to possess and to accumulate goods and advantages at the expense of others. A social system is held to be healthy if it facilitates the acquisition and secure possession of those advantages.

In the Spirit of God, on the other hand, as we heard it said repeatedly in the early chapters of Luke's Gospel, food and clothing are to be shared, the hungry are to be fed. When Jesus said his mission, fulfilled that day in Nazareth, was to "proclaim the acceptable year of the Lord," that probably meant the year of Jubilee in which according to the law of Moses land was periodically redistributed.

In the politics of rebellious mankind, we are ready to sacrifice persons to causes, even to ideas. General labels like "freedom" or "justice," "socialism" or "capitalism," "order" or "humanism" become positive or negative values in their own right, causes to combat for or to destroy. The modern word for this is "ideology." The biblical word that fits best is probably "idol."

In the Spirit of God, the jealous God who wants us to serve none other, there is no such disincarnate or ideal value worthy to demand the sacrifice of the concrete personal and communal values of our real neighbor. Those abstractions will remain valuable in the measure in which they help us better serve our neighbors. They become sinful when we are asked to sacrifice our neighbor to them.

In the politics of rebellious mankind we trust that there must be some way to survive without judgment. If things get bad enough, those in charge can jettison a few of their benefits in order to save the rest. Often the word "negotiate" is used, as we have seen in the aftermath of Camp David — for the fine-tuned process of haggling and hassling to determine how one can give up as much as one has to, but without yielding anything essential, without sacrificing control, without needing to die. There are those who think that the purpose of religion is to postpone or avoid judgment or sacrifice or deep change. There are those whose hope for SACLA is that by raising the voltage of prayer and praise South Africa's power structures can postpone paying the price of reconciliation, or at least break it down into easy installments. They say, and they pray, "Let us avoid deep trauma and profound change."

In the Spirit of God, on the other hand, it is at the house of God that judgment begins. As Michael Cassidy showed us yesterday, regarding the prophets, and Jesus supremely, the Servant of the Lord undergoes the judgment which others merit. He does not ward it off. He pays the price, and he calls his disciples to carry a similar cross. If SACLA makes sense, it is with the hope that the inevitable wrenching reckoning will come sooner, not later; that it will be faced honestly, defenselessly, with faith in the God who raises from the dead.

In the politics of rebellious mankind one seeks to avoid not only sacrifice but also repentance. It would mean a loss of "face" or of momentum to admit that one had been wrong. Every change of course must be explained as a minor adjustment confirming how right one had been before. A manufacturer or an educator never admits that his product is not the best.

The Spirit of God, on the other hand, enables repentance, change of direction, reconstruction of relationships, and the implementation of the lessons learned from the previous errors. Instead of avoiding loss of face one proves one's openness to facts. Instead of maintaining momentum one reduces the damages of a wrong course by changing it sooner. Repentance is a blow to a person's (or an institution's) pride but not to his (or its) dignity, but not so great a blow as the evil we bring about if we refuse to change.

The specimens I have identified are very broad:

- forgiveness
- servanthood
- readiness for concessions
- truth telling
- hope that finds new ways
- the equal dignity of all
- sharing
- the rejection of ideology or idolatry.

If I were not a guest from across the globe, I would have the right to say more precisely just now that this same pattern of difference should apply in South Africa to specific laws, specific institutions, specific customs, specific policy choices, etc.

V. Relocating the Duality

Our first need has been to deny a dualism, to reject the splitting apart of territories separating the political from the nonpolitical. The duality which is real instead is a difference of responses separating obedience from rebellion. Then there is also a difference which sets apart from others those who — in all their abiding ignorance and weakness — confess Christ as Lord (a political title). The Bible calls them *ekklesia*, which we translate "church," but which in Greek means an ordinary public decision-making assembly, a town parliament. This new kind of community deals with all the choices we've observed above:

- vengeance or forgiveness
- domination or servanthood
- rigidity or concessions
- truth telling or misinformation
- determination or hope
- manipulation or dialogue
- hierarchy or equality
- ideology or objectivity
- with choices of rank, violence, provincialism, race.

This community does not live unto itself. It is scattered amidst a world full of other systems. There is one system we call the "state," which is not identical with another system we call the "nation"; then there are other systems we call "the economy," "the media," "education." . . . There is the world of the arts, the world of sports, the world of science. . . . No one of these — no more the state than any other — is identical either with the believing community or with the rebellious and fallen world. In the midst of each, in ways varying infinitely according to location and vocation, the presence of the confessing community will raise up signs of the kingdoms. In none of them is the kingdom near enough to realization that those signs can be simple, unambiguous, unbroken.

Sometimes the church will be practically shut out from creative involvement, and the language of dualism will seem appropriate. Sometimes her freedom, even her power, will be great, and the language — but also the temptations — of theocracy will be dominant. There can be no one timeless right way to relate church and state — or for that matter church and university, church and banking, church and the arts — for that other member of the comparison — the state, the economy — has no one firm meaning. What has the nearly unarmed democracy of Costa Rica in common with the crazy brutality of Idi Amin that makes it helpful to call them both "state"? So let us set aside definitions in the abstract, essences, and the idea of the state as such, and look at particular communities, regimes, rulers, in the light of the concrete content of the kingdom. This realism must correct the vision of some according to which these "spheres" could be globally preempted for God in the present age, while at the same time retaining their sovereign claims.

The pattern should be sufficiently clear. There is no special realm of "politics" which Christians, or the church, can avoid and leave to its own resources, or leave to be run by its own rules. True, there are varieties of gifts and divisions of labor in the social order as in the church. It is not the personal gift of everyone to be a leader or a militant in the area of social righteousness, any more than everyone should be an apostle. We should give thanks for every believer whose personal calling is not to be an agent of direct social change, if that person's genuine calling is to be a face-to-face evangelist, or to discharge any other distinct gift. But that is said about the member, not the body. The option of not participating consciously in social change is not available to most of the people in this conference of national leaders.[3] The question is in which way each of us severally and all of us together are directing that change, and whether the daily contributions of all of us, and the special leadership thrusts of many of us, will be governed by the gospel or by the patterns of the fallen world. True, there are societies in which the freedom believers have to participate openly in the political dialogue is far greater than in others. Yet to ask whether, as a believing people, we should be "involved" is hardly ever the right question. The question is on which side to be involved, which issues to give priority to, and what methods to use. Under the Spirit of God, both our means and our ends must (and by his power can) be love: openness, reconciliation, the impatience which calls for repentance and the patience which does not coerce: the dialogue which assures the other, even the enemy, of our respect for his dignity, and the proclamation which assures the world that God's righteousness will conquer in the end.

We need not be surprised that the seer John, on the isle of his exile, wept when (in his first vision, in chapters 4–5 of the book of the Apocalypse) he was told there was no one who could unseal the scroll of destiny. The apparent defeat of the church, the apparent powerlessness of truth and love in the face of imperial tyranny, properly left him doubting God's sovereignty. But then he heard the voice: "Weep not."

---

3. The venue where this paper was read was an invitational "miniconference" within SACLA, directed toward "National and Civil Leaders."

He saw the Lamb, slain yet alive, defeated yet victorious. The Lamb that was slain is worthy to receive power. The path of Christ, the political commitment to truth, servanthood, proclamation, and suffering love, is despite appearances the channel of the power of God.

CHAPTER 12

Discerning the Kingdom of God in the Struggles of the World[1]

In an age marked by the idea of progress, seen both as a simple fact of history and as a claim to transcendent validation, it has become easy for us to juxtapose hope for the probable cumulative results of human achievement with hope in Yahweh who raises the dead. Thus we cast over our human enterprises the mantle of providential majesty. Even more is this natural when deepening theological analysis suggests:

- that in the Hebraic vision, history more than myth is the vehicle of God's presence;
- that the history of salvation unrolls in the same world as the history of Pharaoh, Assyria, and Rome, not in some other world or on some other plane;
- that even in the apparent powerlessness of diaspora existence the faithful are called to seek the peace of the ("secular") city;
- that world history, including the unification of the globe in a Western idiom (technology, world communication, the modern

1. Reproduced by permission from: *International Review of Mission* 68 (October 1979): 272. The title was assigned by the editors of the *IRM* as part of the preparation for the Assembly of the Division of World Mission and Evangelism (DWME) of the World Council of Churches, to be held in Melbourne in 1980 under the theme "Your Kingdom Come." Allusions within the text refer largely to conversations in the context of the DWME.

237

state, the concept of rights), is derived from the desacralizing effect upon cultures of the proclamation of Yahweh's invasion of human experience;

• that the world mission of the church is inseparable for good and for ill from the creation and propagation of Occidental values.

No surprise, then, that we feel driven to interpret our life and commitment in kingdom language, to see our hopes and successes as God's own. But can we move from generally affirmative visions of "history" at large to claiming God's specific partisanship in contested issues? Can we choose confidently, generally, between gradual and rapid social change? Between personal and collective or between economic and political definitions of human rights? Can we justify such preferences on normative grounds not reducible to our interests or our particular tastes? Can we choose between competing definitions of decolonization? No surprise, then, that in recoiling from the dangers of provincialism and self-righteousness, others seek to safeguard the objectivity, transcendence, and dignity of the kingdom by renewing the ancient dichotomies of time versus eternity or body versus spirit, from which follows a refusal to correlate God's struggle too closely with ours.

We could write the history of theology, especially of missionary theology, and especially in our age, as the history of this problem. Impressed by the newness of our times, how do we read the world's story and find the meaning of our mission within it?

We have been invited by some to find guidance in the way in which "revolution" has become the leitmotiv of our age. This has been done: today by the "theologians of liberation," but also by Josef Hromadka two decades ago and by E. Stanley Jones as long again before that. We have been shown the parallel between secularity and the technical view of reality on one hand and the gospel message on the other; each frees mankind from chaos, stagnation, and cosmological pluralism to make the world orderly and effort worthwhile. Each undercuts the conservatism of religious worldviews: thus A. van Leeuwen, but also the early ecumenical missiologists Mott and Speer. Hans Hoekendijk called us to replace ecclesiocentric visions with cosmic visions of kingdom proclamation. "Church growth" analysts, while ecclesiocentric in terms of immediate mission policy, lean heavily on their reading of secular cultural trends to perceive where the gospel can count on a hearing. The Mexico Commission on World Mission and Evangelism (CWME) Assembly called us to look beyond ourselves to discern and to join in "what God is doing in the world." The next Assembly in Bangkok sought to discern the shape of "salvation today" in terms of the general agenda of human yearning. Some say progress-oriented language now needs to yield to apocalyptic imagery since ecological disaster and world starvation are more credible than any other extrapolation of our world's fate.

Can one say anything about such a broad spectrum of concern and communication where there is not space to survey it all fairly? It will have to suffice, but it is also proper, however unsatisfactory for our systematizing propensities, that what I can propose here should be a handful of slogans, rules of thumb, proverbs, and not a broad programmatic yardstick or a single key theory.

In 1961 the commission created by the Department of Missionary Studies to cap its three-year study of "The Word of God and the Church's Missionary Obedience" stated as the first of its "omnibus questions":

What is the relation between the Course of the Gospel and what is going on in the world? What is God's redemptive purpose in and for world history? What do we expect as a result of missions?[2]

The editors' preface to this summary said that this question "is of vital importance because the contemporary crisis of Christian missions calls for interpretation of the Christian understanding of history itself": already a predisposition of the question. To say at some specific time (without needing to detail its indices) that there is a "contemporary crisis" that can "call for" some answer is already to have begun reading history in a particular way.

The ten paragraphs of response provided in that document did not speak as pointedly as we might now wish to the thesis that "God's work in the world" can be neatly discerned and simply celebrated, but they did survey the abiding agenda. We may begin our list of rules of thumb with their response to the strongest challenges, namely, to those other movements in history which promise a salvation of their own:

---

2. "The Missionary Task of the Church: Theological Reflections," *Division of Studies Bulletin* 7, no. 2 (autumn 1961): 6.

If new messianic movements arise, offering to mankind, in some name other than that of Jesus, the total healing and the peace for which men long, this should be no matter of surprise to Christians.[3] The Church has neither to fear nor to surrender itself to such promises and claims.

It is fitting that we should discern in the great movements of the age not mere potentiality, "power" waiting there "neutrally" until it be claimed and channeled for good or ill, but rather "Powers," antimessiahs, alternative pretenders to saviorhood. If they can be rendered usable in humanity's service, they need to be sobered, demythified, disenchanted through the proclamation of Christ's lordship. Their claim to adequacy and autonomy must be overruled in order for them to align with "what God is doing."

"What God is doing" in the world is often not a ratification of our good intentions but a judgment on our unfaithfulness. God does not condemn our ecclesiocentricity as such: God too is ecclesiocentric. That is why he condemns our failure by letting another messiah fill the gap we left: not in order that we should follow after that substitute but in order that the church be restored as proclaimer of all his righteousness.

The "omnibus questions" had concluded, "What do we expect as a result of missions?" The response drew back from providing such a simply instrumental conception.

> The Church knows that God is at work within the events of history, and that He calls His people to participate in the struggles of life in the name of Christ, so that through their obedience — whether in partial victories or in faithful defeat — they are enabled to be signs of the ultimate victory of Christ.

"Sign," rather than "instrument," describes more properly how our words and deeds "work." We proclaim; our humanizing deeds signify. Others, or rather Another, will determine whether success or sacrifice better represents the Lamb's lordship. "Whether here and now the

---

3. "The Missionary Task of the Church," p. 8. The drafters intentionally did not provide an example here, but the primary example of a "new messianic movement" they had in mind at the time was Marxism.

churches are given power, wealth, and great numbers, or whether they have to serve in weakness, poverty, and contempt, is for their Lord to determine." The beginning of accountability in our discerning "where it's at" is our confession that power and progress, consensus and trend, are ambivalent indices.

There is no Christian faith (or for that matter no Jewish or Muslim or Marxist faith) that does not proclaim in one way or another the meaningfulness under God of ordinary human experience: marrying, dying, prospering or becoming poor, winning or losing wars, etc. Yet because the God before whom events have meaning is confessed as truly God and not a distillate from or a summary of human opinions, that meaning is not evident on the surface of the events. It must be discerned prophetically. The prophecy which makes this meaning manifest is itself a gift. It is therefore not subject to determination by majorities or by kings, although some particular persons may, with time, be recognized by their hearers as more specifically prophets than others.

Nor is the word of prophecy, despite all its transcendent claim, self-authenticating. It too is subject to criteria. There seem to have been some people at Corinth who thought that Spirit utterance was so self-authenticating as to be unaccountable. The apostle had to remind them (1 Cor. 12:3) that the Spirit does not blow every which way but only in harmony with the confession of Christ's lordship. The same point is made when 1 John speaks of testing the spirits (4:1) or when Peter says prophetic interpretation must not be private (2 Pet. 1:20) or when Paul adds (1 Cor. 14:29) that those who utter prophetic declarations are subject to the evaluation of others. What things mean, what is to be spoken, must be tested at the bar not so much of relevance as of resonance. It must echo the meaning of Jesus.

It would be unbelief for us to be embarrassed by the simplicity of this statement. Whatever echoes the confession of Christ's humanity is recognizable as the spirit to listen to. Whatever denies that normativeness and that particular humanity is not to be heard. The Christ by whose standard the spirits are tested, as 1 John 4 makes especially clear, is the earthly Jesus.[4] Our criteria must be not merely "christological" in some vague, cosmic sense, but "jesulogical." We properly must test

---

4. Modern doctrinal debate has often been about the deity of Christ. For this author the humanity is what counts.

"what is going on in the world" by the substantial criteria Jesus asked to be judged by (Luke 7:22ff., echoing 4:18ff.): namely, concrete deeds of servanthood. Sloganeering professions of loyalty to liberty or justice, peace or plenty, are brought down to earth in the sharing of bread and the washing of feet.

The temptation soon arises to be freed of the limits of Jesus' earthliness, Jewishness, and cross. We often speak of this temptation as "gnostic," because one of its early forms sought to describe a "larger Christ than Jesus" by incorporating into a speculative system the contribution of other paths to wisdom. But there are analogies to gnosticism as well in the advocacy of "larger" views of the historical process. Some appeal to the Father, others to the Spirit, others to the "Cosmic Christ" or to the Trinity as a whole[5] as warrants for learning from "creation" or "nature" or "history" other lessons than those of the incarnation. Have we other standards than those of the crucified rabbi to recognize what we shall accredit as "liberation" or as "humane"?

To this the apostolic witness (John 1; Colossians 1; Hebrews 1) responded with the insistence that any "larger" claims for Christ as preexistent, as creator or cosmic victor, must not be disengaged from the man Jesus and his cross.[6] "What God is doing" will have to be discerned in the same light tomorrow. Where oppression gives way not to counteroppression but to servanthood, where suffering is accepted and not imposed, where human dignity commands respect not alone through anger but through the re-creation of community (which may very well not be attained without anger and confrontation), there the claim "God is at work" may not be presumptuous.

The discernment of God in history demands ideologically ecu-

---

5. One widely echoed form of this argument is the appeal of H. Richard Niebuhr to the Trinity in his *Christ and Culture* and in occasional essays; cf. my summary in "How H. Richard Niebuhr Reasoned," especially pp. 61ff., in Glen H. Stassen et al., *Authentic Transformation* (Nashville: Abingdon, 1996), and the notion of "other lights," appealed to over against the earthly Jesus, in my *The Royal Priesthood: Essays Ecclesiological and Ecumenical,* ed. Michael G. Cartwright (Grand Rapids: Eerdmans, 1994), pp. 186ff.

6. I have written more fully about the temptations to subject Jesus to one's own notion of what would be bigger or truer, and about the response of the apostolic theologians; cf. my *The Priestly Kingdom* (Notre Dame, Ind.: Notre Dame University Press, 1985), pp. 49-54.

menical conversation. This may be the realm of our deepest abiding division. Denominational diversity will long plague us, but it is being progressively overcome as we meet issues for which the old differentiae are irrelevant. National divisions are deeper and are deepening, but at least in theory Christians know they are committed to a supranational communion. It is far more difficult to define and sustain the notion that Christians might (or might be obliged to) transcend the conflicting world-spanning meaning systems by which we have been trained to read history. It would be again gnostic to want to define just one true non-provincial view of all history, which would transcend and condemn all the others. Yet at the least we must pledge that as we each read all history from within our own ideological skins, we must juxtapose to that reading those of churches in other worlds and other times.

What God is really doing will usually be a surprise. Our very tools for identifying meanings distort them. Futurology before the Club of Rome extrapolated economic growth rates within stable-system assumptions, without much consideration of the thresholds where cumulative quantitative changes add up to systemic upset or collapse, or of the depletion of scarce resources. Theologians began proleptically adjusting to the triumph of immanentist materialism and the death of God, when a new religiosity was already growing. How clearly was continental China once thought to have been irreversibly stamped with the imprint of Mao's thoughts? Behind modesty in prediction comes modesty in goal-pointed practical decisions based upon predication. Especially must this apply to projections of liberation through violence, of economic renewal through long-range manipulation of sacrifices by workers and consumers, or to the subordination to partisan political goals of civil and personal rights. Even if the promise "guns today, rice tomorrow" were true, the trade-off would be dubious; but it is a prediction that will not work out, and that not only because the violence of the means resorted to to achieve it will be self-defeating.

"The kings of the nations . . . let themselves be called benefactors, . . . but it shall not be so among you. . . . I am among you as a servant." The irreducible historicity of Jesus' servanthood protects us from two quite natural misinterpretations of historical responsibility. One of them moves from substance to form, considering as right that which is rightly intended. "Love" is a positive subjective intention, which may be called on to justify any action done in its name. The other moves from deeds to goals. "Intention" in an objective sense is then the goal sought, justifying any means claiming to reach it. Whether the "benefaction" claimed by those who lord it over the nations be objective or subjective, Jesus' servanthood undercuts the claim to justification by intention. His call is not to "intend" well in either sense, to will the good or to achieve it, nor to be justified, so much as to be present as servant.

The criterion of servanthood is substantial, not merely formal. It throws an especially clear light on one monumental kind of "discernment of the kingdom in history," namely, identifying events of statecraft as preeminently worthy of recognition. "God has done it" inaugurated the confusion of Constantine's peace with the reign of God. "God wills it" sent the crusaders off to the Near East. The error was not that no meaning should have been ascribed to events, but that nonservant criteria reversed the relation of church and world.[7]

Good news is no news. Who is in high office or what laws are written will make less difference for many indices of where things will have gone by the year 2000 than the cumulation of an infinity of tiny deeds: mothers who feed their children, children who learn their lessons, craftsmen who finish a job, doctors who get the dosage right, drivers who stay on the road, policemen who hold their fire. The lunge for the large view is often the beginning of self-deception. The predilection to see one's own small deed as significant or as right when and because it can be shown to contribute to some overall victory scenario overburdens punctual responsibility in decision and undervalues the continuities of character and covenant. The kingdom is like the grain growing while no one watches (Mark 4:26f.), like the hidden leaven silently taking over the flour bin (Matt. 13:33). Contrary to the proverb, watching a pot does not keep it from boiling, but it does misdirect the pot watcher's creativity.

God makes men's wrath praise him (Ps. 76:10), yet men's wrath does not accomplish God's righteousness (James 1:20). In that paradoxical sovereignty which classical theology called "providence" and the earlier fathers called lordship or *sessio ad dextram*, there is a nonreversible relationship between our deeds, which may be evil, and God's use of them for ultimate good. God's sovereignty, which includes wrath,

---

7. Cf. in *The Priestly Kingdom*, pp. 138-42 and note 15 there on the temptation to identify one's own government as bearer of the meaning of history.

can integrate the works of human rebellion without rendering those actions morally good. That YHWH used Assyria's troops to chastise his own people (Isa. 10:6ff.) did not make those deeds into good works, nor were the Israelites called to celebrate them or to help with them. That God reserves vengeance to himself and may then "delegate" that vengeance to Cyrus or to Caesar (Rom. 13:2, 4 and Isaiah 45) is grounds for his people to renounce human vengeance (Rom. 12:19 but also Deut. 32:35) rather than claiming to be his instruments. The same applies to the place of Pilate in the crucifixion.

Discerning the kingdom in our struggles must then distinguish between what events ultimately mean and the desire to get ethical instruction from them. This is the distinction not always recognized when a decade ago currency was given to phrases like "discern, celebrate, and join in what God is doing in the world." Providence remains inscrutable. Our estimates of how to help history along, whether they claim to be guided by prophecy or by secular common sense, are still only our guesses, always limited by our point of view and usually by our interests. They can never replace the Torah or the incarnation as moral guides.

"We reject the false doctrine that the Church can and must acknowledge as a source of its proclamation, beside and in addition to this one Word of God, other events, powers, forms and truths as the revelation of God" (Barmen Declaration, Article 1). The warning of the Barmen confessor is still needed. If Jesus Christ is God's word, then no other event can be, in itself, firmly or finally either a revelation or an achievement on the same level. The course of events in the world can give us cues (signals as to when to speak) and clues (hints of larger meanings). It can offer echoes or it can project images of the gospel of the kingdom coming. As echo and image, it sends us back to the original, sends us back the more firmly in the measure in which we take the present seriously as the real terrain of an authentically ongoing saving work.

Index of Names and Subjects

Index of Scripture References

See also individual writers' names in Index of Names and Subjects